MUSLIM VOICES IN SCHOOL

Narratives of Identity and Pluralism

Özlem Sensoy
Simon Fraser University, Burnaby, British Columbia, Canada

Christopher Darius Stonebanks
Bishop's University, Sherbrooke, Quebec, Canada

SENSE PUBLISHERS
ROTTERDAM/BOSTON/TAIPEI

A C.I.P. record for this book is available from the Library of Congress.

ISBN: 978-90-8790-955-0 (paperback)
ISBN: 978-90-8790-956-7 (hardback)
ISBN: 978-90-8790-957-4 (e-book)

Published by: Sense Publishers,
P.O. Box 21858, 3001 AW
Rotterdam, The Netherlands
http://www.sensepublishers.com

Printed on acid-free paper

FOR JOE

TABLE OF CONTENTS

ÖZLEM SENSOY AND CHRISTOPHER DARIUS STONEBANKS

INTRODUCTION

Voice & Other Acts of Insubordination

I'm also troubled by, not what Senator McCain says, but what members of the party say. And it is permitted to be said such things as, "Well, you know that Mr. Obama is a Muslim." Well, the correct answer is, he is not a Muslim, he's a Christian. He's always been a Christian. But the really right answer is, what if he is? Is there something wrong with being a Muslim in this country? The answer's no, that's not America. Is there something wrong with some seven-year-old Muslim-American kid believing that he or she could be president? Yet, I have heard senior members of my own party drop the suggestion, "He's a Muslim and he might be associated with terrorists." This is not the way we should be doing it in America...I'm troubled about the fact that, within the party, we have these kinds of expressions.

Former Secretary of State Gen. Colin Powell, Oct 16, 2008, *Meet the Press*

There was a time in my life as an educator when I did not speak about politics and education. It was my most naïve moment...For me, now I say that education *is* politics. Today, I say education has the quality of being politics, which shapes the learning process. Education is politics and politics has *educability*.

Paulo Freire, 1986. p. 61

"Contrary to what a lot of people think," Jimmy Yan told me when I called him to discuss the case, "most of the racism in our society happens to the most vulnerable members in our public schools."

Moustafa Bayoumi, 2008, p. 109

Politics and schools are inexorably intertwined. The politics and education about Islam, Muslims, Arabs, Turks, Iranians and all that is associated with the West's popular imagination of the monolithic "Middle-East" has long been framed within problematics. In schools, we, as other non-powerblocs (Kincheloe & Steinberg, 1997), are a *problem*.

In *How Does it feel to be a Problem* Moustafa Bayoumi tells the story of Yasmin, a young, smart, Muslim girl of Arab and Filipino heritage. Yasmin lives in Brooklyn, struggling, perhaps more appropriately fighting her way through the high school public school system. Her simple desire to join the student governance, with her platform of "I'm here to help *you*" (p. 89) is at first embraced by her peers, but when it becomes clear that her faith requires some accommodation for her performance of her elected duties (she offers to set up and clean up for the school dance but on religious grounds can not participate) she is dismissed from her elected position by each level of the school's institutional brain trust. In brief, to the school structure, she is a problem.

We are (as are and were others) a problem. Playing with Canadian and U.S. collective memory, Waubageshig (1974) titles his book *The Only Good Indian* tempting his reader to complete the sentence with U.S. Civil War General Philip Henry Sheridan's reputed sentiment, "...is a dead Indian." Ward Churchill's (2004) book *Kill The Indian Save the Man* confronts the sentiments of indifference in Canada and the U.S., institutionally and interpersonally, to the residential school era and its legacy. Bayoumi's (2008) Brooklyn hookah café Arab-American participant naively and incorrectly remarks "We're the new blacks ... You know that, right?" (p. 2); and when this perspective is juxtaposed against popular Aaron McGruder's (2001) *The Boondocks* cartoon, "We're number three! We're number three!!" in the context of a *Newsweek* article stating that Arabs and people presumed to be from the Middle East (read: brown) now superseded Black Americans as the most hated racial group, it is difficult to ignore the triangulation at work among: people of the Middle East, other "others," and the racialized and now globally-situated vocabulary of violent, evil, foe, *problem*. It wasn't long ago that U.S. General William Boykin described his combat in Somalia in a biblical good versus evil trope, popularly stating (and subsequently amending) that while in pursuit of his self described Muslim foe, "I knew that my God was bigger than his. I knew that my God was a real God and his was an idol." From the Crusades to Gulf War 2, we, as that diverse group of people that represents the West's *Islamic World*, whether "over there" or "right here" and "home grown" are a problem, and perhaps nowhere does this problem discourse play out more intricately than in schools and other non-formal locations of education.

Muslim youth in the West wherever they are on the continuum of secular to orthodox, continue to struggle in negotiating intersecting, and sometimes dissecting, meanings of self– their religion, race, ethnicity, culture, way of life, community and knowledge. This struggle occurs alongside the current War on Terror political climate, the multitude of media entertainment images (Shaheen, 1984, 1991, 2001) a news media (FAIR, 2001) and a schooling system (Kincheloe & Steinberg, 2004) that consistently and systematically represents a homogenous and myopic Islamic faith, Muslim culture and people. The 2005 riots in France in which Muslim youth were predominantly positioned as perpetrators, the outrage and protests of Muslims regarding the Danish *Jyllands-Posten*'s publication of demeaning caricatures of the Prophet Mohammed, the banning of hijabs in schools, the denial of Muslim prayer spaces at universities, the continued detainments and implications of terror intents about countless Muslim young men in North America, and other incidences that so widely sanction the debasing of human rights and human dignity have left non-Muslims confused, angry, and poorly informed about their fellow citizens, while once again reducing all Muslims to being defined by a media that allow no diversity of voice, no understanding of context, nor space for complexity.

With this book, we seek to advocate the use of "counterstory" narratives (Nelson, 2001) utilized to empower and repair damaged group and individual identities that emerge from dominant-group constructs of Muslim people. Our goal is to push back against the reductive mainstream "stories" that have been told about us for generations if not centuries, in mainstream schools (al-Qazzaz, 1975; Said, 1979; Suleiman, 1977, 1983; NAAA, 1980; Sensoy & DiAngelo, 2006; Sensoy, 2007; Stonebanks, 2008) and in media (Ghareeb, 1983; Said, 1997; Shaheen, 1984, 1991, 1997, 2001; Stonebanks, 2008; Stonebanks & Sensoy, 2007; Steet, 2000; Kincheloe & Steinberg, 2004). The chapters are authored by Muslim acculturated authors, and tell a multitude of experiences about Muslim student experiences in Western schools. Through this collection, we hope that non-Muslim readers will have an opportunity to read a diversity of perspectives about Muslim experiences. We expect these counter-narratives to facilitate the repair of damaging, hegemonic narratives that have permeated the Western dominant consciousness and collective memory (Kincheloe & Steinberg, 1997). Through the sharing of these more diverse, contextual, and complex stories, these chapters become "...narrative acts of insubordination" (Nelson, 2001, p. 8).

> But enough about you, let me tell you about me...
>
> Michael W. Apple, 1996, p. xiv.

We began this book with the intention of gathering readable, accessible, compelling, varied, voiced, passionate, real, textured, multi-faceted, hybrid, fearless, fearful, cautious, bold, modest, and inspired accounts of living Islam in relation to mainstream schooling in the West. We believe that the authors of these chapters represent these qualities, and that the collection together helps to make the diverse experiences of Muslim students both contextual and complex. Our intention is that *MVS* be a "handbook." Each of the twelve chapters can be used separately, or alongside of other readings referenced with discussion questions at the end of each chapter. The book is organized chronologically from elementary through university experiences of Muslim students. In chapter 1, Mona Abo-Zena, Barbara Sahli, and Christina Safiya Tobias-Nahi describe the narrative experiences of Muslim students participating in an essay contest about courage. We say without shame that our favourite passage in the whole of this book is written by sixth grader, Osama who writes, "Imagine having a meeting with the President of the United States. Would you be late? Of course not. Well I had a meeting with the Creator of the Universe...you wouldn't want to miss that meeting." The authors share Osama's and other Muslim students' stories of courage, and offer a nuanced analysis of how these students navigate stereotypes, post-9/11 fears and other dynamics of school and social life.

In chapter 2, Shaza Khan offers us a glimpse in to the lives of adolescent Muslims involved in a youth program. Through her interviews and conversations with these students, Khan describes the complex set of challenges that youth face as Muslim students attending predominantly non-Muslim schools in the U.S. Khan writes, "Crisis has often been thought of as a central aspect of adolescence and identity formation. For Muslim American youth, there have been systemic efforts to locate the crux of their crisis in the "clash of cultures" which is perceived to be inherent in their backgrounds as practicing members of the Islamic faith and residents of a democratic and secular United States." Khan's discussion gives a sense of the breadth and depth of mainstream school ignorance about the lives and experiences of Muslim students, and also the strategies many Muslim students adopt to cope with these challenges.

In chapter 3, Seema Imam continues the theme of ignorance of Muslim student life by pulling front and center, and examining, the discourse of separation of church and state in relation to schools. Imam catalogues some of the central and persistent aspects of the school curriculum (both the formal and informal curricula of schools). Her chapter gives us a sense of the volume of dominant societal messages that Muslim youth must navigate. Imam writes, "[M]any schools still tell Muslim parents that "we" cannot cover religion because "we" observe separation of church and state …In interviews, the participants shared stories about how they themselves or their children were deeply involved in the religious activities of other faiths while in school, in spite of the discourse about the separation of church and state [such as]…Children are asked to sing Christmas songs including religious ones for assemblies; Children were required to make Christmas tree decorations and take them home for their own Christmas trees." The detailed account that Imam offers gives readers a cogent sense of the prevalence and endurance of Christianity and Christian-privilege in school culture.

In chapter 4, Nawell Mossalli gives us a deep look in to the life of a Muslim teenager in small town, adding "voice to the cold statistics," as Mossalli puts it. In addition to Rana's story, Mossali describes the various school-based experiences of other Muslim students such as fifth-grader Hashim who is forced to repeatedly contest to his classmates that they didn't just ride camels in his home country, or of Kareem, a second grader, who has a piece of ham waved in his face by his teacher, arguing "it's not going to bite him!" These stories while easily dismissed as isolated incidences, as a collective become difficult to ignore. Rana's story invites readers to examine the question, if Rana is successful as a "typical" American teen, at what cost was this success achieved? A sobering question, and one that demands our attention as educators working in pluralistic societies.

In chapter 5, Özlem Sensoy investigates the construction of "textbook Muslims" in school settings. It is well-known in critical education circles that in the absence of personal experiences with groups who are different from oneself, our primary source of education about "others" is the school curriculum and media. Sensoy examines the kind of education about Muslims that students will obtain if their only source of knowledge is the "textbook Muslim." She offers this analysis alongside of mainstream discourses about Muslims (and those thought to be Muslims). She writes, "The images of textbook Muslims in this sample conveyed an overall sedentary nature of life among Muslims. This, in and of itself, may seem like a small point. However, I would argue that this type of depiction of sedentary-ness functions to uphold another familiar binary discourse in the West. "Rolling up one's sleeves" to "get down to work" and "hammer out agreements" are more than metaphors. They are core elements to explaining mainstream Western experiences of advancement, progress, and modernity." This chapter challenges us to consider what part of our knowledge about Muslims is actually knowledge about "textbook Muslims."

Chapter 6 is Dalia al-Houseini's personal account as an immigrant Canadian of Arab heritage. She discusses how school-based discourses influenced her self-image and self-concept as a Palestinian and Muslim Canadian. The chapter is organized in to vignettes that unfold like scenes in a life narrative about identity negotiation and flux. Among the most compelling parts of the chapter is al-Houseini's discussion of her experiences with other Brown students in her high school. She writes, "As I befriended the brown group, I felt more welcomed. We had more in common. I remember one of the first things I was ever told by them was that I was *Brown*. Sometimes we would joke that I was *beige* because I looked White, but my ethnicity was not White. We would always discuss diversity issues such as foods we have in common, similar traditions and similarities in language. We all felt that we shared tradition and a common experience of oppression. We never outright said to each other that race is playing a major factor in our friendship, perhaps no one had taught us the language to express what we all knew, but we would find other ways to communicate our feelings." There are some profound lessons to be learned here about the value of fostering safe spaces for students with shared group identities to talk about, and develop the language to examine their racialized experiences.

Chapter 7 is about sexual orientation identity among Muslim students. Younes Mourchid offers us a detailed look at the experiences of the Muslim LGBTQ community by examining the narratives of gay and lesbian Muslim university students. The complexity represented in this chapter is deeply educative. As one of Mourchid's participant's says, "The 'shit' hit the fan with the events of 9/11 and my identity as a Muslim kid fossilized... I became associated with everything America was angry about...I began to distance myself from my religious identity and the baggage that came with it... I asked my parents to move somewhere else where no one knew we were Muslim... I just wanted my faith to be a private matter and question for me." This stance is brought in to tension: as the events of 9/11 fuel unfavorable sentiments about Islam and Muslims, many young gay and lesbian Muslims who Mourchid writes about describe having to make sense of their sexual orientation identity within the framework of existing narratives about being gay in Islam and also post 9/11 narratives about Arab and Middle Eastern peoples.

In chapter 8, Shabana Mir offers us an analysis of three students navigating their personal and school-based experiences at university. The call for (or boasting about) a "diverse university student body" is not uncommon to those of us who work at universities. Mir examines how Muslim students negotiate being part of a "proper body politic," which often means "White-majority-with-White-influenced-minorities." Mir writes, "As students of higher education, it is essential for us to grapple with the difficult question of how minority students may preserve identities, while we seek to promote diversity and inter-racial and inter-cultural exchange on campuses." Mir argues that such contexts can create circumstances that put minority students' identities at risk. The stories of the three undergraduate women she recounts give insight in to how such risk manifests.

Chapter 9 is about navigating intersecting minoritized identities. Author Samaa Abdurraqib describes her experiences as a university student navigating what it means to be an African American Muslim woman. She discusses the complex intersections and readings of her body: as foreign, as Black, as other, and explores the marginalization of her body as Muslim. She captures this tension in this way, "When Islam is discussed in the classroom, the assumption is that I am not necessarily speaking from a position of knowledge or authority, and thus my experience of being Muslim and the knowledge that stems from that experience are not perceived as valid. On the other hand when race and Black-ness is discussed, I am immediately afforded a position of authority." What are the effects, causes, and functions of the eclipsing of her Muslim identity and centralizing of her Black-ness? How and why this occurs is the topic of her essay.

In chapter 10, Carolyne Ali Khan offers us a creative essay that draws the reader closest in to what it might be like to "feel" the experience of being Muslim in the West. Her essay situated in her own school-based experiences (as student, as well as teacher) connects these experiences to mainstream discourses about Islam. She juxtaposes her own, personal, family-anchored education about Islam with the popular mainstream narratives. She writes, *""What is that in your hand?" "Nothing Dad...just some leaves, from the bush." "Let me see." I opened my small hand. "Ahh," (my father sighed, shaking his head gently) "Look at how perfect even this tiny leaf is. Beautiful. That little plant in your hands was growing outside peacefully. It is one of God's creations, just like you...* It is not uncommon to open a Muslim newspaper (in Pakistan, Jordan and Egypt where I have lived) and find an article or photograph that expressly illustrates the connection between God and nature. In keeping with this, the Islam that I learned from my father, regards the sensual, (with the joys of food/drink, music, and love of nature), as a way to be respectful of God's perfection as it is mirrored in a rich world. I have yet to see a representation of Muslims as embodied and sensual beings in the news or in school curriculum in the U.S." Ali Khan's essay embodies what it means to navigate hybrid spaces for Muslim students.

In chapter 11, Christopher Stonebanks examines pop culture narratives about Muslims and considers them alongside of conversations had with two Muslim teacher education students. He begins his analysis by asking, "What space, if any, has the teaching profession created, facilitated, or even allowed for Muslims to actively participate in the public school system?" His discussion bridges mainstream narratives and values attributed to Muslims with the perceived incompatibility between those values and Muslims in school contexts. The discussion with participant, Abdul, is illuminating, Stonebanks writes, "Abdul, who noted his visible Muslim-ness, joked how in his first year introductory course to teaching, the professor cautioned the students on the reality of judgement concerning proper attire and appearance while attending their in school field experience. [Abdul said], 'Yeah, they always use that word, "be well groomed." As I look at myself in the mirror, I'm not well groomed according to your definition. (Starts to laugh) According to the definition centuries ago, I'm very well groomed!' ...On the one hand, the field of education prides itself on its "acceptance of diversity" while on the other hand, this young Muslim man has to navigate preconceived notions of a beard or clothing that he knows is sadly associated with "one of those prototypical terrorists." This chapter closely examines how such narratives of incompatibility can influence the experiences of Muslim teachers in school settings in the West.

Chapter 12, by Imran Mogra describes the life stories of two Muslim teachers in the U.K. The chapter offers a holistic story encompassing the early lives, school experiences as students, and as teachers in mainstream schools. The narratives Mogra describes communicate the juggling that occurs when teachers navigate their religious identities in schools. While for one teacher, "the positive response from her current head teacher suggests that the school is empowering her as she is attending courses, sharing her expertise and demonstrating her competency and has offered herself for promotion." Other, "teachers experience prejudice, ridicule and hostility in their work place and in society ...[and] unfortunately are pushed to consider alternative careers." Avoiding a unilateral story of "the" Muslim teacher experience, Mogra's chapter describes both the successes and challenges of Muslim teachers engaged in teaching.

> Because education is politics, it makes sense for the liberating teacher to feel some fear when he or she is teaching.
>
> Paulo Freire, 1986, p. 61

Transgressive knowledge and classrooms do not come without risk. The authors within this book present experiences and voices (their own as well as of their participants) that may make some readers uncomfortable with what is being offered and unsure of whether or not they should bring such perspectives in to the class. After all, it is *easier* to use the multitude of resources framing Muslims in a neo-liberal "caring" perspective of being in need of support, resources, or care than it is to present the possibility that *the problem* may require much more inward gazing and reflection on the part of mainstream structures of schooling. We, Christopher and Özlem, as editors believe strongly that this book, and its intent to present voices in schools that are otherwise muted, is part of a tradition of critical scholarship that is rooted in the works of scholars such as Paulo Freire, Frantz Fanon, Edward Said, Henry Giroux, bell hooks, Shirley Steinberg, Ira Shor, Gayatri Chakravorty Spivak, Tariq Ali... and most specifically for this book, from the work of and dialogue with Joe Lyons Kincheloe.

The idea for this book took hold on the McGill University campus at the corner of Dr. Penfield and McTavish. Contemplating for a moment, the Department of Integrated Studies in Education's Canada Research Chair in Critical Pedagogy, Joe, gently responded to the question I (Christopher) had just posed with his own, *What do you think we should do next?* It was after dinner and we had just stopped at the stone stairs on our way back to our cars parked at the top of McGill's infamous steep climb to the Education building. This was a kind of halfway rest stop en-route to the peak of K2 mountain, and an opportunity to continue our conversation. On that late spring evening, while students busily navigated past us, to and from their university business, we talked for over an hour about a common vision we had for schools. My own deeply influenced by Joe's work:

> A regressive politics of knowledge helps produce a technicist education that is more concerned with "how to" than "why" questions. (...) Imagining *what could be* — a central goal of any critical pedagogy — has no place in such regressive schools. (Kincheloe, 2008, p. 4)

Imaging what could be...

Joe had a profound vision of what could be, but he also had pragmatic knowledge, from years of experience working in the trenches across the United States, of what primarily existed in schools. When promoting what could be, Joe was always quick to point out the "wonderful" and "brilliant" teachers and classrooms he had encountered (Kincheloe, 2003), but mindful of the realities of what was and unfortunately continues to be the norm. Joe had spent a lifetime observing and responding to social injustices. He was a child of the Cold War, segregation, the civil rights movement and a volunteer medic (exempted for medical reasons) in the Vietnam War (to pre-empt his eventual draft into a conflict he protested against) – all of which contributed to his examination of the manner in which schools produce and legitimate some knowledge, while disregarding others and other forms of knowledge production. Joe came into his academic stride during his country's military foray into the Middle East in the early 90s. During this time of continued miseducation and media-driven knowledge about the history, ideological, social, psychological, emotional and even pathological values and current conditions of the peoples of the Middle East, Joe's dedication to social justice could not divert from addressing the dehumanization and marginalization of Muslims in both formal and non-formal locations of education. In conversation with Joe, the Tonkin Gulf distortions that facilitated consent to the Vietnam War had direct connections with the public relations' fabricated account from a tearful 15 year old girl of having witnessed Iraqi soldiers killing Kuwaiti babies by pulling them from their incubators and tossing them onto the hospital floor. Why, we would discuss, was little learned from one moment in history and not transposed to the present?

Although he was fascinated with the way such knowledge was constructed, he never overlooked the ultimate purpose of his research: to reduce human suffering. Little escaped Joe's attention of how knowledge and consciousness were produced and served to function as a means to either alleviate or add to human suffering. From the manner in which the conquest of the Americas was taught in North American schools to the seemingly trivial Geico, "so easy a caveman can do it" advertising campaigns, with the punch line that *some people* are ridiculously oversensitive to stereotypes in the media was a slogan he could easily connect as complacency towards marginalization and oppression. "Christopher," he said, "I'm *fascinated* by those commercials." Everything for Joe held possibility as a teachable moment; where something, for better or worse, could be "learned" and it was those "why" questions of what was being taught, either overtly or covertly, that would engage him deep in dialogue. Ever and always present, was his concern with how such knowledge affected people.

Post 9/11, the often hidden curriculum that has long existed in Western schools with regard to the Middle East, Islam, and Muslims became an important area of research and writing for Joe. *The Miseducation of the West: The Hidden Curriculum of Western-Muslim Relations* (2004) a book he co-edited with Shirley Steinberg, primarily examined the covert manners in which both formal and non-formal locations of education contributed to the acceptance in the Western consciousness of a backwards, monolithic, Muslim East where they were in need of civilization, by whatever means necessary. It is important to mention that the *Miseducation of the West* was being developed prior to the second invasion of Iraq, in a climate where statements like, "you're either with us, or against us", were politically the norm and anything else was politically risky. Whatever the risk, again ever present was Joe's concern for people. Already influenced by Joe's work, through a simple stroke of luck, I (Christopher) was asked to contribute a chapter to the *Miseducation of the West* and wrote of my experiences as an elementary aged student of Iranian descent in an overwhelmingly White, Christian suburb of Canada. I was humbled that Joe had asked me to contribute and he was humbled that his work had not only made me a better teacher, but answered so many questions of my own experiences as a minority in schools. A few years later, sitting on those steps at McGill, I asked Joe what his plans were to follow up *Miseducation of the West* and he responded, "What do you think we should do next?" This book, *Muslim Voices in School*, is the product of that discussion. This book was mostly conceptualized in that conversation, as a natural progression from the *Miseducation of the West*, where a diversity of Muslim and Middle Eastern voices representing a diversity of perspectives, perhaps as a professor, teacher, student or parent contribute their scholarly voices about the experience of Muslim youth and schooling in the West.

It is important for us to also note that Joe's allyship was not limited to his scholarly production. In the early stages of this book's development, I (Özlem) communicated with Joe primarily over email, me in Vancouver and he in Montréal. In one particularly relevant exchange, I shared my concerns about speaking "for" (or being perceived to speak for) all Muslims, and the ease with which even relatively tame work was misunderstood and even assaulted by academics (as mere opinion and not scholarship), and also by non-academics (as anti-government, anti-nation propaganda). I told Joe that my name had been posted on a conservative watchdog style "here are the Muslim lovers" hate blog that included a multitude of (specific and violent) allusions against me and (more so) a colleague I had worked with. I wrote to Joe, "As a new academic, I'm pushed to publish in academic journals, yet I also see how important it is for us to speak to the broader public, yet the costs are so high. How can these bloggers rationalize guarding their own anonymity so closely with mysterious user names like, "wisconsin republican" or "stake of the oppressor", not signing names to their hate speech, while simultaneously using the web to dig deep into our lives to find evidence of our radicality, including my colleague's wedding photos posted online for friends??"

This event was disturbing and frightening because as public scholars we could not hide behind anonymity. It was also personally disturbing because a year earlier

I had received threatening letters through campus mail for a different publication. I could feel myself frightened in to conformity and had inadvertently stepped in to knowing another way in which power circulates and manages any critique (however openly expressed). Joe was no stranger to these realities of doing critical work. He himself endured criticisms that would crush many and that walked a wobbly professional/personal line. In response to my frustration and fears as a novice doing counter-hegemonic work, he bore witness, "it's overwhelming. when i talk to most people from dominant cultural backgrounds, even those who think of themselves as progressive, they don't get that these things happen and the pain they cause. Sometimes such ignorance just overwhelms me. so, i do understand. know that i am an ally and will always attempt to do whatever i can. we'll keep on fighting."

Joe ended his email with his familiar valediction, "In solidarity." To Joe, "in solidarity" was anything but a slogan. The weaving together of the personal with the pedagogical, challenging the artificial disconnect of scholarship from "real life" were central commitments in Joe's work. In his last book, he wrote (2008):

> [C]riticality does not promiscuously choose theories to add to the bricolage of critical theories. It is highly suspicious of theories that fail to understand the malevolent workings of power, that fail to critique the blinders of Eurocentrism, that cultivate an elitism of insiders and outsiders ("we understand Foucault and you don't"), and that fail to discern global system of inequity supported by diverse forms of hegemony and violence. It is uninterested in any theory – no matter how fashionable – that does not directly address the needs of victims of oppression and the suffering they must endure. (p. 28).

This stance wasn't about propaganda or popularity – for he moved with ease in and beyond the spectrum of discourses from the most sophisticated academic ones to the most sophisticated "down home". What he believed was that any criticality must be in the service of more than itself. It must be engaged with exposing the institutional and historical structures that have held the status quo in place, and that it must connect to the lives of the oppressed. As another scholar whom Joe admired, Edward Said (1996) wrote, our role as critical scholars is to confront orthodoxy and dogma, and "to represent all those people and issues that are routinely forgotten or swept under the rug" (p. 11). Joe's work was embedded in these theoretical and personal commitments.

With *Muslim Voices in School*, he was always supportive, he enjoyed hearing about the development of each chapter and about the authors who have contributed their work to this collection. Eager to submit the completed manuscript to Joe and Shirley for their review, we were dotting the final "i"s and crossing the last "t"s in December. On December 19, 2008, while on vacation in Jamaica, Joe suffered a heart attack and died. If he were still alive, he more than most would have appreciated this collection, and the chapter authors' collective desire to *imagine what could be* in school where it is all too common not to ask the *why* questions.

For a man who committed his scholarship and his life to contribute to easing the suffering of others and who passionately believed in the possibilities that schools hold to contribute *to what could be*, we dedicate this book to Joe, a colleague, friend, and mentor, a brother and an ally to Muslims and the people of the Middle-

East. We miss him deeply and hope that this book captures the spirit of his dedication and helps to move another step forward in our collective work to harness scholarship to serve the betterment of humanity and the end to human suffering.

In solidarity...

REFERENCES

Apple, M. W. (2004). *Ideology and curriculum* (3rd ed.). New York: Routledge Flamer.

Apple, M. W. (1996). *Cultural politics & education*. New York: Teachers College Press.

Bayoumi, M. (2009). *How does it feel to be a problem: Being young and Arab in America*. New York: Penguin Press.

Churchill, W. (2004). *Kill the Indian, save the man*. California, CA: City Lights Books.

FAIR (Fairness & Accuracy in Reporting). (2001). "This isn't discrimination, this is necessary" Beware the "Arab-looking". [www document] URL. Retrieved from http://www.fair.org/index.php?page=1081

Freire, P., & Shor, I. (1986). *A pedagogy for liberation*. Westport, CT: Bergin & Garvey.

Ghareeb, E. (Ed.). (1983). *Split vision: The portrayals of Arabs in the American media*. Washington, DC: American-Arab Affairs Council.

Kincheloe, J. L. (2008). *Knowledge and critical pedagogy: An introduction*. New York: Springer.

Kincheloe, J. L., & Steinberg, S. R. (2004). *The miseducation of the West: The hidden curriculum of Western-Muslim relations*. New York: Greenwood Press.

Kincheloe, J. L. (2003). *Teachers as researchers*. New York: Routledge Falmer.

Kincheloe, J. L., & Steinberg, S. R. (1997). *Changing multiculturalism*. London: Open University Press.

McGruder, A. (2001, November 7). *The Boondocks*. Universal Press.

National Association of Arab Americans. (1980). *Treatment of the Arab world and Islam in Washington metropolitan area junior and senior textbooks*. Washington, DC: Author.

Nelson, H. L. (2001). *Damaged identities, narrative repair*. New York: Cornell University Press.

al-Qazzaz, A. (1975). Images of the Arabs in American social science textbooks. In Abu-Laban (Ed.), *Arabs in America* (pp. 113–132). Wilmette, IL: The Medina University Press International.

Said, E. W. (1979). *Orientalism*. New York: Vintage.

Said, E. W. (1996). *Representations of the intellectual*. New York: Vintage.

Said, E. W. (1997). *Covering Islam: How the media and experts determine how we see the rest of the world*. New York: Vintage.

Sensoy, Ö. (2007). Pedagogical strategies for disrupting gendered Orientalism: Mining the binary gap in teacher education. *Journal of Intercultural Education, 18*(4), 361–365.

Sensoy, Ö., & DiAngelo, R. J. (2006). "I wouldn't want to be a woman in the Middle East": White female narratives of Muslim oppression. *Radical Pedagogy, 8*(1).

Shaheen, J. G. (1984). *The TV Arab*. Bowling Green, Ohio: Bowling Green State University Popular Press.

Shaheen, J. G. (1991). The comic book Arab. *The Link, 24*(1), 1–11.

Shaheen, J. G. (1997). *Arab and Muslim stereotyping in American popular culture*. Washington, DC: Center for Muslim-Christian Understanding.

Shaheen, J. G. (2001). *Reel bad Arabs*. New York: Olive Branch Press.

Suleiman, M. W. (1977). *American images of Middle East peoples: Impact of the high school*. New York: Middle East Studies Association of North America Inc.

Suleiman, M. W. (1983). The effects of American perceptions of Arabs on Middle East issues. In E. Ghareeb (Ed.), *Split vision: The portrayal of Arabs in the American media* (pp. 337–344). Washington, DC: American-Arab Affairs Council.

Steet, L. (2000). *Veils and daggers: A century of national geographic's representation of the Arab world*. Philadelphia: Temple University Press.

Stonebanks, C. D. (2008). Spartan superhunks and Persian monsters: Responding to truth and identity as determined by Hollywood. *Studies in Symbolic Interaction, 31*, 207–221.

Stonebanks, C. D. (2008). An Islamic perspective on knowledge, knowing and methodology. In N. Denzin, Y. Lincoln, & L. T. Smith (Eds.), *Handbook of critical and indigenous methodologies* (pp. 293–321). California, CA: Sage Publications.

Stonebanks, C. D., & Sensoy, Ö. (2007). Did we miss the joke, again? The cultural learnings of two Middle East professors for make benefit insights on the glorious West. *Taboo: A Journal of Education and Culture, 11*(1), 41–51.

Waubageshig (1974). *The only good Indian*. Ontario: New Press.

PART 1:

VOICES & EXPERIENCES OF MUSLIM STUDENTS IN THE K-12 SCHOOL YEARS

MONA M. ABO-ZENA, BARBARA SAHLI AND
CHRISTINA SAFIYA TOBIAS-NAHI

TESTING THE COURAGE OF THEIR CONVICTIONS

Muslim Youth Respond to Stereotyping, Hostility, and Discrimination

INTRODUCTION

Anti-Muslim sentiment and discrimination targeting Muslims are on the rise, and school communities are not immune. While school systems strive to prepare students for responsible social and civic participation by promoting respect for diversity, educators often struggle to determine whether Muslims' beliefs conflict with Western values. This conflict may seem particularly volatile given the U.S.-led "War on Terror" and post 9/11 tensions that repeatedly link Islam, and Muslims in general, with terrorism. The underlying narrative presumes that Muslims and their values are rightly deserving of disdain, mistrust, and fear. This presumption places the burden on individual Muslims to disavow the actions and rhetoric of terrorists, or risk being viewed as supporting them.

Muslim youth are not exempt from this burden. Faced with misunderstanding and at times hostility, some Muslim youth try to defend themselves and their faith by explaining what they understand to be the principles of Islam to their teachers and peers. Others try to disassociate themselves from the generalized blame by attempting to conceal their Muslim identity. Still others experience dissonance between the values and behaviors of their families and those of their peers. Tensions and misunderstandings are further compounded by the difficulty in untangling myths about Islam and Muslims from realities. The dearth of diverse mainstream Muslim voices to receive attention highlights the need to explore the narratives of ordinary Muslims, particularly those of youth.

As Muslims working in educational settings and witnessing these escalating burdens that children and youth face, we recognize that the challenges did not begin on September 11, 2001. Even in our own lifetimes, we have witnessed and ourselves experienced the challenges of simply "being" Muslim. Our differing experiences and locations give us each a unique professional and personal point of entry into the topic.

Mona M. Abo-Zena is the daughter of Egyptian immigrants raised in a small town in Iowa. *Growing up, I was keenly aware that being Muslim made me different from my peers. Like other individuals from non-dominant social groups, I still catch myself doubting my own professional worthiness. My own experiences with marginalization led to my commitment to critical multicultural scholarship*

Ö. Sensoy and C.D. Stonebanks (eds.), Muslim Voices in School: Narratives of Identity
and Pluralism, 3–26.

and practice as a way to create inclusive school environments for all youth. As a teacher and administrator in both public and Islamic schools, I realized that I finally had the opportunity to validate the young girl who had been embarrassed to speak Arabic in public, and who guiltily mouthed the words to Christmas carols during music class. Through the use of diverse materials and the design of alternative classroom experiences, I have tried to create learning environments that recognize every individual in the learning community and emphasize both the limitations and opportunities surrounding feeling marginalized.

Barbara Sahli is an American-born convert to Islam. *From this perspective, I learned first-hand that fortitude is needed to reveal oneself as a practicing Muslim in a society that often holds negative connotations of Islam and Muslims. My inner journey towards Islam in adulthood was tempered by the knowledge that others would misunderstand. My decision to accept Islam strained family relationships and altered some professional ones. Being Muslim was akin to being an alien, a traitor. Years later, I made the choice to wear a hijab after prolonged internal deliberation. While I viewed it as an outward sign of my inner conviction, I understood that others would view my dress not as a sign of strength but of weakness. I realized wistfully that I would never again be "anonymous"—able to slip inconspicuously into a gathering and blend into the crowd. I knew that now I would stand out, be noticed, be known (or presumed to be known). Sometimes this was an advantage, as when curious individuals felt comfortable enough to approach me to ask questions about Islam, which I welcomed. At other times, in the supermarket, behind the wheel, or walking in the park, I occasionally received startled expressions, hostile gestures, or hateful glances. Frequently, strangers ask where I'm from, and my reply of "America" is usually greeted with, "Yes, but where are you really from?" To be a Muslim in America is to be perceived as an outsider, even if this is one's homeland.*

Christina Safiya Tobias-Nahi is an American who converted to Islam in France over a decade ago while pursuing a graduate degree. *There, I witnessed the furor over the l'affaire du foulard or the state ban against wearing the hijab in public schools and watched as a handful of young women decided to study on their own rather than be forced to give up their religious convictions. Similarly going through my own debate about whether to don the veil given how others might view me, I was inspired by these young women who were willing to forgo a formal diploma at whatever risk to their future careers, believing that ultimate success is not bestowed by others (teachers, employers) but by their Creator. At the same time, I was frustrated that a state would so readily marginalize some of its members simply for their religious dress. Like other freedom fighters before and since, they resisted the injustice and took a stand. The outcome of their decision is still unresolved, and the tensions still persist, both in France and in other countries including the United States.*[1]

SOCIO-CULTURAL FRAME OF ISLAM IN AMERICA

Like other youth, Muslim youth vary in terms of the salience of religious beliefs and practices in their lives. Further, the various national and ethno-cultural origins of Muslim youth, whether indigenous, immigrant, or refugee, give rise to cultural, ethnic, racial, gender, and socio-economic variation. The history of Islam in the United States is documented to have appeared during the time of slavery when a percentage of Africans captured and taken aboard slave ships were Muslim (Austin, 1997; Diouf, 1998; Alford, 2007). While there is evidence of isolated Muslim slaves maintaining their religious practice, the institution of slavery inhibited the free practice of religion and establishment of religious communities. Subsequent to such beginnings, voluntary immigrants of Muslim heritage started entering the United States during the late 19th century, largely from the Levant, which today includes Syria, Jordan, Palestine, and Lebanon (Haddad, 1987). After a decline in the practice of Islam by freed slaves, there was an Islamic resurgence among African Americans in the 1960s led by prominent Muslims such as Malcolm X. Simultaneously, the passage of the Immigration Act of 1965 marked an influx of Muslim immigrants, which transformed the American landscape with respect to religion (Eck, 2002). In addition to earlier waves of immigrants and their extended families, the largest percentage of Muslims in Western countries is comprised of relatively recent immigrants who represent more than 100 countries of origin. Understanding the plurality of Muslim history and experiences in the United States adds a nuanced dimension to the perceived homogeneity of Islamic history, beliefs, and practices. Muslims have some shared identifications based on religion, but also represent a tremendous racial, ethnic, and cultural diversity (Sirin & Balsano, 2007).

Like other ethnic or racial minority youth who must respond, either internally or externally, to negative images about their group (c.f. Spencer & Markstrom-Adams, 1990), Muslim youth face qualitatively different identity tasks than do many of their peers. Feelings of defensiveness and of being under attack or scrutiny because of their religion are widely considered to be part of the fabric of a Muslim youth's life experiences, and thus this psychological dimension and fear of being an outcast is an aspect of their lives within the school context (Kahf, 2006; Beshir, 2004; Zine, 2001). Hostile behavior and bullying in school settings is a common reality for Muslim students, evidenced by incidents of discrimination that have occurred nationwide in the classroom, in the cafeteria, during extra-curricular activities, and on the school bus, where the perpetrators have been not only students, but also teachers and other school personnel.[2]

THE CONTEXT OF FEATURED YOUTH NARRATIVES

This chapter shares and studies the narratives of personal courage written by Muslim sixth graders as part of the Max Warburg Courage Curriculum[3], a regional competition for public and private schools in the greater Boston area. The humanities program memorializes Max Warburg, a sixth grader who exemplified courage as he lived with and died from leukemia in 1991. The program encourages students to recognize examples of courage in their own lives. The curriculum includes a selection of novels that illustrate the courage of young protagonists, some of whom faced racial, ethnic, and religious discrimination (e.g., *Roll of Thunder, Hear My Cry, So Far from the Bamboo Grove,* and *Number the Stars)* and culminates with students drafting their own personal narratives of courage. Students are particularly motivated by the fact that one narrative from each participating school will be published in the annual collection of essays, featuring a portrait of each young author. Finally, all students whose essays are published, along with their teachers and parents, are hosted at a gala luncheon held in a hotel banquet hall with guest speakers including the Mayor of Boston.

As with any curriculum, the degree to which any given teacher follows it or incorporates it into the classroom environment varies. Having taught this unit for several years at an Islamic school, one of us (Sahli) noted the enthusiasm with which students approached this particular writing assignment. Indeed, students produced their best writing for this project, perhaps because the personal narratives gave them permission to consider examples of courage in their own lives – examples that often go unnoted, but that nonetheless require considerable inner strength. Her introduction to the writing process began with a discussion of the meaning of courage and emphasized that true courage did not require a superhero, but rather it could be exhibited by ordinary individuals who overcome their fears in their daily lives. She modeled her own "courage" by sharing her personal story of deciding to wear the hijab despite the negative reaction of others. Students brainstormed other examples of courage, such as standing up for a friend who was being teased, facing a fear, or fasting during Ramadan while in public school. After listing several ideas for examples of their own personal courage, each student selected a focus and drafted her or his narrative. Through peer editing and teacher conferencing, each essay went through multiple revisions in order to fine-tune vivid word choice, supporting details, and sentence fluency. All the finished essays were placed on display at school and reflected the students' hard work and pride in the endeavor.

Some students chose topics that reflect experiences common to a broad spectrum of youth, such as dealing with the death of a family member or overcoming shyness. Others highlighted aspects of their experiences as Muslims, such as responding to stereotyping and being characterized as "other" because of their belonging to a marginalized group. In order to draw the marginalized voices to the center, this chapter features essays[4] describing how youth respond to alienation and includes published and unpublished narratives of Muslim students from both Islamic and public school settings. The stories highlight the diversity of Muslim youth voices and introduce native born, immigrant origin, and refugee youth from at least seven countries spanning three continents. While their voices reflect the hybrid nature of their backgrounds, they share an important similarity: through a range of behaviors, these students publicly and actively self-identify as Muslim. Consequently, the narratives provide an opportunity to consider the *meaning* of religious practices to those who observe them. Furthermore, the students' voices starkly reveal how some Muslim students negotiate their religious identity and religious practice in a context that often includes explicit ‹ themes of misunderstanding, fear, and marginalization. The stories of stigm may be a result of religious discrimination, or because of one's race or ethnicity, or when a youth's religious practices distinguish him or her from non-Muslim peers. This chapter reflects on what narratives may mean to the youth themselves given the stories that they choose to share.

> "We construct our identity through the stories we choose to tell about ourselves. Stories reach across culture and establish meaning. Stories form a language beneath our other languages. They place authority in the heart of the listener. Stories help us locate ourselves in time and place" (Storytellers and Listeners for Peace and Healing, 2008).

Finally, the chapter concludes with practical suggestions on an individual, classroom and school or policy level.

FEELING MARGINALIZED BY RELIGIOUS DISCRIMINATION

While an individual Muslim youth's responses to negative images about Islam may vary according to a number of factors (e.g., level of religious commitment, quality of friendships and family support), youth who are faced with negative portrayals seek to develop adaptive responses where they utilize their personal resources of resilience to meet the challenges of the context (Lerner, 2002).

Sixth-grader Jelani tells the story of being caught in a quandary where he is at once confused and terrorized by the 9/11 attacks, but at the same time feels compelled to prove his religion's innocence:

> ...Before September 11th, I remember my mother and other Muslims talking about the Oklahoma City bombing. They held their breath hoping and praying that Muslims were not involved. Immediately, Muslims were unjustly targeted. After the arrest of Timothy McVeigh the Muslim community was relieved.

> However, September 11th proved to be something different...I wanted to keep using the word horrible because horror is what I felt. I kept on thinking how evil; whoever did this thing was evil. Then I found out that the people who perpetrated this evil claimed Islam (the religion Muslims follow) as their way of life. Islam–this beautiful religion, the way I have lived and known the world all of my life, was being charged with the taking of thousands of innocent lives....

> For us Muslims, this act of violence was a heavy burden to carry, knowing that people now saw me and the rest of the Muslims as targets for anger, targets for revenge, and targets for retaliation. I knew that people gave me dirty looks and yelled hateful things and sometimes even killed people who wore clothes that represented the Muslim religion or appeared to be from Middle Eastern descent; it was from their own ignorance they reacted this way.

7

The Muslims in America could not let the portrayals of hatred stop them and I couldn't let it stop me! It just wasn't the same life as it was before. It took courage just to walk out of the house. One day I was walking down a street in my neighborhood when a car started to follow me. I didn't let that scare me. I just kept on walking. I glanced and the person driving glanced away. Then all of a sudden I heard a glass bottle break right behind me; then the car drove off. I wasn't hurt, but I was terrified! I knew I couldn't give into that fear. I wasn't going to let anybody's ignorance affect me.

People yelling hateful things don't [sic] affect me like it did a couple weeks after the attacks. Most people got it through their heads that the people who crashed the planes into what was once the World Trade Center and some of the Pentagon building did not represent the principles of Islam...I have to be courageous to be a Muslim in America."

Jelani Lynch, 6th grade male, public school, 2002

Educators in mainstream institutions would generally agree that it is problematic for students of minority religious, ethnic, or cultural groups to be spotlighted to speak for or otherwise justify what "their group" thinks or what members of their group do. There is acknowledgment of the tremendous diversity within the group and the potentially harmful effects of such spotlighting on the children. But in reality, particularly after 9/11, many Muslim youth have been asked to explain the motivation for the attacks, as though they could speak for the perpetrators of terror. As Jelani's story recounts, his mother and her friends held their breath, knowing that if the perpetrators were Muslim, they would be held to account. It is common for many Muslims to feel 'guilty by association' because often Islam is implicated as part of the problem. Although current events often reference abhorrent acts committed by individuals belonging to all kinds of groups, basic fairness generally prevents holding an entire group responsible for the actions of individual members. To cite a well-known example, the sex abuse scandal within the Catholic Church did not result in a broad backlash of hatred towards ordinary Catholics or even towards all priests. Blame was placed squarely on those priests who committed the acts and on those in authority who covered up the crimes and allowed them to continue. Faithful Catholics who were outraged and pained by the crimes did not have their pain compounded by a barrage of attacks on their religion and their persons or the ensuing slander, surveillance, and suspicion that Muslims have faced.

While Jelani's narrative indicates that he found the courage to deal with religious discrimination, not all youth have such positive outcomes. Consider the tragic story retold on National Public Radio (NPR) of a fourth grade Muslim girl who was deeply traumatized after her teacher presented an inflammatory book to 'educate' the class about the 9/11 tragedy.[5] The young Muslim girl relates how her classmates' attitudes towards her changed: "They all saw me as a different person – like before reading the book [they thought] I was just a normal child and then [after reading it, they thought] I turned into an Islamic extremist who hated the world and wanted to kill everybody.... All my friends were starting to question me— 'Why does your mom wear that on her head?' 'Are you sure you're really not related to him' [Osama bin Laden]?" Students began taunting her, calling her "loser Muslim" and "Osama." The young girl was so traumatized by the situation that she suffered deep harm; her father's inability to cope with his daughter's devastating encounter with prejudice led to the eventual breakdown of the family unit. This story is an extreme example of the effect classroom marginalization can have on a student's identity.

Muslim youth may feel marginalized simply because they are Muslim. If they are teased by their peers because they *are* Muslim, or because they *are not* Christian they may in turn feel ashamed of their religion or internalize a negative religious group image. Even more extreme, they may disassociate from outward demonstrations of religious practice in order to minimize the apparent differences between themselves and their non-Muslim peers. Muslim youth may feel pressured to keep secret, deny or even abandon their Muslim faith in an attempt to blend in. Perhaps as a coping mechanism, some youth may adopt practices or behaviors that they (or their families or religious communities) feel are not in line with Islam. Such responses to religious pressure and discrimination are explored in a large scale study of religion in the lives of adolescents in the U.S. where Smith and Denton (2005) found that religious minority youth are more likely than peers from mainstream religions to incorporate aspects of other religions into their own values.

While such openness to religious pluralism may be considered a "normal" part of religious exploration in the U.S. context, such scenarios put Muslim youth, and other religious minority youth at risk because for them, the norms at home may conflict with the norms at school. How does one develop a sense of coherence and stability when "fitting in" at home and school may require opposite or different actions? One author (Abo-Zena) states, *I recall telling my kindergarten teachers that my parents would be upset if I touched the piglet[6] that for some reason was a guest in our classroom. The teacher reassured me that it would be fine. At home, my mother and I shared the routine conversation about what I had done at school. I can still hear the disgust in my mother's voice as she repeatedly told me to wash my hands. Unlike the promises of my teachers (whom I trusted unconditionally), it was not fine (at home) to have touched the piglet. Although the subject of contention varied throughout my childhood, the central theme remained: what was "normal" at school was not "normal" at home, and vice versa.*

While there are Muslim youth who maintain high levels of religious commitment, it is important to note that even they extend a large amount of energy to process the overall negative appraisals of their religious group. Even though Jelani reports rebounding after experiencing religious discrimination, we must remember the countless youth who face similar challenges, but whose stories have less fortunate endings.

MARGINALIZED BY IMMIGRANT STATUS, RACE, AND RELIGION

The various images used to describe the assimilation process for U.S. immigrants (e.g. melting pot, salad bowl, mosaic) outline the task for the immigrant and the host community; the "melting pot" implies a degree of cultural heritage loss, but it does not explain the fate of those who cannot or choose not to "melt." Immigrants who are religious minorities may also be racial minorities or have cultural values and behaviors that seem divergent from some mainstream values and behaviors, further heightening their sense of being outsiders. Consider Adam's writing on how he dealt with immigration status, race, and being Muslim:

...In the first grade, I was not a person who spoke English that well. I spoke my native language, Somalian. In my class, I was the only person that was from Africa. I did not want people to dislike me because of the country I was from or because of my religion, so I did not say anything. The fear of being an outcast was overwhelming.

One day, I thought that enough was enough. I announced it to everyone in my class. I told them that I was a Somalian and a Muslim and that I was proud of it. Some kids did not know what a Muslim or a Somalian was, due to their limited knowledge of the world.

I want people to say, "I don't care what you say or where you're from because I will still love you."

Adam N. Farah, 6th grade male, public school, 2006

Adam's fear of being without close friends and generally disliked because of his religion and being from Somalia could negatively impact his school performance through underperformance (Steele, 1997) and his inability to make and maintain friends, a key element of social adjustment (Paley, 1992; Tobias-Nahi & Garfield, 2007). Adam's narrative reveals that while his emerging English language skills may have been perceived as a deficit by his classmates and teacher, he recognized his knowledge base exceeded that of the peers who, as he says, "had little knowledge of the world"; he had fluency in another language and knowledge about aspects of the world that his classmates lacked. While they may have dismissed him and isolated him due to his inferior English skills, his announcement to the class about his religious and ethnic identity was a brave proclamation that demonstrated self-esteem impressive for a first grader. It is also noteworthy that when asked to narrate a story of personal courage as a sixth grader, Adam recalled this formative experience from five years earlier. In his young life, this makes the point startlingly clear how significant these moments of identity challenge and articulation are.

Particularly for the immigrant child, the uprooting experience and journey to the new home are important aspects of the personal narrative that contain intricate details about challenges and opportunities the child and family face (Igoa, 1995). While the current school climate characterized by high-stakes testing evaluates proficiency through standardized tests, schools and their assessment measures seem not to value the real-world skills and character possessed by many of the students (e.g., proficiency in languages other than English, strength developed in dealing with a traumatic situation). While Adam's story highlights the negotiation of identity in a new location, Kowsar shares a "coming to America" story punctuated with violence and disruption:

> I showed courage the time I left my country. It is not easy leaving your home but I had to because of a war between my country, Somalia, and another country. Many people died and their homes were destroyed.
>
> It all began in 1990 when my family and I were eating dinner. We heard a gunshot. We all ran in one room, looked out the window, and saw people running. My father said we had to leave. We packed the important things we needed and we left the house. At that time my mother was pregnant. I had to stay strong for my younger sister and brothers. We walked far into the woods. That night, we slept in a little cave. About a week later we came to a place called Kenya. We stayed there with my grandfather. I thought we were going back to Somalia.
>
> After a year my father said we had to go to America. I was sad leaving my country and my friends, but I knew it was for the best and I didn't want my younger sister and brothers to feel sad too. It took a lot of courage to be strong.

Kowsar Haji, 6th grade female, public school, 1999

Kowsar's identity as a Muslim can be assumed by noting her name and nation of origin, and observing her photograph published alongside her essay where she dons the hijab. Instead of explicitly discussing her identity as a Muslim, though, Kowsar's narrative focuses on other key contextual circumstances. A war in her native country of Somalia forces her family to become refugees and they had to relocate at least twice. Being the oldest, Kowsar not only had to deal with her own abrupt dislocation, but had to lead her younger siblings and assist her parents during a transition phase that took years. The adjustment to living in a new land included the need to master another language. While both immigrant and refugee students share the challenges of adapting to a new country and the likely separation from extended family, refugee youth have additional challenges that often include exposure to war and other violence and a likely long-term, if not permanent, separation from their native land and sometimes their nuclear and extended family. Unlike immigrant peers who are able to maintain heritage language and other aspects of culture as well as personal relationships during regular or occasional travel to their homeland, refugee youth are largely cut off from travel to their native country and are more likely to experience downward socio-economic mobility than immigrant peers (Suárez-Orozco & Suárez-Orozco, 2001). Kowsar's narrative resists prevailing assumptions that characterize refugees as helpless, pitiable figures in a state of loss. Instead she shows the sacrifice and strength needed to endure a violent disruption of her life.

FEELING MARGINALIZED BY PUBLIC AND "DIFFERENT" RELIGIOUS PRACTICE

Students who strive to maintain their religious identity and practice in a non-Muslim country negotiate a balance between their beliefs and what is considered normative in broader society. Ritual prayer, one of the pillars of Islam, is performed five times per day at designated time windows that correspond to the position of the sun. In this way, a practicing Muslim's routine is punctuated by brief intervals of prayer throughout the day. Because Osama's family believes that prayer at its designated time is a priority, he regularly takes 5 to 10 minutes to perform prayer in any permissible place that includes home, school, the mosque, or a public place.

In his essay written in early 2001, Osama describes his adherence to the prayer schedule as an obligation to keep an appointment with the Creator:

> Imagine having a meeting with the President of the United States. Would you be late? Of course not. Well I had a meeting with the Creator of the Universe. Being Muslim means you have a different life than most people. You have to pray five times a day. When you pray to Allah (the Arabic word for the one God) you wouldn't want to miss that meeting.

> Once I got into a situation when the time of the meeting came and I didn't think I could make it. My family was going to Canada and the time for prayer came. My dad stopped at a rest area with a gas station and a restaurant. After lunch, I went to the bathroom to make *wudu*. (Wudu means washing up in a special way to became clean for prayer.) While I was making wudu, eyes were on me longer than they needed to be. I felt uncomfortable because I knew that behind my back people were thinking, "Who is this maniac washing so strangely?" I couldn't wait to leave the bathroom, so I quickly finished washing.

> Then the hard part came. I would have to pray in front of everyone. My dad told me to pray in the Arcade room. I knew that's the place all the kids would be. I went in and there were some kids playing. I tried thinking of things I could do to avoid praying in front of them. I could go and lie to my dad and say that I prayed, or not pray and not tell my dad, or pray in the car. But I knew I had to pray so I pushed all those sneaky thoughts away and started praying. One kid stared at me for a while. I thought he must have been thinking, "Who is this crazy kid bowing to an arcade game?" I couldn't stand it any longer. I wanted to stop and run out of the room, but my conscience kept telling me to keep at it. Knowing I had to pray kept me from breaking away. After a while, the kid was losing interest in me and started focusing on his game. This gave me a big boost in trying to complete my prayer.

> As I finished praying I learned that I could pray anywhere, even if someone was watching me. If I find myself in that situation again, I would know what to do. I learned that praying to Allah is much more important than worrying about what other people think.

Osama Duwaji, 6ᵗʰ grade male, Islamic school, 2001

In his story, Osama faces a difficult moral choice. After an initial struggle, he pushes past his conflict between following his beliefs and his awareness that observers may not only scrutinize his actions but also ostracize him. Since 9/11, the unfortunate linkage of terrorism with religious practices has affected ordinary Muslims. Misunderstandings arise, as in the well-publicized incident of six imams who prayed at the airport before boarding their plane and aroused the fear of some fellow passengers, resulting in their removal from the flight (Conlon, 2006). Muslim youth, particularly males with identifiable Muslim names or beards and females who veil, experience marginalization caused by hate speech such as being told to "go back to your country." Osama recounted his trip to the public library weeks after the 9/11 attacks. After he routinely provided the librarian his library card, she noted his name and, perhaps involuntarily, gave him an apprehensive look. Osama concluded that this is not a good time to be named Osama. He and other Muslim youth have already been socialized to realize that others see them as threatening. How do adult caregivers begin to erase or replace the negative images being internalized?

Further, like parents of racial minority children (McLoyd, Hill, & Dodge; 2005/2007), parents of Muslim children must navigate issues such as cultural socialization and preparation for bias so that their children are equipped to deal with the unfortunate realities of religious and ethnic profiling and surveillance. One author, (Abo-Zena) recalls listening to an NPR feature about Muslims with her then five year old son. *My son perked up when he heard the radio announcer refer to Muslims and asked me what the story was about. I hesitated before answering. How much should I share with such a young boy? I worried that he might have picked up on the negative tone of the broadcast, whether or not either of us were ready for the conversation. If I didn't answer him explicitly and reflect the tone of the story, how would my son interpret feeling that I was evading him and his questions? I heard myself answer that, "Some people don't like Muslims very much." When he asked why, I replied that most probably don't know much about us, so we'll have to show people that we are good. Unfair as it is, I have to prepare my children for the reality that our humanity is not assumed, and we have to work actively to persuade others of it.*

Because of fears of being the victim of a religious hate crime or of being targeted due to increased surveillance or religious and ethnic profiling, Muslim youth are challenged to maintain the basic practices of the religion, as Munther illustrates:

> It was a few weeks after September 11, 2001 and my family was going shopping in the ...mall.... While we were walking, I saw everyone looking at us as if we were terrorists. You wouldn't notice it at first, but every one who looked at us was pointing fists at us. One even mouthed a swear at me. My dad didn't notice, but I did.

> Then my dad stopped dead in his tracks because he remembered we had to pray. I was hoping that we could pray at home. Unfortunately, we went to pray next to the most popular store there. I felt as if I was trapped in the

middle of a circle and there was no way out. When we started praying, I felt the bare floor with my forehead. I was really scared. I thought that people were exchanging looks of fear and hatred, or thinking we had a gun or a knife. I was panic-stricken but I kept saying in my head, "I can survive this." I knew I couldn't move until I finished the prayer. Then finally the prayer was over. I felt as if there were crowds cheering. My dad noticed the happiness on my face and said, 'That's my boy.'

We headed home and it was the best day of my life because I showed a lot of courage by standing up for myself and doing what my religion tells me to do even though other people might not understand....

Munther El-Alami, 6ᵗʰ grade male, Islamic school, 2003

While Osama worries that others will view his ritual washing and prayer as strange, Munther is scared that others will interpret his prayer as a sign he is a terrorist, and feels physically threatened. It seems an oxymoron that prayer – a highly spiritual and meditative activity – could be viewed instead by onlookers as threatening and dangerous. But as the stories of both boys demonstrate, the meta-narratives associating Islam with terrorism, backwardness, and fear circulate broadly in mainstream U.S. society, such that the most "ordinary" of activities in a Muslim's day are misconstrued as being "deviant" and frightening.

MARGINALIZED BY GENDER AND VEILING

As in many religious communities, the style of dress in Islam is mediated by cultural as well as regional norms with secular, practicing, and orthodox Muslims expressing a diversity of dress styles. For some Muslim females and males, modesty of dress and behavior are an integral part of their faith, each gender following particular guidelines for dress (al-Hilâlî & Khan, 1404). Because many in the West tend to judge Islamic dress in relation to *Western* norms (especially norms of gender relations) and separate from the broader and multiple contexts of Islam, adherents to Islamic dress guidelines are often interpreted within a framework of Western ideas about what Muslim dress (especially dress for women) *means*. Despite mainstream perceptions that all Muslim girls and women are forced by oppressive Muslim men to wear a scarf, the following narratives reveal a great deal of agency. Taking a principled stand with respect to one's position and values is not without consequences, though. Afnan, for instance, details her choice in her decision to cover:

Courage is doing the right thing without fear and compromise. A short time after 9/11 many Muslims were afraid of expected discrimination and harassment as a consequence of biased media coverage. Some Muslims were too afraid to even go shopping, go to work, or to the mosque. Even worse, some Muslim women were afraid to wear their hijabs outside their homes. It was a painful, fearful time for Muslim individuals and families. During this time my mom started writing a book on hijab. Many times I overheard her discussing book chapters with her friends about the importance, merit, and benefits of hijab. Her words attracted me and I believed in it more. I wanted to wear hijab, but I was hesitant. It took me three stages to reach my final decision. First I asked my parents for their opinions, but they said that I was free to do what I wanted and they were not going to force the hijab on me. Second, I thought hard about it. I considered the benefits and the good deeds I would be rewarded, then of the disadvantages of how I would be treated in public. Finally, I made my decision; with courage and no hesitation, I decided on wearing the hijab. Nowadays, I feel very proud of myself that I made the right decision and was able to practice my religion with freedom and courage.

Afnan Nehela, 6th grade female, Islamic school, 2007

In contrast to the rational tone of Afnan's story that recounts her deliberative process in making her decision, Amina tells the story of how she felt disempowered because of her experience with veiling in a public school and how this feeling changed in the supportive environment of an Islamic school setting:

It all started when I was in 3rd grade. I wore a hijab (a headscarf) to school one day and every one stared at me. They kept asking me what I was wearing and why, so I never wore it again. It made me feel self-conscious. I wear it because it is for religious reasons. It shows modesty in my religion.

The next year I wore it in 4th grade in an Islamic school and I felt much better and I didn't care about what people said about what I wore. Now I wear it everywhere I go and I wear it with confidence and I stick up for what I believe in.

Amina A. Zekeria, 6th grade female, Islamic school, 2007

For some Muslims like Amina, their manner of dress starkly marks them as a religious other. Although Islamic dress for women is an outward display of an internal faith decision, it is often misinterpreted by the West as a sign of oppression and generally perceived as something foreign and undesirable. Thus, it can make Muslim youth and their families the objects of alienation, glares, and suspicious glances, and sometimes even the targets of hateful speech and action. The girls who cover with whom we have worked discuss the countless questions of curiosity they field in order to justify their physical appearance:

"Do you have to wear that at home?"

"Don't you get hot?"

"Do you wear that in the shower?"

While some questions may be asked with innocence, they exist in the context of epithets propagated by the media such as the Hollywood movie *Towelhead* (2008) based on the novel with the same title. While the content of the film and book were not the point of contention voiced by Muslims, there was opposition to the use of a slur as a title. As CAIR-LA Executive Director Hussam Ayloush said,

"Mainstreaming a bigoted term in this manner will only serve to legitimize and normalize anti-Muslim prejudice in our society" (CAIR, 2008).

The misunderstanding surrounding the veil may alienate Muslim girls from peers, particularly non-Muslim ones. Non-Muslim students who wish to befriend Muslim peers may struggle to reconcile their friendships with the often negative mainstream discourses they hear from their own parents and society around them. For example, Fatimah's story illustrates how subtle and covert the process of alienation can be:

> The way I show courage is by wearing my *hijab* (head scarf) full-time. A girl who wears her hijab full-time is called a Muhajaba. I became a Muhajaba in 2nd grade. Wearing a hijab was hard at first, but I got used to it. When I told my classmates that I wore my hijab full-time, they asked me why. They asked if I was hot with my hijab on. I replied that it was hot sometimes, but I want to please God.

> Sometimes I participate in camps and educational programs with non-Muslims. The kids in these programs ask, "Why do you wear that rag on your head?" I tell them that it is not a rag, it is a scarf, and I wear it because of my religion. I am a Muslim. The kids respect me for being strong. In one science camp, I received an award for being a "Model Camper." A Model Camper is one who has good behavior and treats others well.

> Some of my friends' mothers were attacked for wearing a hijab after the World Trade Center was bombed in September. Some of my friends who used to be Muhajabas stopped because their mothers were afraid for their safety. I had many thoughts about changing my mind, but I stuck with my decision. Obeying God is what gives me the courage to be a Muhajaba.

Fatimah Mahdee, 6th grade female, Islamic school, 2002

As these girls' narratives reveal, wearing a hijab routinely provokes condescension, discrimination, fear, and anger, reactions which are not ordinarily directed toward the outward faith expressions of other religious groups. A possible explanation for the disparity in treatment may be that mainstream Westerners know little about Muslim females' reasons for dressing modestly and covering their hair, but the reality is that they have received a great deal of negative messaging about the hijab. Unfortunately, the messages seem to convey themes of oppression, violence, and lack of choice. As one Muslim girl experienced, females who choose not to display themselves in public may encounter insults and resentment:

> Last summer, I went to the zoo with my friends and we were all wearing hijab....I overheard a man who was working there saying, "They cover their heads because they're ugly inside." I was shocked and frightened. I just wanted to shout and yell at him that we don't wear it because of that. Then I remembered that I chose to wear it even though I knew people would say ugly insults and do mean things (Tobias-Nahi & Garfield, 2007, p. 90).

Muslim females who cover confront assumptions about their weakness, oppression, lack of freedom and perceived lower status in Islam. Indeed, Westerners, and in particular, Western females, view Muslim women as "the archetypal oppressed woman in stark contrast to their own perceived liberation," not recognizing or considering their own oppression (Sensoy & DiAngelo, 2006, para. 3). Some examples of Western women's oppression include how females still receive unequal pay for equal work, how they routinely confront sexual harassment in the workplace and in other social interactions, and how the fashion, media, and entertainment industries dictate norms about sexuality and physical attractiveness, promoting an unrealistic image of beauty that pressures women to appear ever-thinner, ever-younger, and ever-sexier. Alternately, many Muslims who cover report feeling liberated because they reserve their sexuality and beauty for their husbands and are free from uninvited sexual attention and obsession with appearance. Rather than allowing others to judge their physical appearance, they expect to be valued for their deeds, character, and intelligence. Thus, these narratives about the hijab actively counter and respond to discourse that is deeply engrained in popular society regarding gender and veiling.

Through more accurate and personal exchanges with the 'other,' encounters both inside and outside of school can be facilitated. One such illustrative narrative involves Ruqayya, a girl who loves sports but hesitated to participate because of her concerns about how others would react to her hijab. She explains:

> ...Every year when my mother registered my brothers for their teams, she would ask me if I wanted to play and I always said, "no" though I really wanted to play. You see, I have always gone to an Islamic school and all of my friends are Muslims.
>
> I never really communicated with non-Muslims, so I was kind of nervous because sometimes people treat us badly because we look different. They would make fun of the way we dress and call us names. I thought that if I were to play on a soccer team with them, they would do the same. Also, I would have to get special permission [from the coach] so that I could wear pants instead of shorts and my headscarf, which is called a hijab.
>
> This year when my mom asked me, I gathered up all the courage I could find and decided to try out for the team. The first day was really hard. I was nervous just walking up to the field. I expected to hear laughing and whispering behind my back. Instead, a few girls came over and said hello to me. I was too nervous to do more than whisper a response.
>
> They asked a few questions about my religion, but that was OK. I went to practice a few times, and then realized that not all people treat Muslims badly. Some people can be very nice and friendly even if they are totally different. If I had not tried out for the team, I would not know how strong and courageous I could be.

Ruqayya El-Asmar, 6th grade female, Islamic school, 2004

By overcoming a reluctance to participate in new experiences for fear of the reactions of others, barriers can be broken down and there is potential for the positive development of Muslim and non-Muslim youth. Friendships that involve diverse religious and/or ethnic groups provide a solid foundation for the construction of allies who can support each other in addressing issues of civic equality. For example, in a series of incidents in Canada (Myers, 2007; Scott, 2007), referees prevented Muslim girls from playing soccer while wearing a hijab purportedly for safety reasons, although previously they had been allowed to play without incident. In response, the entire team and sometimes other teams in the league were willing to forfeit the match in protest of what the girls and their supportive coaches and parents recognized was a thinly disguised case of religious discrimination. Unlike passive types of learning, experiential knowledge and authentic interactions such as these are often powerfully instructive in creating empathy and providing meaningful lessons in character development (Sahli, Tobias-Nahi & Abo-Zena, 2009).

AT THE MARGINS: WHETHER TO AFFIRM ONE'S MUSLIM IDENTITY

Some Muslim youth may acknowledge their religious faith internally, but may think carefully about whether and when to reveal their faith to others. Muslims who are not recognizable as such have the option to decide whether to self-identify as Muslims, which is a choice that may be perceived as both a privilege and burden. The responses to negative images about Islam may lead to a variety of outcomes, including maladaptive responses where youth develop behaviors and approaches that are inconsistent and appear disingenuous because of feelings of shame or being conflicted (al Jabri, 1995; Zine, 2001). This is different from bicultural competence where youth generally develop different knowledge and skills for different contexts and can readily "switch" between settings maintaining a positive identification with both or all aspects of their social group membership (LaFramboise, Coleman & Gerton, 1993) During the "carefree" days of summer, Yacob struggles with fears of social isolation and worries about violating his religious beliefs.

> I was running though the woods when they spotted me. They started to chase me, so I ran off the trail. Thorny bushes scraped my bare arms and mosquitoes were eating me alive. I was lost and got stuck in a swamp. I was knee deep in water and couldn't find my way out. How did I get into this situation? My parents had decided to send me to a YMCA summer camp. I hated the idea because I wanted to stay home and play Sony Playstation. It would be a change for me to be around people other than Muslims because I went to Muslim school.

> When I got to the YMCA on my first day of camp, butterflies swarmed in my stomach. A thousand thoughts passed through my mind. I wondered if I would make friends. As I looked around the waiting room, it seemed like a big reunion. Most of the campers knew each other. When I got onto the bus, I felt like getting off, but I made sure to take care of my younger brother.

After arriving at camp, we started the day by playing manhunt. I was a little afraid because I did not know these woods. That's how I got stuck in this swamp. When I managed to get out, I was covered in mud. I was afraid everyone was going to laugh at me. But they did not. They were curious about what had happened to me. After that I did not dread camp.

I made lots of friends over the summer. Then one day my friends asked me what religion I believed in. I felt like lying to them because I was afraid they might tease me. I found the courage by remembering that people should not lie about their religion. I was still the same person inside. I stuttered and told them, "I am Muslim." Then they started to get interested and asked questions about Islam. Finally I realized camp was not so bad after all. I think it took courage for me to tell them what religion I believed because I could have just lied to them, but instead I told the truth.

Yacob Eid, 6th grade male, Islamic school, 2003

Parents, educators, and a range of public and private stakeholders share the imperative to create inclusive school and broader environments so that all youth find a welcoming and safe place to develop.

OTHER LAYERS OF VISIBILITY AND INVISIBILITY

Not all Muslim youth are forthcoming about their religious beliefs and values. Many Muslim youth are visible because their names, dress, or nation of origin "mark" them as Muslim, but their beliefs and practices may or may not be consistent with their ascribed identity. While research suggests that the importance of faith for youth tracks fairly closely with the importance of religion to the parents (Smith & Denton, 2005), there is limited discussion of inter-parent and intra-parent variability in religious practice, or parents who do not belong to the same religious tradition or denomination. Like youth of other religions, Muslim youth experience this variation and discontinuity within the nuclear family and beyond it. Other Muslim youth are difficult to identify (e.g., females who do not cover, students whose names and family histories are not associated strongly with Islam), and these youth may stress their Muslim identity selectively based on the context and other factors. Many other Muslim youth choose or feel forced to keep their Muslim identity invisible. Some may not have strong religious convictions, while others feel that being perceived as a practicing Muslim may put them at risk of being isolated or looked down upon. Finally, like other aspects of development, religious identity is a dynamic one and closely interwoven with other aspects of their context and identity, and thus shaped by the accumulation of experiences. As described by a researcher of minority youth development and schools, "Identity-building in cultural and social spaces is not a one-time process, but involves a continual negotiation and renegotiation between children and schools" (Nassir, 2004, p. 155) and other salient aspects of their social context.

SUGGESTED ACTIONS FOR EDUCATORS

While it is important to sustain an inclusive learning environment throughout the year, teachers could particularly reinforce the inclusiveness of the classroom at the start of the school year. With increasing numbers of immigrant and refugee students, the classroom has become a testing ground for contact between different cultures. Teachers could use multiple strategies to actively affirm and reflect the contributions and challenges that students and their families bring to the learning process. All levels of school context (e.g., classroom and school policy, curriculum, materials) could attend to the multiple levels of students' identities; particular attention should be made to highlight backgrounds that may have been omitted from positive portrayals and include the language biography of students, aspects of race and ethnicity, family constellation, and a child's "coming to America" story. In addition, inclusiveness should go beyond token or superficial acknowledgements of diversity that merely display the artifacts of different social or cultural groups and actively explore what the artifacts mean to the people who use them.

Furthermore, there is a clear need to work with teachers to examine their own lenses and assumptions so they are better equipped not only to deal proactively with their students, but also to guide students in the same critical self-reflection of their biases in order to "interrupt the perpetuation of inequality" that can occur when the sources of our knowledge and beliefs about others are left unexamined and unchallenged (Sensoy & DiAngelo, 2006). Such approaches to the learning environment can occur through a multicultural and anti-bias curriculum, while setting a vigilant tone with zero-tolerance of actions and speech that threaten students physically or psychologically.

On a school or institutional level, educational contexts should strive to accommodate Muslim youth who wish to fulfill religious obligations while at school. School systems should consider adopting an inclusive religious accommodations policy (CAIR, 1999). This may include arrangements for modifications of physical education dress requirements, compliance with dietary laws in the breakfast and lunch program (e.g., putting an image of a pig on foods containing pork products in the lunch line so that emerging-literate children can easily identify food content), and accommodations for fasting students or those observing prayer. For students who wish to pray in school, parents and school staff are encouraged to meet to discuss provisions for adequate prayer space during the designated times. Within a study of world religions, teachers could make use of resources within the community by inviting practicing members of a faith tradition to help understand the religion in context.

In language arts and social studies curricular contexts, teachers can support students to critically analyze written and multimedia images. Consistent with tenets of multicultural educational standards, educators should select literature and class materials that provide inclusive role models for all children (Style, 1988). For example, an exploration of current events, religion, or gender images in the media may include how and why individuals of different faiths have represented their religion through dress historically and in contemporary times. Such discussions can help diffuse tensions before they erupt into verbal or physical confrontations.

Consequently, youth will have been prepared to recognize religious dress and behavior outside their religious tradition, making such future interactions less awkward for all participants.

CONCLUSION

Due to religious discrimination and a frequently ill-informed societal environment, Muslim youth, their families, and their support networks need to develop adaptive strategies to negotiate the constant barrage of myopic images and experiences that demonize Islam and Muslims. Given this state of affairs, it is not surprising, then, that the students mentioned in this chapter have reflected so eloquently on the theme of courage needed in their young lives just to be themselves. Their narratives illuminate that Muslim youth can challenge the dominant perception of Muslims as terrorist, fanatical, suspicious, backward, insular, anti-Western, anti-democracy, and of Muslim women as oppressed, submissive, powerless, abused, and uneducated. By resisting these unjust perceptions and replacing them with truer ones, Muslims can repair their damaged identities and be re-identified as morally worthy rather than contemptible (Nelson, 2001). Thus by telling their own stories, students can alter oppressive perceptions of Muslims, improve their own self-perceptions, and refuse to be further victimized and vilified.

As authors, it has been liberating to incorporate our voices with the narratives of the students in order to counter the dominant narrative about Islam and claim the privileged position of telling our own stories. It is empowering to learn to use one's voice to communicate externally what one is experiencing internally. To expect any racial, religious, or ethnic group to automatically rebound from such a negative climate reduces the urgency that stakeholders such as public officials and policy makers address the toxicity of certain perspectives, practices, and policies. Educators, in particular, are in an optimal position to bridge the distance between "us" and "them." As long as there are disenfranchised groups, such advocacy in its many forms is needed. One effective strategy to strengthen bonds within communities and build bridges across communities is the use of narratives:

> Stories connect us to each other. In ways that polemics and polls cannot, they can reveal our conflicts within ourselves and our vulnerabilities to each other. Stories can describe why certain choices are made and others are passed over, and they can reveal the colors of our emotions. Stories have the capacity to convert a line drawing into flesh, to dislodge the power of the presumption and prejudice (Bayoumi, 2008, p. 12).

Stories such as the narratives presented in this chapter can enable readers to identify both with those who are separated by barriers of race, class, culture, and religion, and also with contexts and situations to which they may bear witness yet until now have not responded. Words have substance and power. They wash over our consciousness and become part of our landscape. To neutralize the words that harm and humiliate, we must amplify the voices, stifled for too long, of those attempting to repair and restate their own identities. It is then up to those who actively listen to respond with recognition, to readjust their own perceptions, and finally to share their newfound understanding with others.

DISCUSSION QUESTIONS AND EXTENSION ACTIVITIES

(1) What views, assumptions, feelings, or thoughts did you have about Muslim youths' experiences that did not match the accounts in this chapter? What is the most surprising difference between your assumptions and the narratives of the youth? What are the most likely reasons for these differences?

(2) Which of the experiences in the narratives can you relate to, and which can't you? Consider a time when you felt:
– different because of your (or your family's) language, race, or ethnicity;
– different because of how you dress;
– wrongfully blamed or just guilty by association;
– even your parents could not understand what you are going through;
– afraid that if you told others something about yourself, they may reject you, but also felt uncomfortable about keeping a secret;
– proud or embarrassed by your family's "coming to America" story?

(3) What experiences are unique to particular groups and which ones may be common across groups?

(4) What political and social conditions contribute to the mistreatment of particular social groups? How is this mistreatment both interpersonal (name calling, localized micro-aggressions) and also institutionally structured (laws and systems of control and monitoring)? How is it justified?

IF YOU LIKED THIS CHAPTER, YOU MAY ALSO ENJOY:

Khan, S. (2009). Integrating identities: Muslim American youth confronting challenges and creating change. *In this book.*

Mossalli, N.N. (2009). The voice of a covered Muslim-American teen in a southern public school. *In this book.*

Banks, J.A. (c.1975/2003). *Teaching strategies for ethnic studies*, 7th ed. Boston: Allyn and Bacon.

Council on Islamic Education (1995). *Teaching about Islam and Muslims in the public school classroom.* Fountain Valley, CA: Council on Islamic Education. Lesson plans and other resources available from http://www.cie.org/index.aspx

Global Connections on-line resources for parents and teachers retrieved 9 February, 2009 from http://www.pbs.org/wgbh/globalconnections/

Gardner, R. (Producer & Director). (2004). *Islam: Empire of faith* [documentary]. United States: Gardner Films, in association with PBS.

Kronemer, A. & Wolfe, M. (producers), & Schwarz, M. (Producer & Director). (2002). *Muhammad: Legacy of a Prophet* [documentary]. United States: Kikim Media, in association with Unity Productions Foundation, and PBS.

Muhammad: Legacy of a Prophet
Additional materials including lesson plans available at http://www.pbs.org/empires/islam/eduk12plan.html

NOTES

[1] In the 2008 presidential campaign, Barack Obama, who has family ties to Islam felt compelled to distance himself from the religion, so much so that on at least two occasions his staffers asked covered Muslim women to remove themselves from his proximity so their images would not appear in any campaign related photographs. See Smith, B. (2008, June 16). Muslims barred from picture at Obama event. Retrieved from http://www.politico.com/news/stories/0608/11168.html

[2] The Council on American Islamic Relations (CAIR) reported that 7% of all reported discrimination cases towards Muslims during 2006 occurred in schools (CAIR, 2006). This does not represent the countless unreported events of bullying or hostile behavior Muslim youth endure. Most examples included insensitivity or aggression by peers, as in the case where an Arab boy was found bound and locked in a closet in his New York elementary school (Marzulli, 2007) or when Somali girls were chased by their peers into a bathroom in a Boston high school and had their hijabs pulled off, leaving one student hospitalized (Vaishanav, 2001, Tobias-Nahi & Garfield, 2003, 2007). In the example where the Muslim girl was asked by her teacher to remove the hijab in front of her peers in the cafeteria, we see that even educators, the adults in charge of creating the space, may alienate Muslim youth and contribute to a hostile learning environment (CAIR CA, 2007). Consistent with other religious minorities, Muslim youth report frequent bullying in Western schools (Elsea & Mukhtar, 2000). In response to a report indicating that teachers acknowledge that attacks on Muslim students have risen, state and federal governments have developed specific measures to address faith bullies and incorporated them into general anti-bullying initiatives (Milne, 2006). Measures have included passage of the Safe Place to Learn Act (AB 394) that require California's education department to play an active role in ensuring full and proper implementation of existing anti-discrimination laws that apply to schools (CAIR, 2007), and similar initiatives in other states.

[3] http://www.maxcourage.org/home.php

[4] Seven of the ten essays in the chapter were previously published as part of the Max Warburg courage curriculum. Here are the references to read their essays in their entirety:
El-Alami, M. (2003). Courage in my life. In *The courage of Boston's children, Volume XII* (pp. 78–79). Boston, MA: The Max Warburg Courage Curriculum, Inc. and The Boston Public Schools.
El-Asmar, R. (2004). Courage in my life. In *The courage of Boston's children, Volume XIII* (pp. 22–23). Boston, MA: The Max Warburg Courage Curriculum, Inc. and The Boston Public Schools.
Duwaji, O. (2001). Courage in my life. In *The courage of Boston's children, Volume X* (pp. 58–61). Boston, MA: The Max Warburg Courage Curriculum, Inc. and The Boston Public Schools.
Farah, A. N. (2006). Courage in my life. In *The courage of Boston's children, Volume XV* (pp. 42–43). Boston, MA: The Max Warburg Courage Curriculum, Inc. and The Boston Public Schools.
Haji, K. (1999). Courage in my life. In *The courage of Boston's children, Volume VIII* (pp. 30–31). Boston, MA: The Max Warburg Courage Curriculum, Inc. and The Boston Public Schools.
Lynch, J. (2002). Courage in my life. In *The courage of Boston's children, Volume XI* (pp. 50–53). Boston, MA: The Max Warburg Courage Curriculum, Inc. and The Boston Public Schools.

Nehela, A. (2007). Courage in my life. In *The courage of Boston's children, Volume XVI* (pp. 46–47). Boston, MA: The Max Warburg Courage Curriculum, Inc. and The Boston Public Schools.

[5] http://www.thislife.org/Radio_Episode.aspx?sched=1163

[6] According to the Qur'an, eating pork is *haram* (unlawful) because it is unclean or harmful (c.f. Qur'an 2:173, 6:145). Although touching a pig is not explicitly prohibited, some individuals may wish to avoid the animal altogether out of concerns that it is impure or unhygienic.

REFERENCES

Alford, T. (1977, 1986, 2007). *Prince among slaves*. New York: Oxford University Press.

Austin, A. D. (1997). *African Muslims in antebellum America: Transatlantic stories and spiritual struggles*. New York: Routledge.

Bayoumi, M. (2008). *How does it feel to be a problem? Being young and Arab in America*. New York: The Penguin Press.

Beshir, S. (2004). *Everyday struggles: The stories of Muslim teens*. Beltsville, MD: Amana Publishing.

Conlon, M. (2006, November 11). U.S. Muslims outraged after imams kicked off plane. *Reuters*.

Council on American-Islamic Relations Research Center. (1999). *A model for school district religious accommodation policy*.

Council on American-Islamic Relations. (2006). *Results that speak for themselves: 2006 annual report*. Retrieved from www.cair.com/Portals/0/pdf/2006_Annual_Report.pdf

Council on American-Islamic Relations CA. (2007, November 21). Rising harassment of minority students in school. Retrieved from http://www.cair.com/ArticleDetails.aspx?ArticleID=23813&&name=n&&currPage=1&&Active=1

Council on American-Islamic Relations CA. (2008, August 25). CAIR asks studio to change 'Towelhead' film title. http://www.cair.com/ArticleDetails.aspx?mid1=777&&ArticleID=25369&&name=n&&currPage=1

Diouf, S. (1998). *Servants of Allah: African Muslims enslaved in the Americas*. New York: New York University Press.

Downey, G., Eccles, J. S., & Chatman, C. (2005). *Navigating the future: Social identity, coping, and life tasks*. New York: Russell Sage Foundation.

Eck, D. L. (2002). *A new religious America: How a "Christian country" has become the world's most religiously diverse nation*. San Francisco: Harper.

Erian, A. (2005). *Towelhead*. Emeryville, CA: Simon & Schuster.

Eslea, M., & Mukhtar, K. (2000). Bullying and racism among Asian schoolchildren in Britain. *Educational Research, 42*(2), 207–217.

Haddad, Y. Y. (2004). *Not quite American? The shaping of Arab and Muslim identity in the United States*. Waco, TX: Baylor University Press.

Haddad, Y. Y., & Lummis, A. (1987). *Islamic values in the United States: A comparative study*. New York: Oxford University Press.

al-Hilâlî, M. T., & Khan, M. H. (1404). *After Hijrah Translation of the meanings of the Noble Qur'an in the English Language*. Madinah, Kingdom of Saudi Arabia: King Fahd Complex for the Printing of the Holy Qur'an.

Igoa, C. (1995). *The inner world of the immigrant child*. Mahwah, NJ: Lawrence Erlbaum Associates.

al-Jabri, H. (1995). Profile: Double youth, the split personality syndrome. *The Message-Canada, 19*(8), 28.

Kahf, M. (2006). *The girl in the tangerine scarf*. New York: Carroll & Graf Publishers.

LaFramboise, T., Coleman, H., & Gerton, J. (1993). Psychological impact of biculturalism: Evidence and theory. *Psychological Bulletin, 114*(3), 395–412.

Lowry, L. (1989). *Number the stars*. New York: Bantam Doubleday Dell Publishing Group, Inc.

Marzulli, J., Einhorn, E., & Divito, N. (2007, July 31). NY: Arab boy bound & beaten in class, suit Says. *New York Daily News*. Retrieved from http://www.nydailynews.com/news/crime_file/2007/07/31/2007-07-31_arab_boy_bound__beaten_in_class_suit_say.html

The Max Warburg Courage Curriculum. Retrieved from http://www.maxcourage.org/home.php

McLoyd, V. C., Hill, N. E., & Dodge, K. A. (Eds.). (2005, 2007). *African American family life: Ecological and cultural diversity* (The Duke Series in Child Development and Public Policy). New York: Guilford Press.

Milne, J. (2006, November 10). Plan to beat faith bullies. *Times Educational Supplement*, (1), p. 5.

Myers, S. (2007, November 26). Hijab and soccer. Another red card. *The Montreal Gazette*. Retrieved from //www.canada.com/montrealgazette/news/story.html?id=a4aa0281-fcd3-4a00-9363-13946df4264e&k=43032

Nasir, N. S. (2004). "Halal-ing' the child: Reframing identities of resistance in an urban Muslim School. *Harvard Educational Review*, *74*(2), 153–174.

Nelson, H. (2001). *Damaged identities, narrative repair*. Ithaca, NY: Cornell University Press.

Paley, V. G. (1992). *You can't say you can't play*. Cambridge, MA: Harvard University Press.

Rudin, S., Carey, A., Rajski, P. (Producers), & Ball, A. (Director). (2008). *Towelhead* [Motion picture]. United States: Warner Independent Pictures.

Sahli, B., Tobias-Nahi, C., & Abo-Zena, M. (2009). Authentic interactions: eliminating the anonymity of otherness. In Y. Haddad, F. Senzai, & J. Smith (Eds.), *Educating the Muslims of America*. Oxford University Press.

Scott, J. (2007, February 27). *Hijab red card sparks uproar in Quebec: No tempest over turbans but hassle over hijab & a Canadian mask on an alarming global trend toward fear-mongering and racism*. Retrieved from http://www.saltspringnews.com/index.php?name=News&file=article&sid=15807

Sensoy, Ö., & DiAngelo, R. (2006). "I wouldn't want to be a women in the Middle East": White female student teachers and the narrative of the oppressed Muslim woman. *Radical Pedagogy*, *8*(1).

Sirin, S. R., & Balsano, A. B. (2007). Editors' introduction: pathways to identity and positive development among Muslim youth in the West. *Applied Developmental Science*, *11*(3), 109/111.

Sirin, S. R., & Fine, M. (2007). Hyphenated selves: Muslim American youth negotiating identities on the fault lines of global conflict. *Applied Developmental Science*, *11*(3), 151–163.

Smith, C., & Denton, M. L. (2005). *Soul searching: The religious and spiritual lives of American teenagers*. New York: Oxford University Press.

Spencer, M., & Markstrom-Adams, C. (1990). Identity processes among racial and ethnic minority children in America. *Child Development*, *61*(2), 290–310.

Steele, C. M. (1997). A threat in the air: How stereotypes shape intellectual identity and performance. *The American Psychologist*, *52*(66), 613–629.

Storytellers and Listeners for Peace and Healing. (2008, September 28). Retrieved from http://dorianhaarhoffwriter.homestead.com/community.html

Suárez-Orozco, C., & Suárez-Orozco, M. M. (2001). *Children of immigration*. Cambridge, MA: Harvard University Press.

Style, E., & McIntosh, P. (1988). Curriculum as window and mirror. In E. Style (Ed.), *Listening for all voices* (pp. 9–12). Summit, NJ: Oak Knoll School.

Taylor, M. D. (1976). *Roll of thunder, hear my cry*. New York: Puffin Books.

Tobias-Nahi, C., & Garfield, E. (2007). An Islamic school responds to September 11. In Books, Sue (Ed.), *Invisible children in the society and the schools* (3rd ed., pp. 81–102). New Jersey, NJ: Lawrence Erlbaum Associates.

Vaishanav, A. (2001, November 12). Somali parents aim to end school violence. *Boston Globe*.

Watkins, Y. K. (1986). *So far from the bamboo grove*. New York: William Morrow & Co., Inc.

Zine, J. (2001). Muslim youth in Canadian schools: Education and the politics of religious identity. *Anthropology & Education Quarterly*, *32*(4), 399–423.

Mona Abo-Zena
Eliot-Pearson Department of Child Development
Tufts University

Barbara Sahli
Outreach Consultant for Understanding Islam
Boston, Massachusetts

Christina Safiya Tobias-Nahi
Islamic Relief USA
Alexandria, Virginia

SHAZA KHAN

INTEGRATING IDENTITIES

Muslim American Youth Confronting Challenges and Creating Change

IDENTITIES, CHALLENGES, AND CHANGE

In the context of post-9/11 America, stereotypes about Muslims have become commonplace and discrimination based on one's religious and national background has become politically sanctioned (van Driel, 2004). Muslim youth growing up in this socio-political climate must contend with the reality that their identities- either those they consciously express or those that others project unto them- will also be contributing factors to the challenges they face in school and society. Identity formation is an on-going process that occurs throughout one's life. Individuals actively construct and negotiate multiple and fluid identities in historically-situated, socio-cultural contexts (Rogoff, 2003). Rather than having static and fixed notions of what it means to be oneself, these identity formations and expressions change depending on the individual and the ways in which his or her race, ethnicity, religious or sectarian affiliation, gender, and socioeconomic status are valued and viewed within a specific context (Schachter, 2005; Yon, 2000).

One of the more common stereotypes about Muslims, which regained prominence after September 11, 2001, was that Muslim values and beliefs were in some manner inherently incompatible with Western cultures. In response to this, after September 11, 2001, I began to consciously portray my "American" identity along with my "Muslim" identity by coupling a hijab, the Muslim headscarf, with blue jeans and long-sleeve t-shirts. Prior to this, in an effort to maintain Islamic modesty, I typically wore my hijab with long dresses, ethnic Pakistani clothes, or the long dark overcoat associated with women in Saudi Arabia, called an abaya or burqa. My decision to change the way in which I expressed my multiple identities (a Muslim female, U.S. born citizen, second generation Pakistani-American) was a direct reflection of the political and social climate in post-9/11 America. Through clothing alone, I attempted to counter the stereotype that being a Muslim American was somehow an oxymoron. This example illustrates how identities are affected by the historical, political, and social contexts of an individual, and how identities are multiple, fluid, and context-specific.

Several challenges are also associated specifically with Muslim identities in North America. Some of these have been highlighted in the emerging research on Muslim experiences in North American schools. This literature reveals how stereotyping, systemic discrimination, and school cultures that are incongruent with

Ö. Sensoy and C.D. Stonebanks (eds.), *Muslim Voices in School: Narratives of Identity and Pluralism*, 27–39.

Muslim values and beliefs lead many Muslim students to experience alienation, marginalization, and a sense of "othering" (i.e. van Driel, 2004, Zine, 2001, chapters in this volume).

As one of the few Muslims in my public high school in Western New York, I relate personally to these findings, having experienced many of these emotions only a decade earlier. In particular, I often felt singled out by my teachers to represent the opinions of all Muslims regarding religious and political matters. I can remember numerous occasions, for example, when teachers asked me to talk about or formally present aspects of my Pakistani heritage or Muslim religion. At times, I welcomed this as an opportunity to educate my peers about my background, such as during "International Night" in elementary school; but there were also numerous occasions when the burden to educate my peers and teachers about Islam and "other" cultures was overwhelming, particularly as I myself struggled to make sense of the intricacies of religious teachings.

I never quite figured out the perfect way to respond to such requests, especially when made by teachers (as opposed to peers) at my school. Raised by immigrant parents who instilled a deep respect for teachers and for formal education, I felt it was somehow inappropriate to deny their requests. Instead, I attempted to push aside my insecurities and come to class with information and artefacts in hand. There is no doubt that I learned a lot about my cultural background and religious traditions through these experiences. Nevertheless, I also began to feel resentful of being singled out as "different" by teachers, even when I felt I was just as "American" as my White and African American peers.

Traditionally, theories of adolescence and identity formation have positioned youth as passive and helpless victims of their conflict-ridden surroundings (Damon, 2004). Yet reflecting on my own efforts to navigate these challenges, and based on my interactions with Muslim youth in various professional capacities over the past eight years, I am keenly aware that such projections are inaccurate. Instead, I have found that despite being troubled by their challenges, most Muslim youth are able to resist, encounter, or overcome their obstacles.

In this chapter, while I discuss some of the challenges Muslim youth face in their schooling contexts, my focus remains on their responses to these obstacles. I do this in an effort to steer away from traditional depictions of crisis-ridden adolescents and to illustrate how youth are actively involved in transforming the marginalizing factors in their environments. I conclude with an examination of contextual elements that have helped some youth successfully work through their challenges.

It is my hope that this discussion will give readers insight into the potential of youth to be active agents of change in their own lives and in society. I purposefully draw heavily on direct quotes from Muslim youth who are discussing both the challenges they face in their schooling contexts and also their responses to these obstacles. As religious and often ethnic/racial minorities, these youth are used to having to validate their views and experiences. Here, however, I attempt to provide a space in which their opinions are accepted as valid representations of their own lived experiences. I also hope to provide concrete ideas for educators to help create and foster spaces in which youth have the opportunity to construct hybrid identities without being fearful of mockery, disrespect or disregard towards their religious or cultural backgrounds.

CONTEXTUALIZING THE RESEARCH

Between March 2006 and April 2007, I conducted a qualitative case study that explored the role of a youth program on the identity formation and adolescent development of its Muslim participants. The youth program is an interscholastic tournament of competitions and workshops held across the United States and Canada that aim to give participants a better understanding of Islam and Muslims. Although the tournament welcomes high school students of all backgrounds to partake in its activities, including non-Muslims, attendants are predominantly Sunni Muslims, second generation Americans, and of Arab, South Asian, and African descent.

Altogether, eight semi-structured individual interviews and sixteen semi-structured focus group interviews were conducted at the program's regional and national tournaments held in Atlanta, Georgia, Houston, Texas and College Park, Maryland. There were seventy-six participants whose ethnic and sectarian composition mirrored that of the tournament population with an equal number of male and female participants. Focus groups were comprised of two to eight interviewees and were fifteen to seventy-five minutes long with the average lasting approximately forty minutes.

Although participants were not asked to elaborate on how closely they followed Islamic practices and beliefs, through the course of the interviews, many indicated that they attempted to observe the five Muslim prayers on a daily basis, to fast during the lunar month of Ramadan, and to adhere to Islamic norms of intergender interaction. There were a minority of participants who revealed that they did not observe these religious practices on a daily basis, instead highlighting a social or political identity as Muslim.

The high level of adherence to Islamic practices and norms amongst my participant pool was unusual compared to the larger population of Muslim American youth, many of whom do not pray regularly, wear a hijab, or follow norms of gender segregation. On the other hand, given the context of the study, in which interviews were conducted at a tournament focused on Islam and Muslims, this is not surprising. Most importantly, it means that the data obtained for this study represents in large part the views of Muslim youth who are consciously striving to learn about and implement Islam in their daily lives.

EXPLORING CHALLENGES

In this section, I describe some of the challenges youth faced as Muslim students attending predominantly non-Muslim public and private schools in the U.S. Concurrently, I discuss how participants understood these challenges in relation to their identities as Muslim Americans. I then explore some of the methods they used to work through the challenges and conflicts associated with these identities.

Challenges in School

Students in this study who chose to identify themselves as Muslims and those who were ascribed this identity from outside were plunged into various roles, challenges, and scenarios based on the connotations others associated with their Muslim identity. In many instances, the Muslim identity was ascribed to them due to their teachers' and peers' conflation of their ethnic and religious identities. In some cases, participants said that because they were identified as Muslims they were mistakenly presumed, particularly by their teachers, to have knowledge about Islamic religious practices, other countries and cultures. While some participants invited these reactions, others felt frustrated, annoyed, or concerned that being identified as a Muslim could hold such implications.

Rehan[1], a student of South Asian descent who attended public high school in Atlanta, described an experience he had when a teacher asked him to explain to the class "the five pillars of Islam." He asked, rhetorically,

> Why would I know [about the five pillars] and everybody else doesn't know? I find that kind of, you know, kind of segregated type of thing, cause like she [the teacher] sees a brown guy and she assumes that I'm Muslim so I should know.

Rehan appeared to believe that the teacher conflated his South Asian ethnicity with a Sunni Muslim identity. However, Rehan did not adhere to traditional Islamic practices, and furthermore, as a Shia Ismaili, his belief system did not reside solely on the five pillars of Islam. Thus, the metanarrative that his teacher relied upon to construct her definition of Muslims revealed her perception of Muslims as a monolithic group, all of whom were devout worshippers and therefore suitable representatives and authorities of their religion. This perception overlooked the potential that her Muslim students could construct a social or political identity as a Muslim in the absence of adhering to Islam's religious tenants. Moreover, it overlooked the fact that one could be an ethnic minority descending from a predominantly Muslim country yet not identify oneself as Muslim.

Rehan's reference to feeling segregated in class was echoed by several other study participants as well. In particular, these participants felt that being identified by peers and teachers primarily through their religious or cultural backgrounds cast them as 'others' in their classroom and indicated that their identities as Americans were being overlooked. Madeeha, a female student who wore the hijab to her school in Raleigh, North Carolina explained,

> People ask you, "In other cultures, [do] they do this?" and then he [the teacher] will be like, "Right?" I mean, I'll be like, "I was born here all my life. I don't know."

Madeeha expressed frustration at the assumption that she was somehow an authentic spokesperson for "other cultures." In order to expose the underlying assumption in her teacher and peers' questions regarding 'other cultures,' she pointed out that she, like most of them, was born in the U.S., and therefore knew as much about these other cultures as they did.

On the other hand, particularly for female students such as Madeeha who wore a hijab to school, there was a sense of obligation to answer others' questions about Islam, despite the assumptions of "otherness" that their inquiries implied. This is similar to findings in Zine's (2006) study on Muslim females in Canada who wore a hijab to high school. She found that despite not always wanting to represent their community of Muslims, the young women recognized that their prosocial behaviour could confound others' stereotypes of Muslims and in turn proactively assert a new and positive image of Islam.

An exchange between Madeeha, Samar, Zainab and Amani, all female students who wore the Muslim head scarf to their public and private schools in Raleigh, reveals the pressure they felt to respond accurately to questions, even when they were absurd or offensive:

Madeeha	I mean we try to be morally open to like *dawah* [inviting people to Islam], but some questions, we don't know how to answer. Like there's one kid in my math class, he was like, "Oh yeah if you don't wear your scarf, will you be like condemned, or what will happen to you?" And I was like, you know… I can't decide, God will decide, and he was all confused.
Samar	Yeah they don't understand but–
Madeeha	Yeah they wonder like why do people cover their whole faces and then, why don't people just show their neck. And I was like, well people have like different levels of, you know, beliefs. And they don't really understand.
Shaza	So it sounds like people come to you all as though you're authorities for Islam. Do you like that or does that bother you?
Zainab	Sometimes it bothers me.
Madeeha	We don't always know what the best answer is.
Amani	It puts pressure on you.
Zainab	You don't want to say the wrong answer.

Even though they were bothered by their peers' questions, many felt that as one of the few Muslims in their schools they were obligated to inform people about their faith, which they acknowledged was misunderstood by many.

Central to all of my participants' comments about the challenges and conflicts faced as Muslim American youth was the experience of being a religious minority in the United States and in school. The extent to which they practiced Islam had an affect on, but was not always indicative of, the ways in which they experienced themselves as Muslims within these contexts. In other words, while being a Muslim typically held some religious connotation, it also took on social and political undertones as well.

As a result, many student interviewees who talked very little about practicing Islamic rituals still expressed concern about reactions they received from peers and teachers simply because of their perceived identity as Muslims. Their skin colour, ethnicity, and religion, which they explain were often conflated, were enough to trigger anti-Islamic, or Islamophobic, sentiments as they went about their daily lives. The identity of "Muslim" therefore became ascribed onto many youth participants by others despite a lack of outward religious expression, causing them in turn to respond and act on this identity in a social or political manner.

RESPONDING TO CHALLENGES

In this section, I discuss how some youth in this study used Islamic symbolism, jokes and humour, and Muslim peer groups and associations to help respond to and address several of their challenges. The examples I draw on reveal that as the youth worked through these challenges, they were also engaged in a constant (re)construction, (re)interpretation, and expression of their identities as Muslim Americans.

Islamic Symbolism

One of the most documented methods used by Muslim students in the U.S., Canada, or Great Britain to respond to their challenges includes the use of the hijab, which is a symbol well recognized as a marker of Muslim identity. For example, Dwyer (2000) found that several Muslim females in Great Britain were "able to construct an alternative identity through their dress, which challenged parental assumptions about appropriate attire but could also confound the expectations of others" (p. 481). The females in her study were able to resist static notions of what it meant to be both Muslim and British by projecting hybrid identities through their clothing, which involved wearing a hijab with traditional Western attire, such as jeans and long-sleeve t-shirts.

Many of the female participants in my study also talked about their use of hijab to respond to their challenges, including responding to stereotypes about Muslims, resisting peer pressure, and constructing a "Muslim space" for themselves in their schools. For example, despite the absurd questions they received about their religion and scarves, the five young women from Raleigh felt that the hijab gave them an opportunity to teach their peers about Islam. Interviewees who did not wear hijab also had their own ideas about how it helped Muslim females. Ansar, an African American male who attended a predominantly Black high school in Atlanta, discussed how males at his school had more respect for females who wore hijab than those who did not, stating "They don't even try to mess with them."

Bilal, who attended school in Atlanta as well, further explained:

They talk about other girls in their face and call them like all these bad names, all these bad names of girls getting around or whatever, but they won't tell a Muslim that, not that I've ever seen, not a Muslim girl. They respect Muslim girls. They be like saying "What's up" to them and whatever and just walk away cause they know, hey, keep your distance.

Ansar and Bilal's statements illustrate how hijab helped females effectively convey that they were not interested in physical interactions with their male counterparts. The ability to do so further indicates their ability to create a "Muslim space" in which Islamic norms of modesty and intergender interaction were recognized and respected by even non-Muslim peers.

For Muslim males, there were similar benefits to using Islamic symbols to identify oneself as Muslim. For example, Ameen, an African American male from Atlanta who often wore a *kufi*, a cap sometimes worn by Muslim males, to school was quickly recognized as a Muslim by his peers. This made it easier for them to approach him with questions they had about Islam. Although some Muslim students would be uncomfortable with these questions, Ameen welcomed this as an opportunity to teach others in his school about Islam, something he felt passionate about.

Ansar also mentioned that by explicitly telling his peers that he was Muslim, some of them refrained from doing un-Islamic activities around him. He said,

Like I tell a lot of my friends I'm Muslim... and they be like "Oh, I'm not going to do this around you, you're Muslim."

As an African American, Ansar stated that most of his peers did not immediately identify him as a Muslim. Yet, instead of wearing a physical symbol to represent his Muslim identity, Ansar vocally declared his identity as a Muslim to many of his peers. Given the prior knowledge and assumptions they had about Islamic beliefs and practices, this pronunciation of faith gave his friends insight into the types of social activities he would not participate in, helping Ansar proactively resist common forms of peer pressure. In this instance, assumptions held by Ansar's peers about Islamic practices worked in his favour, as he did not have to engage in lengthy explanations of his religion, which he indicated he was uncomfortable doing given his limited knowledge of Islam.

Jokes and Humor

Muslim students used jokes and humour in different ways to confront challenges they faced. While some used humour in witty ways to address stereotypes held by peers in their schools, some joked with non-Muslim peers in an attempt to avoid otherwise confrontational scenarios.

For example, when Iman, a high school student from Panama City, was asked if she was hot wearing her hijab and full-sleeve clothing, she answered her peers by saying, "I'm hot with or without these clothes." This response helped Iman directly answer the question she was asked while drawing on a pun—"being hot"—to overcome the stereotype that she could not be fashionable or attractive in hijab.

Rana, a high school senior in a public school in Atlanta, told her peers she was going to dress up as a terrorist for Halloween. After an awkward moment of silence from her peers, she laughed and told them she was just kidding. During her interview, she explained why she used such jokes with her peers, stating that it was an effective means of shattering stereotypes of Muslim students as serious, uptight, and/or extremist:

> I mean like people still take it lightly if you joke, like take it as humour and people they see that you're comfortable you know. They're not going to think you're this uptight religious girl whose extremist probably; you know, they're not going to think like that.

Mustafa explained that he also made jokes about Islam and terrorism because:

> We don't want to hurt somebody, no we don't want to fight. So like okay [if] someone was like "You're a dirty Muslim," I'm not going to be like "Yo, say that again and I'm going to punch you in your face." No, I'm just going to… make fun of it, just play around with it.

Mustafa's comments point out that joking was used by some as an alternative to responding violently to potentially offensive comments, muting and/or reducing the sting of the stereotypes from which the comments were derived.

The initiation and acceptance of these jokes by the Muslim participants in my study seemed to parallel a tactic similar to what Ajrouch (2004) found in her study on second generation Arab Americans. These students used the term "boater"— a word originally used decades earlier by White Americans to refer to Arab immigrants—to establish an "identity boundary" between themselves and Arab immigrants. This identity boundary emerged due to second generation Arab students' desire to "make clear that although they may be Arab, they are different" from immigrant students who were not yet fully integrated into popular U.S. youth culture (p. 379). Thus, by using the term "boater," they were able to simultaneously claim an ethnic identity that distinguished them from Caucasians while distancing themselves from Arab immigrants in order to assert their identification as Arab Americans.

Similarly, joking provided a safe way for Muslim students in this study to create their own "identity boundary" without purposefully perpetuating hurtful stereotypes about Muslims and/or their ethnic heritages. Instead, it allowed them to express identities as Muslims and ethnic minorities while concurrently conveying to their peers that they were sociable and friendly. Further, these jokes were shared by peers whom they knew and with whom they had established positive rapport. Given this context, it is possible that their jokes highlighted the absurdity of the stereotypes they drew upon, such as those regarding the inherently violent nature of Muslims, or the notion that all Muslims were terrorists.

Though their use of such stereotypes could also be interpreted by many as internalized racism, a topic discussed by several scholars regarding the use of the "n" word amongst African Americans, the Muslim students in my study had clear reasons for why they chose humour to respond to potentially offensive remarks made by peers. Specifically, rather than feeling hopeless about the pervasiveness of stereotypes about Muslims in a post-9/11 society, they felt jokes and humour could create counter-images of Muslim Americans that were positive, friendly, and funny.

Muslim Peer Groups and Associations

In her study on Muslim students attending public schools in Toronto, Zine (2001) found that her participants differentiated themselves from peers of other faiths through their involvement in Islamic organizations, such as a Muslim Student Association (MSA), and Muslim-only peer-groups. By doing so, they were able to resist peer pressure that could have caused them to compromise elements of their faith.

This was a strategy that many of my study participants also relied upon to resist peer pressure, address stereotypes, and educate others about Islam. Specifically, one female student talked about the role of MSA in helping her and her Muslim peers respond to insults by peers who made negative comments about Islam and Muslims.

> When we're in school and like say someone is saying something like bad about the Muslims or... maybe you get dirty looks for like wearing a scarf. But right then in MSA you come back and you report it to your [Association's] president and the MSA [will] right then use it as an opportunity; we'll make an open house at the masjid, or like we'll go to the library and we'll set up a display about the hijab.

Her explanation illustrates that the MSA was an organization that Muslim students could depend on for immediate and effective responses to Islamophobia, while having the benefit of being seen as a legitimate and "professional organization" by school officials and peers. In this manner, MSA helped many students transform potentially marginalizing factors in their schools while working to create a positive image for Muslims through organized efforts.

Other efforts included group-sponsored community service and organizing and participating in interfaith events. MSAs that put on such events helped create forums in which Muslim students could interact with peers of different faiths and openly but respectfully discuss their beliefs, opinions, and practices with one another. Lena and Maryam, two students from Atlanta high schools, felt that this helped them "break down barriers between the religions." Thus, for many, being involved in their school's MSA gave them the opportunity to formally educate their school and broader communities about what it meant to be a Muslim, in turn helping them proactively reduce the sense of mystification that surrounded their Muslim identities.

The president of an MSA at a public high school in Houston also talked about the benefits of being in an MSA. He stated:

I go to a public school so there are a lot of non-Muslims that I'm surrounded with. So it's really hard to integrate your Muslim self with your American self or whatever other culture you're from because it's so easy to give in to peer pressure and to do what your friends are doing... But MSA gives you a way to connect with the Muslim students in your school and it helps you to not have to hide yourself and you can just be who you are.

His statement explains how these associations helped Muslim youth become more confident in their beliefs and practices while providing a convenient source of peer support in the face of challenges associated with their religious identities.

HELPING YOUTH CONFRONT THEIR CHALLENGES

Given the nature of my study, participants often discussed the challenges they faced in their interactions with teachers and other school administrators. Yet, it was clear from talking to several of them that they felt that educators could play a positive role in their schooling experience as well.

For instance, Talal, who attended a suburban high school in Atlanta, discussed how his teacher explicitly told him he could leave class whenever he needed to for prayer. As a sophomore, he had already established a reputation that helped teachers trust him and respect his religious practices. His discussion revealed that his teachers helped prayer become an integrated part of his daily activities, allowing him to practice Islam without casting a spotlight on his differences.

The ability to respect students' unique identities, practices, and beliefs without making them feel "different" from their peers was something several students desired. Samar, a student who went to high school in Raleigh, talked about how she felt when teachers stopped in the midst of a lesson to ask her to verify information being taught in class. Such actions, she said, made her feel awkward. She criticized, "it's like they make separate rules for us and we're so like different than everyone else." As a practicing Muslim, Samar wore a hijab, and therefore projected her Muslim identity to others explicitly, but the act of an authority-figure highlighting this unnecessarily was unappreciated.

Instead, participants in this study seemed to value teachers who took time out before and after class to talk to students about concerns they had regarding course materials, assignments, or classroom interactions. Amani's discussion of her own personal experience with a teacher who offended her and discussed it after class is illustrative of this:

Amani   I remember this one incident where I'm taking this medicinal chemistry seminar and the teacher was like bringing out his laptop. And he had a little cover for it and he was like flipping around with the cover and it ended up on his head somehow. And then he goes like this [raising his hands above his head], like look at me. He's a goofy type teacher. And then everyone started laughing, and I was kind of like, I was taken aback, because everybody started laughing. And after class he came to me and he was like I hope that didn't offend you. He was like, I realized that afterwards. I was like, I think it kind of did.

Shaza   And did you tell that to him?

Amani   Yeah. He was like okay, I'm sorry, I was out of line, blah blah blah… I'm actually glad that he came to me because, to be honest, I wouldn't have the confidence to go up to him and say that was wrong.

Given their position of authority, it was difficult for some students to approach their teachers about concerns they had about course materials, assignments, and/or interactions with peers and teachers in class. Therefore, when teachers talked to students privately outside of class, students were often appreciative of their efforts.

Some student interviewees also talked about how they resolved initial challenges to establishing religious practices through the help of a supportive teacher. Basit explains that he was able to find someone in his school who supported his efforts to pray in school, and therefore helped him maintain his religious practice:

> I told one of my other teachers [that another teacher told him learning was more important than prayer], and she said that if she says that again you tell me because she can get kicked out… [and] like if she wants to say something like that she needs to keep it to herself.

In this manner, though the immediate context of Basit's classroom posed an obstacle for him, he was able to find a teacher willing to advocate on his behalf who could help him deal with the situation more effectively.

These brief examples provide some insight into how educators can help Muslim students practice their faith and assert their identities without feeling othered or marginalized in their schools, in turn facilitating the construction of strong hybrid identities as Muslim American youth. Importantly, however, there was no consensus amongst the participants in this study on how this should be done. On the contrary, many students gave ambiguous or conflicting responses to the specific ways that teachers could help them respond to their challenges as Muslim Americans. Still, the discussion points to the fact that while Muslim youth can work by themselves and with one another to respond to their challenges in school, the presence of a supportive and positive school culture can help reduce the occurrence of such problems to begin with. Further, educators who were conscious of the individual needs of their Muslim students and who helped make their religious beliefs and practices an integrated aspect of students' schooling experiences appeared to be successful in helping students feel like integral members of their school community.

CREATING CHANGE

Crisis has often been thought of as a central aspect of adolescence and identity formation. For Muslim American youth, there have been systemic efforts to locate the crux of their crisis in the "clash of cultures" which is perceived to be inherent in their backgrounds as practicing members of the Islamic faith and residents of a democratic and secular United States. My own personal and professional experiences, including the results of this research, illustrate that Muslim youth in fact are actively involved in creating hybrid identities, or identities that are able to simultaneously represent their strong commitments as Muslims and Americans, without falling prey to inescapable predicaments. The combination of their personal drive, creativity, and resourcefulness has helped them resist and proactively address several of their challenges. Educators too have played an important role in helping youth create schooling environments that recognize and respect their religious and cultural backgrounds, in turn helping many create strong hybrid identities as Muslim American youth.

DISCUSSION QUESTIONS AND EXTENSION ACTIVITIES

(1) Recall a time when you shifted the way in which you constructed or expressed your identity/ies due to a change in context. How did your altered identity/ies affect the way in which you were treated/perceived by others? How did it affect the way you felt about yourself?

(2) What specific insights did you glean from the chapter about how schools can be more inclusive of diverse students (Muslim students, but also encompassing other marginalized identity positions)? Consider what initiatives educators could take or implement on their own? What they could do collaboratively with students? What could be done at a classroom level? What could be done at a school-wide level?

(3) The students in this chapter responded differently to their teachers', versus peers', questions about Islam and Muslims. For example, Rehan was offended by his teacher's request to talk about the five pillars of Islam, while Ameen invited the opportunity to teach his peers about his religious practices. What insights did the chapter provide about how educators can navigate how and when to approach their Muslim students about questions they or others have about Islam and Muslims?

IF YOU LIKED THIS CHAPTER, YOU MAY ALSO ENJOY:

Abo-Zena, Sahli, & Tobias-Nahi. (2009). Testing the courage of their convictions: Muslim youth respond to stereotyping, hostility, and discrimination. *In this book.*

Mir, S. (2009). Diversity, self, faith, and friends: Muslim undergraduates on campus. *In this book.*

Cristillo, L., Elamin, N., Hawley, A., & Tawasil, A. (Eds). (2008). *This is where I need to be: Oral histories of Muslim youth in NYC.* New York: Student Press Initiative. Also, online companion to the curriculum guide and book: http://www.thisiswhereineedtobe. com/

Sirin, S.R. & Fine, M. (2008). *Muslim American youth: Understanding hyphenated identities through multiple methods*. New York: New York University Press.

Sarroub, L. K. (2005). *All American Yemeni girls: Being Muslim in a public school*. Philadelphia: University of Pennsylvania Press.

NOTES

¹ all names are pseudonymns

REFERENCES

Ajrouch, K. J. (2004). Gender, race, and symbolic boundaries: Contested spaces of identity among Arab American adolescents. *Sociological Perspectives, 47*(4), 371–391.

van Driel, B. (Ed.). (2004). *Confronting Islamophobia in educational practice*. Stoke on Trent, UK: Trentham Books.

Dwyer, C. (2000). Negotiating diasporic identities: Young British South Asian Muslim women. *Women's Studies International Forum, 23*(4), 475–486.

Rogoff, B. (2003). *The cultural nature of human development*. New York: Oxford University Press.

Schachter, E. P. (2005). Context and identity formation: A theoretical analysis and a case study. *Journal of Adolescent Research, 20*(3), 375–395.

Yon, D. (2000). *Elusive culture: Schooling, race, and identity in global times*. Albany, NY: State University of New York Press.

Zine, J. (2001). Muslim youth in Canadian schools: Education and the politics of religious identity. *Anthropology & Education Quarterly, 32*(4), 399–423.

Zine, J. (2006). Unveiled sentiments: Gendered Islamophobia and the experiences of veiling among muslim girls in a Canadian Islamic school. *Equity & Excellence in Education, 39*(3), 239–252.

Shaza Khan
Warner Graduate School of Education and Human Development
University of Rochester

SEEMA A. IMAM

SEPARATION OF *WHAT* AND STATE

The Life Experiences of Muslims with Public Schools in the Midwest

INTRODUCTION

Living as a Muslim in the Midwest has made one thing evident- that conducting research about the life experiences of Muslims still takes courage. Over a decade ago, the concept of naming the mass media a 'public curriculum' was new to me, and pointing out that it teaches my neighbors about Islam and Muslims in such a way that makes me, my family or my Muslim community unrecognizable to them, seemed a far-fetched notion that wasn't readily supported by any education program of which I was aware. Ten years into my research, and I am still gathering life stories about the challenging experiences Muslims report about raising their families in the Midwest. In this chapter I add my own and the voices of my research participants to revealing and examining these challenges especially in the context of language. As Michael Apple (1990) argues "…much of our language, while seemingly neutral, is not neutral in its impact nor is it unbiased in regard to existing institutions of schooling" (p. 129). This piece examines the language and discourse of mainstream public schooling in the Midwest about Islam, and the impact that language can have on Muslim students and families.

THE RESEARCHER

As an American researcher, I am also a Muslim woman wearing a hijab, a mother, a wife, a grandmother, and an educator with sixteen years of classroom experience in Chicago public schools, five years as a founding principal of one of Chicago's first Islamic schools, and twelve years as a teacher educator working as a university professor in teacher preparation. All of these experiences and lenses from the past nearly four decades of adult life have given me multiple perspectives and quite a bit of life experience with which to guide my thoughts and situate this research. Thus by the time I was to begin my doctoral degree research, I knew I had to study the lived experience of Muslims in the midst of the mass media messages, or public curriculum, that so efficiently taught the world about Islam and Muslims.

The insight for this research is contextualized within my own lived experiences. Coming from a Midwestern farming community with a population of just over a thousand, I chose Islam in 1971 at the age of seventeen, at almost the same time

Ö. Sensoy and C.D. Stonebanks (eds.), Muslim Voices in School: Narratives of Identity and Pluralism, 41–54.

that Cacious Clay and Cat Stevens chose to follow Islam and became, respectively, Muhammad Ali and Yusuf Islam. I was not old enough or experienced enough to realize that I was about to put America's freedom of religion discourse to the test. A few years later I changed my name from Martha to Seema. I was eager to do this, proud of *my* Islam and eager to perform the hajj.

I set many goals for myself as I began to practice Islam. I wanted to build a strong Muslim identity, create a plan for raising an American Muslim family with a strong Muslim identity in my homeland, and contribute to the education of Muslims in America. In elementary social studies I had learned about freedom of religion and freedom of the press. In Sunday school at the Methodist Church I had attended, I'd learned that God was the creator of the entire world and that God loved all the people of the world, red, yellow, brown, black, and white. I was a very proud American child. The fact that I had taken these lessons *literally* allowed me to feel free to explore a new religion and it made it easy for me to embrace a world of people. Six months after choosing Islam I married a Pakistani Muslim, and traveled to meet my in-laws in Pakistan, a place I visited twice within a five–year period of time. This was a significant period in helping me to understand and to implement my own family goals. It had not yet occurred to me that I would face tremendous challenge trying to raise an American Muslim family in my homeland. In fact moving to a position outside the mainstream religion would mean that I would come face to face with the so-called "separation of church and state." The First Amendment to the U.S. Constitution secures freedom for the establishment and practice of any religion. Yet while the dominant religious tradition is discussed, and even overtly celebrated and practiced in the school context, for most other religious discussions, I was to repeatedly hear that in American schools we have a "separation of church and state" and therefore we simply can't actually engage in discussions about religion, recognize any other holidays, or even have children make cards and decorations. This "separation" door would be so tightly shut, it would take years before I was able to even name and simply talk about it.

The trips overseas, the life goals and the name change helped me immediately to begin sorting Islam from culture, and culture from Islam. I wanted to know what God expected of me as a Muslim in order to attain the hereafter. Within a few short years in 1978 with two young children, we traveled to perform hajj. It was perhaps the greatest chance to witness the only event or place in life where people of every economic status, people of every race, speaking every language of the world come together annually and stand together in faith. It is a place where each day, everyone you meet feels like an old friend. It was indeed a life changing experience, surely a golden moment. It was the only religious gathering or crowd I have ever witnessed (with the exception of my second hajj in 2006) filled with people from all over the world. My childhood had been built upon a relatively homogenous, White life of spirituality and service to God and I had found the road I would journey through life, through Islam, on "the straight path" as it is says in the Qur'an.

Many learning experiences began to surface after the 1978 hajj trip. I began to wear a hijab. Soon after the hajj, the Iran hostage crisis took place and my first child had started attending public school. My view of the world was now through the eyes of a Muslim American, a *hajji*[1] and now the world looking back at me, saw a Muslim woman wearing a hijab. By the time I began to do research about the Muslim experience, in 1998, I had experienced nearly three decades as a Muslim in the Midwest.

The years that had passed can only be described as having had my feet in two communities. I had grown up in the American mainstream as a White American. Those experiences had never left me but in fact intersected with a new Muslim American identity, which had become the dominant one. As others who began their lives in another religious community but made the choice to embrace Islam may agree, one may never feel *completely* adjusted. This is an area of constant reflection for me. Perhaps, because I seem no longer to be considered one hundred percent American, and likewise just short of being perceived as one hundred percent Muslim in the Muslim community. Life experiences are really priceless. All of these experiences have helped me to understand participant voices and the role of power and position within a community, within larger society, and within schools.

When I began to take a careful look at the experiences of Muslims in the Midwest, it weighed heavy on my heart, even in the pre-9/11 days. Those around me made comments that revealed how much they believed the mass media lessons, which had been troubling me for a decade. I had all of this before me and I wanted to research it, to dig into it. At several junctures in my studies, colleagues and professors close to me wanted to impart their "good advice." For example, one said, "Why not just do research on vocabulary development or something, then you'll be done." From the Muslim community came other advise, "We're immigrants and we're guests, it's okay if they do this with us because our religion is not known much to American authorities." But, the knot deep in my American heart kept bursting forth to the tune of my sixties youth, with John Lennon singing the soundtrack, "You may call me a dreamer, but I'm not the only one." America is a good place. Americans are good people and I am not a guest. I dreamed of sharing the stories so the public would know that Islam is a legitimate faith and that Muslims are, like all people of the world, *good*. Little did I know that post 9/11 would compel me to do more in sharing the lived experiences of Muslims in the Midwest, as the landscape, we are told, has been forever changed.

THE PRE-9/11 RESEARCH

In brief, my research was really about giving voice to the stories of six select Muslims living in the Midwest, focusing on their life experiences, perceptions of the negative stereotyping of Muslims, and the public image of Muslims. In effect, trying to reveal what it is like to live in the shadow of what the mass media teaches the world about Muslims and Islam. McLaren (2003) writes, "Critical pedagogy asks how and why knowledge gets constructed the way it does and how and why some constructions of reality are legitimated and celebrated by the dominant culture while others clearly are not" (p. 72). My study sought to explore and hopefully answer some of these questions, specifically in relation to the Muslim American community in the Midwest.

In addition to sharing my own experiences, I studied the stories of five other individuals who were willing to share their "conscious experiences" (Cresswell, 1999, p. 11). They were all American citizens, three by birth and three by naturalization and came from different national backgrounds, three men and three women in total, including the voices of an African American, a White American, an Indian American, a Palestinian American, a Pakistani American and a Jordanian American.

In the letter of invitation in advance of the first interview, I asked the participants to give forethought to media images of Muslims in the Midwest. My opening questions were, "Have you thought about media images of Muslims and Islam? Would you explain the images of Islam and Muslims that you see in the media? Are there examples that you can give?" The women all wore hijab and were all considered practicing Muslims, the men all kept beards and attended Juma prayers[2] regularly and also gave the Friday *khutbah* (sermon) on occasion. While they were not activists per se they were all well-known community members involved in community work.

Reading the Media Image

Below is a list of stereotypical words and phrases shared by the participants in their discussion of the most common media images of Muslims and of Islam. These are likely familiar to you:

Anti-American	Oppressive religion
Antiquated	Really not American
Camel jockeys	Savage
Crazy Muslims	Spreading atrocities
Derogatory	Strange
Distasteful	Suppresses women
Don't respect Western values	Terror
Dumb	Terrorist
Exotic and sexual	Terrorist acts
Extremist	Uncivil
Fanatic	Uncivilized
Fundamentalist	Unliberated
Get real angry	Unsocial creatures
Ignorant	Very angry
Indifferent	Very foreign
Intolerant of minorities	Very negative
Lower class people	Very suicidal
Male chauvinistic religion	Violent
Not educated	

It is important to share this list in order to consider these words and phrases in relation to the discourses circulating in public schools. Muslim children attending public schools sit with students, teachers, and school staff daily, and everyone reads and hears these words in print, on TV, on talk shows, and on the news. Some of these words are even used at times by teachers and fellow students in reference to Islam and Muslims, and are a form of institutionalized knowledge, "deeply rooted in a nexus of power relations" (McLaren, 2003, p. 72). Those words and images create a pervasive disempowering construct, and when I have read or listened to them I have wanted to ask, "Who is that you speak of?"

For a long time, the message about Muslims and Islam in the mass media was loud and clear. One parent reported a disempowering conversation with a teacher in which the teacher wanted the high school student to be allowed to have a girlfriend and told the parent that, "a girlfriend would save him from other kinds of violence because he would have someone." As the interview continued, the parent noted that the teacher sympathetically revealed, "I know your people have these issues we hear about when we turn on the television." The teacher seemed to not comprehend that, the "family values" related to not having girlfriends came from parents making a concerted and conscious effort to raise their child based on particular religious beliefs. The message that this teacher had received from the news was all about the negative violent image of the bad Muslim man and all that this fifteen year old student needed to do was fall in love in order to avoid the feelings of violence that she "knew" were a part of "those people's issues."

The older my own children became, the more I realized how much they were disempowered by the negative misunderstanding of Islam and Muslims that the general public was getting through a media curriculum. The list of stereotypes presented earlier is long and there are also many anecdotes that tell the experiences that people have gone through and schools were a central location for the miseducation about Islam (Kincheloe & Steinberg, 2004).

Muslims in Public Schools

The school experiences as told by participants about their own children, as well as their own public school experience, and in some cases the stories they heard from their friends fell into six categories:

- Muslim children are being involved in religious and secular activities contrary to their beliefs
- Experiences as Muslim students attempt to maintain and practice their own religious beliefs
- Treatment of Muslim holidays in some public schools
- Muslim children have dietary restrictions that are often not respected
- Current events and the school setting
- Muslim children often experience pressure about beliefs and problems with their names

The details of participant responses in these six themes are presented in full in Imam (2002). For the purposes of this discussion, I will share participant accounts from the first two categories: Muslim children involvement in other faith and secular activities; and the experiences of Muslim students as they attempt to maintain and practice their own religious beliefs.

Separation of What? Muslim Children's Involvement in Other Faith Activities

Families grappled with the challenge of category one in a variety of ways. Some ignored it while others offered to come in to the school and talk about Islam. Children were being involved in other faiths during the school day, which led parents to hope that through the school's curriculum and a little effort they might make the strange familiar. While frequently families do come in and share in some schools, many schools still tell Muslim parents that "we" cannot cover religion because "we" observe separation of church and state and therefore "we" won't be needing any holiday things for the Eid holiday; no guest speaker, no treats, no candy, and sometimes not even an Eid holiday greeting.

In interviews, the participants shared stories about how they themselves or their children were deeply involved in the religious activities of other faiths while in school, in spite of the discourse about the separation of church and state. Participants noted the following specific examples:

- Children are asked to sing Christmas songs including religious ones for assemblies
- One Muslim 2nd grader had to memorize, *Twas the Night Before Christmas*
- Children were required to make Christmas tree decorations and take them home for their own Christmas trees
- Children were required to dress up on Halloween
- Valentines were given to a Muslim child and the child was told to sign them and distribute to classmates' Valentine boxes
- Students made a calendar to tear off a page a day until Christmas
- A parent removed her Muslim child from a preschool program when the themes, which revolved around holidays, became too much for her to handle. She had been through Halloween, Thanksgiving and Christmas. When she realized that Valentine's Day and Easter were yet to come, she just gave up

These stories are not uncommon to me. As a university professor supervising student teachers, I regularly observe teaching in the public schools. In the presence of at least 4 Muslim children I heard a first grade classroom teacher introduce approximately 30 holiday books on a November day right after Thanksgiving. The titles were read aloud, and the books were held up. They were about Santa, Christmas, Silent Night, Holy Night, Grandma's Christmas cookies, Christmas mass and Rudolph. Nothing was mentioned about Ramadan, Hanukkah, or Kwanza. The teacher then very enthusiastically said, "In December our room will be filled with Christmas cheer."

The stories of my research participants were about real experiences at open houses, Ramadan experiences, curriculum nights, Christmas seasons and more that had occurred through the public school experience. Stories were told of watching teachers celebrate Christmas for a whole month, asking all children to make tree decorations, memorize, *Twas the Night Before Christmas*, and yet almost never mention—rarely utter, "happy holidays" on Eid. One participant told of her experiences in the public school classroom as a third grader. She expressed it like this:

> In third grade we spent two weeks in art class making an ornament. I told the teacher, I don't need one so why do I have to make one and she said, just make it. So I did but I was bitter about it and I ran home and rang a neighbor's doorbell and told the lady she could have my ornament, cause I did not have a tree. And when we would sing Christmas songs, religiously based ones, about Jesus and Mary, it made me feel very guilty.

As you can see in the stories told by these participants, students start off innocently but then frequently become so involved that they feel guilty. Children grow up in their homes with an identity their parents' help to construct. Many have general religious guidelines that they are to follow. When teachers don't know about the home religion it can be hard for them to involve children in religious activities appropriately. However, too often teachers have made it easy on themselves – by ignoring this religious diversity – at the cost of children made to feel unnecessarily guilty. These holiday stories are far removed from the school curriculum and are about holidays. They go a little bit too far. For example to have to memorize *Twas the Night Before Christmas*, if a child does not serve Santa cookies, wake up to presents, or decorate a tree and so on, the night before Christmas this involvement in the religion of others in a public school has gone too far.

The only way as I see it for these activities to be conducted in school would be to be inclusive of numerous religious holidays at the appropriate times of the year. Even so, I have always preferred thematic teaching through themes other than holidays as the best way to create real community in the classroom because the climate so often created around holidays makes it difficult for students to maintain their own religious practices.

Against the Grain: Attempting to Maintain and Practice Their Islamic Faith

The very strong culture within schools can be noted in the struggle to fit in, it is important to remember that not everyone is trying to "fit in", some are trying to maintain and practice their own faith. Here are examples shared by participants about their struggles to maintain their faith in light of the context above:

– The modesty issue for Muslim girls and boys comes up. Dating isn't practiced by those who adhere to Islam and is often the source of ridicule by students but also by teachers. One teacher told parents, "not to worry, these young boys need the outlet of a girlfriend, after experiences with several girls they can settle down."

47

- Many students are required at all ages to have girl/boy teams or study groups or lab partners.
- A high school gym teacher wanted a female student to just do it, be like others, "just get the swim suit and come in the water."
- Even after several years in the same school or district parents have noticed they have to inform the school or teacher every year of beliefs, practices and holidays as if they are new. The school or district does not include information to teachers on the calendar nor is any effort made so children don't have to do the explaining year after year after year.
- An educational journal omits information that teachers could use. The title indicates a "trio of religions" to be discussed. It turns out to be Christianity, Judaism and Kwanza. It was published in a year the Ramadan was in December.
- Students have sat through many current event lessons from newspapers, which depict their religion as bloody, violent, and one that shows no value for life.
- Students were ridiculed by the teacher for bringing the religion of 'their' country into the classroom on a discussion on abortion where the student mentioned God and the innocence of a baby's life and that abortion is against God's will.
- Prayer rooms on occasion have been made available in schools and then misbehavior caused them to be discontinued, i.e.: other students were running by and making fun of praying Muslim students resulting in the Muslim students being reprimanded.
- A teacher has told students in class that their God whom they call *Allah*, is not God. One teacher told a student when she said to the teacher she is Muslim that there is no such thing.
- A Muslim student in middle school told his mother what a teacher said before the movie she showed, "watch carefully, you are gonna see some ugly people who do ugly things in this movie." The movie was *Not Without my Daughter*. When parents inquired she told them it was a part of her multicultural selections. She fast-forwarded through the *adhan* (or call to prayer), saying, "here we don't have a clue what they are saying." Even though as the participant stated, "the students raised their hands to translate the *adhan*, they were ignored."

Specifically in the last three situations told above, students negotiated how to survive public school life. It takes a great deal of effort to deny someone the right to pray. On many occasions Muslim parents have discussed what to do. In one instance above, an accommodation was made but then retracted because other students ridiculed the prayer. While, in most cases one would assume that an offender of the Muslim prayer should have been the one disciplined, it was the exact opposite. As hard as that is to comprehend, I find the teacher telling a child their, "Allah" is not God is even more egregious. Finally, in the case of the movie and the call to prayer it is simply unprofessional. When we decide to teach we need to understand that our own learning will never stop. There is so much we can learn from students. It is unacceptable for a teacher to mention, "ugly people" and to deny her/his students a voice in their classroom. To ignore a student when we should validate their knowledge in my opinion is a lost seed for world peace. In order to maintain some level of self confidence many students would have to go against the grain in order to participate in their own faith and religious practices.

Another constantly discussed issue was the pressure to "explain how you celebrate Christmas." In fact, Muslims don't celebrate Christmas and won't have a holiday in December on a consistent basis either (because Muslim holidays are cycled according to the lunar – not solar – calendar). Teachers have asked parents to send information to school on how their family celebrates Christmas. Although it may come across as trivial, I can't help but think that it might actually help if, one day, Hallmark stores decided to sell Eid cards. Yes, you can find a small selection of Hallmark e-cards online, but perusing through my local stores leaves me frustrated that it is yet another space in which we do not exist. I have always wondered why there hasn't been a selection of Eid cards when almost every card imaginable is out there and why teachers' stores don't go ahead and sell a few more decorations related to more religions. If we really *are not* separating church from state let us share more religions and portray them all in a more positive light. I would be comfortable seeing information about various religions shared if it was not one religion only and if it was not limited to December and of course if it was presented with every attempt of accuracy with practicing individuals from the various faiths consulted.

THE POST 9/11 RESEARCH

Muslim Parents tell of Public School Students' Experiences

During the weeks and months following 9/11 there were increasing concerns for Muslim students who attend public schools and how much they might suffer as a result of the tragedy. In discussions about how children need to learn about one another I began to gather parents for small focus groups. There was a need for better understanding the Muslim experience during this time.

Over several months I interviewed small groups of parents in focus groups around the city of Chicago and collected surveys from parents about their children's experiences in public schools. This research did two things: First, it provided a fresh perspective from new data as parents answered specific questions about their families' public school experiences and secondly, it provided us with a post 9/11 perspective to measure change given that 9/11, we were told by our president, "changed our world forever." The parents were consistently concerned about countering the public, media-based curriculum so that all children could learn about one another and learn about religion from the followers of that religion. Some noteworthy responses from participants in the focus groups include:

– My child would tell me the chapter on Islam is coming in a few pages. I approached the teacher who told me that she would contact me, however after waiting a few weeks for her to call I reminded her only to discover she had assigned the readings but had completely ignored any in-class discussions and informed students that time was not enough that she would have to continue to move through the book.

49

- Another parent reported her child wanted to pray while at school but the principal told her because of separation of church and state that she would have to pray when she returns home.
- One principal reportedly told students if you want to pray just sit at your desk and pray. He later admitted that he no idea how terrible this was when he realized the nature of the Muslim prayer.
- Several parents offered sweets, decorations and speakers for Ramadan only to have their offers turned down.

There are of course many other stories and scenarios that can be shared to focus on certain aspects of schooling and not enough space in a single chapter such as this. Some Muslims and some educators as well, may not find this topic important, unique, or may even be in denial as to its severity. I have heard some say this sort of thing is not significant, in other words "just get over it." However, I feel strongly that these circumstances need to be addressed and the dialogue needs to be open and frank. The brief yet real accounts, incidences, feelings and emotions that reflect on pubic schooling as it pertains to Muslims in Midwestern public schools are merely a sample for the reader to get a sense of what I consider worth telling.

SHARING THE STORIES IN WORLD EVENT CONTEXT

As the World Turns, Some Schools Tick

Current event stories came up a lot during the course of this research. It was surprising how world events were echoed in the stories being told about what happened in schools. From experiences as far back as 1979 when hostages were taken in Iran and Ayatollah Khomeini's name became a household word, the Oklahoma City bombing, current day stories related to women of Afghanistan, the day that Saddam Hussein's statue was toppled, and even the stories of non-Muslims who are self proclaimed authorities on Islam and Muslims.

In the days when Islam and Muslims were hardly spoken about in any context other than foreign ones, a first grade class copying assignment was given as the whole class participated in 1979 in an all school, "letters to Khomeini" project. The whole world was watching as college students in Tehran took American hostages and held them in the U.S. embassy. The first graders copied, "your country is wrong, Ayatollah. Your Moslem[3] people should not hold Americans who come in peace and love." One Muslim child related it to her parents. The parents could not decide what should be done and so they silently, did nothing.

One parent reported an incident with her own son after hearing a news story that came out about a school essay assignment on the Oklahoma City bombing (which was concluded after much speculation otherwise, as not to be related to Muslims). Her son was told by a friend to remember to write down in the essay that 'your religion kills' while other religions, 'love.' In the reported news story it was the teacher who had reminded a student of what should be included in the essay.

Middle school students in the Chicago suburbs discuss women, their wages and rights to vote as an American tradition during the month of March (women's history month). However, studying about women and freedom probably was not the pervasive theme of one suburban school bulletin board in 2000 titled: "March is Women's History Month, Wonder How the Women in Afghanistan will be Celebrating?" It depicted a bulletin board display with a life-size-cloaked, burlap-sack face-covering with holes for eyes. Across the bulletin board were details about women in Afghanistan seeing only women doctors, having coverings on their windows, getting less education, only going out when accompanied by a man, and more. A culture club sponsored the bulletin board. Perhaps little analysis is needed, we can all understand there are issues, by the same token, many American women prefer seeing female doctors, most people have curtains and blinds on their windows and equity for women in America is still a debate. The interview participant who told this story questioned its real purpose in a school where thirty percent of the students were Muslim and some girls wore a hijab. The mere appearance of the bulletin board was startling to some. The faculty sponsor defended it by saying, "It is good for our students to see that they have freedoms and choices."

During the Saddam Hussein years of turmoil from the first Gulf War onwards, many students with the same last name were ridiculed and taunted. Sometimes it was worse for girls, particularly if they wore a hijab. In numerous cases it went rapidly from name calling to pulling off of the hijab and one parent told a story of a girl, who toppled out of her chair just weeks after the statue of Saddam was pulled down by American troops. The student who pulled her chair out from under her said, "we'll just topple Saddam's daughter."

The examples cited above are straight from schools and are about the relationship between current world events and religion. Many news stories have fallen upon our ears, stories filled with religious prejudice against Muslims. From self-proclaimed authorities, like Jerry Falwell, Billy Graham's son Franklin and others, we have heard voices of people of authority spreading prejudice. In referencing race, class, gender and religious prejudice, Kincheloe (2005) states "Without an understanding of these specific dynamics, teachers are too often unable — even with love in their hearts and the best intentions — to protect students from the radioactive fallout of hidden structure of racism, class bias, patriarchy, homophobia, colonialism and religious prejudice" (p. 35). It is very complicated I know to say and do the right things all the time, but isn't the impact of these events on Muslims kids in public schools worthy of a serious and sincere response? Such experiences have left some Muslims wishing they were someone else.

CLOSING

This writing only provides a partial image of what Muslim students in public schools are experiencing. It seems to me that the result is very critical since much of it relates to the discourse about the separation of church and state, and for many public schools that's an oxymoron. I hope that teachers, leaders and families find this chapter useful. I hope it succeeded in some small ways at least to bring out the voices of Muslims in the Midwest, lest our reality be forgotten, lost in history perhaps a story left untold.

The accounts shared here are what some Muslim students in public schools tell us. In fact there is much we likely don't yet know. Families who hope their children will be viewed in a good light have made efforts to share their experiences, and have been told that we have separation of church and state and therefore cannot introduce your religion in the school setting. It makes me believe that the discourse of separation of church and state is unclear and needs further attention. The fact that children may not learn about all religions in school is problematic to say the least because when it is omitted it presents students with a message, *that they are not important*. It also denies the general student population an opportunity to gain insights and a better understanding of all people of the world.

As a student I did not learn much about slavery and nothing that I recall about Japanese interment. I admire the matter of fact statement made by Kincheloe (2005), referencing the overwhelming numbers of Africans that the slave trade killed. He writes, "In this context I typically point out that I simply could not trust an institution that routinely ignored such information" (p. 13). Students rely on their textbooks, which become an integral part of the school experience, thus it is equally important to have textbooks that correctly represent – and not ignore – accurate information about Islam and Muslims. For example textbooks have been known to teach that Mohammed, the prophet of Islam, founded Islam, which is counter to the history Muslims believe about him. I still recall learning in fifth grade that his followers were called *Mohammedans*. I had not become Muslim yet and find it funny that I later chose this path and still remember a page in the textbook with a flying carpet. I do think it is a perfect example of how we learn and recall certain facts from textbooks.

Perhaps even what students learn in school about their daily lives indirectly can cause children to lose a bit of their self esteem or positive self concept. My oldest grandson, a first grader in a public school, called me recently and announced he had an assignment. I needed to write him a letter that he would read aloud in class telling about the days when I was young. I wrote him the letter and had fun with it. Later he told me I should have signed it "grandma" and not "dadi" (a Pakistani Urdu word for grandma) since his friends all say grandma. In reflection I see this as the sort of thing that motivates me to search for teaching methodologies that make the strange familiar. He has, at a very young age, already learned from his peers that it is better to conform and be like the others rather than celebrate his own identity and embrace difference.

As a teacher educator I often share with my students that I long for the day when children in classrooms are invited to live confident lives even as they differ in small ways, and that they will work together in great ways with respect and harmony to create a better, more accepting world. I believe that teachers can and do make it possible by creating a community that respects difference. Related to helping teachers understand the dynamics and become comfortable with concepts of religion in their classrooms, I show a video (2007) by First Freedom Center, "The Constitution and Religion in the Classroom" and share a small brochure, Haynes (1999) "A Teacher's Guide to Religion in the Public Schools." To imagine that harmony is possible means that we need teachers in the public schools to teach our children about one another and embrace difference. Doing so sincerely makes the classroom, learning, and life interesting and is precisely what illuminates a schoolroom.

DISCUSSION QUESTIONS AND EXTENSION ACTIVITIES

(1) In this chapter, Imam quotes Kincheloe (2005) by writing, "As a student I did not learn much about slavery and nothing that I recall about Japanese interment… 'In this context I typically point out that I simply could not trust an institution that routinely ignored such information'." What are the implications for this "not knowing"? For one's own knowledge? For one's work in the classroom? For students at all levels of schooling? For advocates? For textbook producers and consumers?

(2) A common analogy brought up for discussion purposes by critical pedagogues is that lesbians and gays are positioned as having to "come out" while heterosexuals are not. Do/Should students (or teachers) who belong to marginalized faith groups have to "come out"? What options are available other than "coming out"?

IF YOU LIKED THIS CHAPTER, YOU MAY ALSO ENJOY:

Abo-Zena, M.M., Sahli, B., & Tobias-Nahi, C. (2009). Testing the courage of their convictions: Muslim youth respond to stereotyping, hostility, and discrimination. *In this book.*

Adam, M., Bell, Lee Ann, & Griffin, P. (Eds.) (1997). *Teaching for diversity and social justice: A sourcebook.* New York: Routledge.

Blumenfeld, W.J., Joshi, K.Y., & Fairchild, E.E. (Eds.) (2008). *Investigating Christian privilege and religious oppression in the United States.* Rotterdam: Sense Publishers.

Nieto, S. & Bode, P. (2007). *Affirming diversity: The socio-political context of multicultural education,* 5th ed. New York: Allyn & Bacon.

Sensoy, Ö. (2009). Kill Santa: Religious diversity and the winter holiday problem. In S. R. Steinberg (Ed.), *Diversity & multiculturalism: A reader.* New York: Peter Lang.

Stonebanks, C.D. & Stonebanks, M. (2009). Religion and diversity in our classrooms. In S. R. Steinberg (Ed.), *Diversity & multiculturalism: A reader.* New York: Peter Lang.

NOTES

[1]   A *hajji* is one who has performed hajj
[2]   Juma prayers refer to Friday prayer or congregational prayers on the Muslim holy day
[3]   "Moslem" was the common spelling at that time for "Muslim"

REFERENCES

Apple, M. W. (1990). *Ideology and curriculum.* New York: Routledge.
Creswell, J. (1999). *Qualitative inquiry and research design: Choosing among the five traditions.* Thousand Oaks, CA: Sage Publications.
Darder, A., Baltodano, M., & Torres, R. (Eds.). (2003). *The critical pedagogy reader.* New York: Routledge Falmer.
Haynes, C. C. (1999). *A teacher's guide to religion in the public schools.* Nashville, TN: First Amendment Center.
Imam, S. (2002). *Six Muslims living in the Midwest in the presence of the negative images of the public curriculum.* Evanston, IL: National-Louis University.
Kincheloe, J. L. (2005). *Critical pedagogy primer.* New York: Peter Lang.
Kincheloe, J. L., & Steinberg, S. R. (Eds.). (2004). *The miseducation of the west: The hidden curriculum of Western-Muslim relations.* New York: Greenwood Press.
McLaren, P. (2003). Critical pedagogy: A look at the major concepts. In A. Darder, M. Baltodano, & R. Torres (Eds.), *The critical pedagogy reader* (pp. 69–96). New York: Routledge Falmer.
Polkinghorn, D. (1995). Narrative configuration in qualitative analysis. *Qualitative Studies in Education, 8*(1), 5–23.
The Freedom Forum Center. (2007). *The constitution and religion in the classroom.* Nashville, TN: The First Freedom Center.

Seema A. Imam
Faculty of Elementary and Middle Level Teacher Education
National-Louis University

NAWELL N. MOSSALLI

THE VOICE OF A COVERED MUSLIM-AMERICAN
TEEN IN A SOUTHERN PUBLIC SCHOOL

INTRODUCTION

The purpose of this narrative is to expose the reader to the experiences of a typical
Muslim-American teenager in a southern public school in Northern Louisiana as
an attempt to inaugurate cultural discussions and understandings concerning
adolescent Muslim Arab immigrants. I had an intrinsic interest in conducting a case
study on a covered muslin teen because I learned very quickly, through my own
experiences as a Muslim Arab-American woman, mother, and teacher, who
recently decided to wear the hijab, that being transparently Muslim in schools
posed several challenges. I experienced extreme anxiety when applying for my first
teaching position which was not eased as the vice superintendent couldn't get past
the fact that I was so well spoken (for someone who wears the hijab). In my pre-
hijabi days, religion was never a topic discussed openly with others. However,
wearing the hijab became an invitation for inquiries, admiration, and sometimes
physical or verbal attacks. My research is guided by my experiences and that of our
community, as I seek to understand the often problematic cultural gap between
Muslims and our public schools.

WHY SHOULD WE CARE?

According to a report released in June from the Council on American-Islamic
Relations (2006), complaints of civil rights abuses increased by 25 percent in 2006.
Meanwhile, according to a *USA Today* poll (2004), 39 percent of Americans
admitted prejudicial feelings against Muslims, while 22 percent said they would
not want Muslims as neighbours. However, while such statistics illustrate, in part,
the attitudes of "adult life", less is known about the forms of oppression Muslim
youth are encountering. Furthermore, although media may report on issues regarding
the freedom to practice religion, the very real problem concerning the freedom to
exercise one's *Muslim* identity is absent.

Muslim Americans attending U.S. schools represent more than 20 countries in the
Middle East and Northern Africa (Schwartz, 1999). They share many similarities with
other immigrant groups seeking to establish an ethnic identity in an overwhelmingly
heterogeneous school system, but they also face additional challenges. Such challenges
include defending one's religion, dealing with stereotyping, and feeling subordinated
and alienated (Jackson, 1995). For example, Anas[1], a fourteen year-old American

Ö. Sensoy and C.D. Stonebanks (eds.), Muslim Voices in School: Narratives of Identity
and Pluralism, 55–70.

boy of Yemeni heritage who I assisted in school, was in the hallway and was joking around with the school's security guard and vice principal when they asked him if *they* could have more than one wife. Anas laughed and responded, "Yeah, just don't get four fat ones or you'll be broke bro!" Afterwards, he shook his head and said, "they ask me that question all the time." My fifth grade Egyptian immigrant student, Hashim, showed signs of quick assimilation to his school's culture when prompted to write an essay for the school's district test. He was asked to write about a favourite hobby. Hashim chose to write about his swim team from Egypt but was reluctant to list the names of his close friends on the team. When asked why, he replied that the scorers of the tests would immediate recognize that he was a Muslim because his friends have common Muslim names. Surprised with his thinking, I asked him what effect did he think it would have if the scorers knew he was a Muslim? He shrugged his heavy shoulders and said, "They'll fail me."

Some may simply dismiss these examples as personal anxieties, however, as I observed other disturbing instances that Muslim students faced, patterns emerged that suggested otherwise. One such incident was of Kareem, a second grade Egyptian immigrant student who I found crying, as a piece of ham was being waved in his face by his teacher. I quickly asked what was going on, and the teacher, showing frustration said, "It's not going to bite him!" Flabbergasted, I informed her that the cafeteria was informed of his religious diet and that he should not be forced to eat something his parents do not wish him to eat. Leaning towards me as though to share a secret, she whispered, "But he comes to school with only a hot dog bun with some white looking cheese in it!"

Another incident occurred while Hashim was taking his monthly social studies test. Hashim grew angered and confused with the last test question and immediately asked me to clarify what he read by translating the text into Arabic. To my astonishment, Hashim's teacher had included a cartoon of two Arab men chewing grass while sitting on camels, with a conversation bubble over their head asking why everyone's enraged about the sudden rise in gas prices. After quietly approaching the teacher, she openly apologized to the class with sincere regret stating that her action was "based on her head and not her heart." She explained that she had chosen the article to serve the purpose of the lesson and overlooked how it might appear offensive to her two Arab students. Besides reinforcing negative stereotypes of Arabs, Hashim and another classmate from Palestine, both close to tears, were forced into the position of repeatedly contesting to their friends that they did not ride camels in their home countries. However, when the next fifth grade class came in, she gave them the same photocopied test. Perhaps her rationale for doing this was that the other class did not have any Arab students and therefore, in her mind, no one would be offended- but I never did have the opportunity to ask her.

MEETING RANA

Rana adds a *voice* to the cold statistics of students of various religious orientations and those with no religious affiliation who are entering U.S. schools in increasing numbers (Haynes & Thomas, 1996). Unlike the immigrant boys I assisted as a translator, Rana expresses a stronger sense of identity and self-confidence, when confronted with similar situations. A Syrian-American girl who was born in southern Louisiana, Rana prides herself in being a radical football fan. Her father is a successful cardiologist and respected Imam for the local Islamic community of approximately 80 Muslim families, and her mother is a medical director at a local hospital servicing low income families. Rana would appear to be a typical thirteen year old if one knew she enjoys being with her family, teasing her four younger siblings, reading Harry Potter novels, and boasting about her ability to eat an entire pizza at one sitting. However, what makes her unique is that during the transition from sixth grade at Bob Petite Elementary[2] to Lincoln High School, Rana decided to cover her hair in adherence to an Islamic practice. I met Rana four years ago with her family at the local masjid and was moved by the solace and peace her tall pre-teen frame demanded compared to her peers.

I decided to talk to Rana for research purposes because I wanted to learn and understand how a teenaged scarf-wearing Muslim girl makes sense of her world. Coming from a small Arab American community, there were only a handful of covered Muslim girls going to public schools, and it seemed that Rana was leading the way. The Muslim boys I tutored in various public schools had their own obstacles, but, in comparison to their female counterparts, they were rarely asked questions related to their religion. I wanted to know, can a girl who has decided to show her devotion to her religion, by wearing a head scarf, thrive in school where Christian traditions are strongly embedded? Are such girls constantly forced to defend their religion? How much weight do they carry on their shoulders to answer with expertise, theological and other practice-based questions? I felt Rana was the perfect choice because she is not only an Arab American who is the product of immigrant parents from Syria, but she is also, according to her school's counsellor and based on her school's assessment measures, a high achieving "gifted" eighth grade student. As a starting point to my ongoing research, it was important to select an intelligent, sophisticated, and respectful participant in order to try and focus on her experiences on a framework of understanding identity (Guido-DiBrito & Chávez, 2003) without the potential distractions of academic frustrations.

THE CASE STUDY

How Do We Discuss Identity?

A framework of understanding identity used by Guido-DiBrito and Chávez (2003) was adopted in the analysis process to focus the findings on five emerging themes from the data: *Sense of Self in Relation to Others, Sensing/Interpreting/Knowing, Ethnic Community Responsibility, Cultural Imprinting,* and *Ethnic/Racial Contrast.*

The first category, *Sense of Self in Relation to Others,* discusses who Rana is and what she believes. The *Sensing/Interpreting/Knowing* category discusses the methodology in how Rana understands who she is while the *Ethnic Community Responsibility* reveals how she feels and, as a result, reacts towards her community.

Cultural Imprinting deals with to what extent is a person immersed in a specific and deeply lived cultural environment and the last category, *Ethnic/Racial Contrast* reveals the experiences that are considered norm in a culture or cultures different from one's own.

Collecting the Data

The data collected consisted of transcribed observations and interviews while immersing myself in Rana's everyday activities by attending Science, English, Reading and Physical Education (P.E.).[3] After school hours, I accompanied Rana to her Muslim Teen Girls (MTG) meetings held for Muslim girls who attend her mosque. As a qualitative researcher, I observed Rana's social interactions during lunch in the cafeteria, noted her body language, and thoroughly recorded random topics that were discussed. My data included written comments in the marginalia of the field-notes, and my analysis strategy was iterative as possible emerging themes were identified in ongoing ways to re-investigate and validate surfacing themes. I interviewed Rana, her friends at school, teachers, administrators, and her neighbours. I also analysed and included popular culture documentation by researching Rana's high school online through the school website and online articles including the local paper for any news regarding Rana's high school in issues related to religion or culture. I also examined the school's physical presence and public notices.

Faithful to a critical paradigm as described by Bogden and Biklen (2003) as the examination of how, "people produce their choices and actions in society" (p. 21) with a feminist ideological strand of wanting to "give voice" to those who may not traditionally fit "the hierarchy of credibility" (p. 17). I tried not to limit my observations to simply the school environment. Thus, I also participated in Rana's religious settings by visiting the local mosque for the Muslim prayers and educational classes she attended, as well as following her and her family as they volunteered their time for charity work. Furthermore, by engaging in a continuous dialogue, I was able to minimize miscommunication and misunderstandings.

Analysing the Data

Since the purpose of this study was to examine Rana's understanding of her world and her place in it, I had to make sure not to force my own perceptions or interpretations and solicit Rana's input throughout the entire process. Comments by the researcher and the participant were noted and analysed continuously to ensure accuracy with Rana's own interpretations.

Our first task during the analysis process was to collaborate in the interpretation process by placing emerging themes into codes. According to a study by Cooper (2005), involving the participant of study in a participatory action research (PAR) process can serve as a, "practical, credible and ethical methodology for research" (p. 463). Thus, I shared with Rana with my ontological, epistemological and methodological beliefs. We continuously discussed issues and themes that emerged as I shared the direction of the study through informal conversations, *Facebook* threads, and e-mail. It was particularly crucial to the analysis and interpretation process to include Rana's input and explanations since the focus of this study is based on her sense of self in relation to her surroundings.

According to the National Centre for Educational Statistics, Lincoln High School has twenty-eight percent of their students eligible for free or reduced lunches in a state where the parish rate is as high as sixty-one percent. Eighty four percent of the students are White compared to a state of average of only forty-eight. Upon entering the school, the smaller number of minorities compared to the other public schools in the state is immediately evident. Rana was the only *muhajiba* (covered) girl in the entire school with 438 students. When I asked the principal if he had ever had a *muhajiba* student during his administrative experiences, he replied that the closest similarity he could recall was a girl who had a rare hair disease. As a result, she wore a hat, then "later decided not to wear anything on her head."

SENSE OF SELF IN RELATION TO OTHERS

Connecting to Others

The *Sense-of-Self* category is a discussion on ethical identity. There has been a great deal of research on ethical identity that discusses theoretical perspectives (Chávez & Guido-DiBrito, 1999; Tatum, 1997) and personal narratives (Brown, 1994) that can provide some explanation as to the psychological and social challenges faced by individuals as they try to figure out who they are. Pinar (2003) suggests that the best way for an individual to explore identity authentically occurs when exiled or estranged. He defines exile as an involuntary membership to a foreign land, or when an individual is perceived as the "other" befitting Rana as a product of immigrant parents and a teenager singled out by the way she dresses. Thus, Rana's sense of self in relation to others is illustrated by two faces: 1. Rana, the Muslim and 2. Rana, the American.

Rana the Muslim

As a Muslim, Rana has a strong sense of self which can be further explored as something rooted in her parents' strong sense of identity, both in cultural and Islamic matters. For example, there is no question in the household that Muslim girls should wear the hijab. While Rana insisted on her spiritual and mental readiness for her decision to wear a headscarf, she was cautioned by her mother who told her that, "it would be a challenge in this [American] culture". When asked if she is conscious of being covered, Rana replied, "sometimes I forget I'm wearing it- like at home I don't take it off right away". In school, Rana is visually distinguished as the Muslim girl who participates in physical education classes wearing a long sleeved shirt under an oversized t-shirt, with long black pants. However, Rana views herself beyond the physical. For example, during the first week of school, Rana self-initiated her exemption from choir as a required elective to avoid singing and performing Christian music, while the parents of the elementary immigrant students I was working with (according to our school Principal) were shy about informing the cafeteria that their children cannot eat pork. Rana is steadfast in her religion and will not compromise by engaging or doing something that she believes distracts her from her faith.

Rana the American Girl

As the American girl is a huge American football fan who enjoys fieldtrips and competing academically. A common American school tradition we might take for granted is student council. Rana was very proud of the fact that she was elected to student council her first year at Lincoln High School. Coincidently, her mother expressed her pride in her daughter for the same occasion, but described in an interview that for Rana "The big encouragement was the first week of school... when a committee was being picked." I realized immediately she was referring to Rana's election as an officer. While Rana is assimilating to the American culture without effort, her mother did not understand some of the common events occurring in school culture (such as the elections of school council officers). Her mother was simply proud because, as she put it, "she was the new kid and seemed like an alien to them. She didn't have a chance to make friends- [but] despite her head cover, she was chosen."

SENSING/INTERPRETING/KNOWING

Where Does Knowledge Come From?

The *Sensing/Interpreting/Knowing* category is defined as an ethnic identity that is validated by how an individual gains knowledge. For instance, "the mind as a primary tool for gathering and interpreting knowledge is likely to do well in traditional learning environments" (Guido-DiBrito, Chavez & Mallory (1996), p. 5). Fortunately for Rana, the pool of knowledge is at her fingertips. Her academic influences are driven by both school and home life, while her Islamic knowledge is acquired through her father's lessons held at the local mosque. Thus, the question that needed to be answered was how does Rana know what is expected from her as both a Muslim and as an American? How has she come to know who she is?

I Think, Therefore I am- Muslim

At home, Rana is defined by her age and her responsibilities since, "...family life is a very important part of Arabs" (Suleiman, 2001, p.16). She is the eldest daughter, a member of a family of seven, sharing responsibilities such as babysitting her siblings and learning the micro-culture modelled by her parents. For example, Rana's adaptation to sensing one's place and expectations was clearly exercised as she was repeatedly reminded by her mother that they should leave the pizza restaurant during her Muslim Teen Girls meeting because the time was drawing near to the *maghrib* (evening) prayer. Rana is not expected, at least by family standards, to miss a prayer due to a social function- even if it is a Muslim social function.

Rana's parents do not pressure her, as her mom stressed in a telephone interview. Rather, the compromise of sensing what is expected and interpreting these expectations is explained to her by suggestions and alternatives presented to her by her parents. Thus, Rana has developed a sense of knowing a reality conducive to her culture and religious expectations, without requiring an explicit "How-to be a Muslim in America for Dummies" manual.

I Think, Therefore I am – Smart

For many Arab Americans, investing in their children through education "…is seen as a social asset, cognitive need, religious duty, and cultural nourishment necessary for both the survival of individuals and groups" (Suleiman, 2001, p.17). Rana knows that her education is important because it is stressed in her religion and her home life. Her mother is a vocal advocate for education in the Muslim community. This is probably one of the factors, that has helped Rana become, not only ethnically unique, but academically exceptional. Rana exhibits individualistic values that "…focus upon individual merit, effort, and achievement" (Pang, 2005, p. 43) simply because she believes she is treated as a rarity at her school. While the rest of her English class were engaged in preparing for the upcoming high stakes tests, Rana would routinely walk to the library, inquire about the arrival of new books and then return to the classroom computer to take several accelerated reading tests in one sitting. She is extremely conscious of the fact that she is responsible for her own academic advancement and vented some frustrations by accusing the parish of making, as she put it, "smart kids take care of themselves".

It is not surprising to witness Rana's self-confidence after being told by one of her teachers that she is "very respectful when asking questions" and, according to her assistant principal, "not a problem child". I also observed frequent and boasting declarations from teachers and friends that labelled Rana as "above average." One of her friends sitting at the cafeteria table was not shy to confess her desire to be "as smart as her [Rana]".

ETHNIC COMMUNITY RESPONSIBILITY

The *Ethnic Community Responsibility* is a construct that entails an individual's feeling or, "…personal responsibility for their own cultural community" (Guido-DiBrito & Chavez, 2003, ¶12). In addition to exploring Rana's ethical self, cultural conditioning is a second factor that was investigated. Cultural conditioning occurs both in Rana's own expectations and the roles expected of her by her surroundings. For example, Rana's peers and teachers are conditioned to a belief system that may force Rana to defend herself, since Arab Americans share with other minorities an, "…involuntary membership, their consciousness of being subordinated, prejudiced and discriminated against" (Suleiman, 2001, p. 7). Suleiman adds that while Arab

American students have, in general, been academically successful in schools, "…contemporary cultural conditioning and historical precedent of misinformation forewarn that we should expect them to be jeopardized in their social and academic growth in the multicultural society" (p. 7). However, Rana's influences from home outweigh that of her school culture. Thus, her personal responsibility can be characterized into the various roles she plays: as a student, a daughter, a sister, and a Muslim girl who feels responsible for her ethnic community.

As a student, Rana behaved with individualistic interests since the school's charitable involvements almost always occurred in the name of a Christian holiday or under the sponsorship of a local church. However, that does not mean that she did not get involved in charitable activities or avoids all of the charities at school. Rather, she is consumed in initiating and participating in charitable undertakings as an extension of the local mosque, fulfilling a community responsibility that is encouraged by her parents.

Although Rana did not join her mother in the room during a visit to a Muslim lady in need at the *Ronald McDonald House*, Rana assisted her mother with her four siblings by getting them ready and loaded in the van in preparation to depart, revealing her responsibility as a daughter. It was like second nature as Rana helped her mother sort through a trunk load of gift bags and presents for the lady, and then she entertained her siblings in the lobby until the visit was over without any difficulties.

In an interview, Rana expressed her responsibility as a sister by explaining that she accumulated a few tardy slips at school because, "I have to help brush their [sibling's] hair, get their shoes on and right socks on." Although she seemed annoyed when telling me this, I asked if it bothered her, she giggled and paused a moment admitting, "It gets really annoying." Instead of venting or complaining, she acted as though this was a necessary and expected responsibility.

Rana also fulfils the role of ethnic community responsibility by serving as the president of the Muslim Teen Girls club (MTG), a group name which she coined. When I asked Rana how she gains a strong sense of her role as a Muslim, she quickly shared that she recently completed reading *Taking Back Islam: American Muslims reclaim their faith* by Michael Wolfe (2004). In a follow up interview in 2008, I asked her if she had read anything else related to Islam, she answered "I haven't read a religious book in a while because I ran out of material". She is a huge role model to the Muslim girls in her group. This was evident when three out of four groups were asked to name an influential Muslim they look up to. I expected the girls to name an influential prophet or figure from the Qur'an and they all wrote "Rana."

Feeling culturally responsible a liaison to stop the stereotyping of Muslim and provide information to non-Muslims even as a sixth grade student as, Rana was anxious to complete a project on Islam to be entered into the parish's competition at a local university. Having a sense of the breadth of Islam and therefore realising it was a broad topic, she, "wanted to do something on Islam so my parents thought women. So, I went along and I did it." This exemplifies how on many occasions,

Rana is able to turn to her parents for guidance and support as she interprets her world to become her own person.

CULTURAL IMPRINTING

Cultural Imprinting deals with the extent of Rana's experiences in a culturally immersed environment. According to the fieldnotes, the cultural environments that set the stage for her experiences, in descending order, include Lincoln High School, the Mosque, and her home. This category infers that the extent of cultural immersion of an individual is indicative of the compromises one will make in the Ethnic/Racial Contrast category. However, despite the fact that Rana may spend most of her day at Lincoln High School, her ethnicity has a stronger imprinting on her identity and she is able to breakthrough certain norms and expectations. This is because Rana identifies herself as one who possesses a collectivist orientation that stresses, "...the importance of group goals over individual goals as well as traditional authority" (Coon & Kemmelmeier, 2001, p. 349) as expected from a Muslim Arab-American, as opposed to functioning as an individualist that Coon & Kemmelmeier claim emphasizes, "...self-determination, pursuit of self-interest, and self-actualization"(p. 349). Thus, it is not surprising that Rana's principal at Lincoln High School made the comment that although he was concerned she would have a hard time at the school, "she was elected for class office the first month or so she came", he said. "[Rana was] up for President or something!" he said, as he waved his arms up in excitement.

Although Rana is unique in being able to actively remain steadfast in her culture and beliefs compared to other immigrant students, one thing they all share is their attempt to avoid cultural imprinting in the American school cafeteria settings. While observing Rana, it became clear quickly that all she ate for lunch was a pack of *Lay's* potato chips. When asked why, Rana admitted that although she enjoys eating traditional Syrian food from home, she cannot blame her mother for not giving her a packed lunch because as she reported, "She [her mother] is in a hurry all the time". Not surprisingly, Rana is member of the *Facebook* group, created in 2007 by a Lincoln High School student, entitled "Why, yes, I am afraid to eat my school's 'food'." A twelve-year old American born Palestinian boy I worked with refused to eat the turkey sandwiches made for him as a substitute for the Friday pepperoni pizza slices because he believed the pink meat is ham. He said he does not trust the cafeteria staff because they don't care. Instead, he would rather starve and wait until he gets home to eat his mom's chicken and rice.

Unfortunately, many of our schools are still very ignorant about Rana's culture and religion. She is culturally immersed in an environment with a huge responsibility of not only representing Syrians, but more importantly, representing her father as the daughter of the Imam and vocal representative of the Muslim community. When attending the Sunday classes offered by her father, Rana is usually the only teenager present, and more often, the only female represented. At Lincoln High School, speaking two languages fluently fascinates her peers, whereas at the mosque, being bilingual is more commonplace, where the Imam lectures in both English and Arabic.

Nevertheless, Rana is able to handle assumptions and stereotypes with ease and patience. An example of this became evident when a close friend of Rana's, Katey, is surprised to learn that the movie she saw of a woman "with a dot on her head. Where she, like, had to marry him, she's not to be dating him, but you know, she gets like too close to him" was not a depiction of a Muslim girl's experience. Politely, defending her religion by correcting her friend with an expert ease that reveals she has dealt with such misconceptions in the past, Rana informed Katey that the dot on the woman's head was indicative of the actress' portrayal of a Hindu and not a Muslim. The misconception brought about further discussions of what Rana's friends learned from the media about arranged marriages and Muslims.

ETHNIC/RACIAL CONTRAST

The *Ethnic and Racial Contrast* category is defined as an individual's own cultural awareness to, "…privilege, oppression, cultural messages and media portrayal" (Guido-DiBrito & Chavez, 2003, ¶22) and the degree to which he or she displays behaviours of a culture or cultures different from his or her own.

Lincoln High School

Educational environments have been found to be socially, culturally, and operationally constructed primarily around specific ethnic, socioeconomic, gender, ideological and personal norms, values, assumptions and beliefs (Freire, 1974). For Lincoln High School, the dominant culture is deep rooted in Christian traditions and activities in organizations that could remain free from religious sponsorship. The "Character Counts" organization that is meant to promote moral character and ethics in students, engages in a yearly "Stocking Stuffer" drive for Christmas while the high school choir performs in local churches, and the local school board continues its tradition of beginning school board meetings with a Christian prayer. When Rana's school district was in a lawsuit after the tradition of a prayer during graduation, the superintendent insisted that "We certainly want to follow the law, but we also believe that it's part of our tradition of our graduation ceremonies. We've done it for years and years … in other parts of the state and the country" ("Webber defends prayer tradition", 2007). Thus, religion in schools for Rana is a norm. Ironically, it is what has empowered her to exercise her own religion.

Religion in Schools

Wearing the hijab or a headscarf is only one step of many for a Muslim woman of age to show her duty to and worship of God. It is also a visual distinction of a Muslim woman's faith in a time where the discussion of religion in public schools is still of much debate. According to Prothero (2007), there are three reasons why religion is avoided in schools: 1. to avoid controversy, 2. misunderstanding of the Supreme Court's decision concerning teaching religion in public schools, and 3. the educational shift of teaching what began as a content-based curriculum to a No Child Left Behind (NCLB) skills-based curriculum. Historically, public education has failed to find a constitutionally and educationally sound role for religion in schools (Nord & Haynes, 1998). However, despite movements in the United States to separate *Church* and *State*, the southern public school Rana attends allows the distribution of Gideon Bibles during instructional time. Lincoln High School also hosts a bible study student group, the Federation of Christian Students (FSC), which meets during a seventh grade math teacher's lunch period. Thus, Rana's sense of individuality as a Muslim is exacerbated by the fact that her school is immersed in activities that are exclusively catered for Christian students.

Local media reported that Rana's superintendent announced that high school teachers could choose how to handle "controversial topics", quoting a school board member who expressed that teachers would be supported who were uncomfortable teaching Darwin's theories of "monkey to man" evolution.

While Rana shows signs of assimilation to the dominant American culture, it is done with minimal compromise to her identity as a Muslim role model to her Muslim peers. For example, signs of assimilation are evident in the language Rana uses. When describing her feelings on *Facebook*, she alludes to street drugs, despite the fact that she is firmly against smoking cigarettes and drug usage. Her *Facebook* thread includes the slang word for smoked cocaine when she writes, "[Rana] thinks that Girl Scout trefoil cookies are secretly loaded with crack........I need more!!! (Facebook, 2008), while Lincoln High School students gossiped about the speculated occurrence of some students being caught for marijuana possession in recent months. Joking around by using the word "crack' is commonplace and outside of Rana's cultural habit. Similarly, Rana always addresses her teachers with the respectful southern vernacular, "ma'am" and "yes, ma'am".

It was easy for me to recognize which activities and functions Rana believed were the dominant, rather than her own, culture's norm. If there was an event or tradition she felt was outside of her culture, Rana would simply exclude herself from it as was done in the example mentioned when she substituted choir with history. Some would think this is a sign of oppression, for what if Rana (or other Muslim students) were *interested* in music. But Rana interprets it as privilege. Numerous occasions interpreted as privilege function as empowering experiences for Rana. For instance, since she was the only student who completed both homework assignments on a particular day, her teacher offered her a library pass. When Rana returned, she, without asking permission or indicating her intentions with her teacher, sat at the classroom computer to begin some Accelerated Reading (AR) Tests. During this observation, the teacher grew frustrated due to the immature behaviour of the class and as a result, demanded the students begin copying the dictionary. However, Rana continued to work on the computer, with occasional glances to the rest of the class, "still whizzing through the tests." She was well aware that the punishment did not include her.

Another incident indicative of how Rana's experiences empowered her sense of ethnicity and race occurred when she verbally announced to her teachers the approach of a Muslim holiday when she would take the day off. It is a cultural norm for Rana's classmates to miss school because they are sick, suspended, or playing hooky. Since Rana takes her class work very seriously, she does not have to act defensively to request a day off. When asked if the teacher was expecting an early announcement or a letter from Rana's parents, I was told by her teacher that Rana is simply required to "make up the missed day. We allow her to make it up. It's no big deal." While Christian heritage students are not required to make up any school days missed for religious purposes (since those days are usually school holidays), Rana stated with confidence, "I told them it's a religious holiday and I had to make up the work when I got back."

While there is "new research on how people's perceptions of racism and sexism still exist but are more hidden than in the past" (Pang, 2005, p. 104), Rana's status as woman and racial outsider has provided her with strength to distinguish how she identifies differently from her peers at school. Thus, it is more important than ever that school children as well as administrators learn to understand and respect the perspectives and religious traditions of others (Nord, 2000) as well as learn how students of non-Christian faiths are coping under pressures of a dominant school culture.

CONCLUSIONS

Describing Rana's experiences and how she defines herself with the themes discussed in this chapter has offered a narrative that hopefully shares a Muslim American teenager's life, experiences, interactions, and feelings. The data revealed that while Rana showed signs of assimilation to a dominant culture, she was still, like most culturally diverse individuals, "seen as an outsider" (Pang, 2005, p. 109). However, Rana proves that by being bicultural, she possesses "competencies and can function effectively in two cultures" (Manning & Baruth, 2004).

Although Rana's mother is more conscious of some of the later challenges Rana could face for wearing the hijab, Rana has been able to thrive and challenge a dominant culture that "holds specific beliefs about race that are usually based on generalized physical characteristics" (Pang, 2005, p. 108).

Some problematic patterns did emerge, especially in relation to how some administrators had limited experience and cautiously engaged in questions that involved race, ethnicity, or religion when addressing Rana or myself. It was only after a long presence in the school that more candid conversations occurred, and I was able to have certain individuals "open-up." Another interesting observation that I became conscience of was the fact that to Rana, I am a "Muslim sister" and that my presence may have affected her feelings of empowerment on certain occasions. I cannot convey to the readers the number of times I was asked by students of Lincoln High School if I was her mother.

Although these final thoughts open up new avenues to explore, I am hopeful that this discussion will provide some helpful insight for educators to help in overcoming the unknown abyss of female Muslim teen students who wear the hijab. I believe Rana's experience shows that adversity prevails as long as we follow her advice to not, "follow the crowd, [and] be yourself." Similarly, I think about Hashim, Anas, and Kareem often, hoping that they will gain the confidence to feel proud of who they are, whether it is identifying with a religion or a culture, and not allow institutional oppression to erode their identity. I believe their steadfast personalities will encourage institutional change that fosters cultural awareness to provide an educational environment where many cultures can co-exist. Hashim will not think twice about writing what he knows, Anas will hopefully no longer have to answer stereotypical questions, and Kareem can openly choose to eat a meal without feeling as though he must defend himself. Perhaps we can all learn something about not fearing who we are and embracing our ethnic identities.

DISCUSSION QUESTIONS AND EXTENSION ACTIVITIES

(1) Mossalli argues that her goals with this project were to offer a glimpse in to the life of a typical Muslim-American teenager. In what ways are Rana's experiences "typical" of American teen life? What are the implications of this for understanding American discourses about a "melting pot" versus Rana's authentic, sustained, and meaningful integration in to her community?

(2) In addition to telling Rana's story, Mossalli offers glimpses in to the lives of Hashim, Anas, and Kareem. These Muslim students are having a somewhat different experience from Rana's in school. The author offers some ideas about why these experiences may be. What are those ideas, and what other ideas could you add?

(3) One of the dominant discourses about America is that one ought to be oneself and not follow the crowd. Compare student experiences accounted in this chapter (and others in the book). Organize them in to moments when Muslim youth conform to dominant behaviours, i.e. when they are "just like (the majority of) us", and when they are *not* conforming, i.e. not behaving "just like us". Analyze your two categories for how being "just like us" or "not like us" are connected to mainstream discourses such as:
- individuality (everyone is a unique individual);
- American exceptionalism (the U.S. is a land of freedom and opportunity for *all*; thus the only factor in your achievements is your willingness if you work hard);
- Neo-liberal diversity discourses (our differences should be celebrated);

(4) How much do you know about the Muslim community in your school, or town, or city? Do a bit of investigation about the size of the community, its ethno-racial make up. Is the community similar to the one Rana lives in? In what ways might numbers matter to the experiences of integration, assimilation, or marginalization that Muslim youth experience?

IF YOU LIKED THIS CHAPTER, YOU MAY ALSO ENJOY:

Abdurraqib, S. (2009). On being Black and Muslim: Eclipsed identities in the Classroom. *In this book.*

Imam, S. (2009). Separation of what and state: The life experiences of Muslims with public schools in the Midwest. *In this book.*

Banks, J.A. (c.1975/2003). *Teaching strategies for ethnic studies*, 7th ed. Boston: Allyn and Bacon.

Blumenfeld, W.J. (2006). Christian privilege and the promotion of 'secular' and not-so 'secular' mainline Christianity in public schooling and in the larger society. *Equity & Excellence in Education*, 39, 195–210.

Gay, G. (2000). *Culturally responsive teaching: Theory, research, and practice.* New York: Teachers College Press.

Tatum, B.D. (c1997). *"Why are all the Black kids sitting together in the cafeteria?" and other conversations about race.* New York: Basic Books.

NOTES

[1] All names are pseudonyms.
[2] All school names are pseudonyms.
[3] For ease of reading, and unless noted otherwise, the quotes are directly from my own interviews and field notes.

REFERENCES

Brown, O. G. (Ed.). (1994). *Debunking the myth: Stories of African-American university students.* Bloomington, IN: Phi Delta Kappa Educational Foundation.

Chávez, A. F., & Guido-DiBrito, F. (1999). Understanding the ethnic self: Learning and teaching in a multicultural world. *Journal of Student Affairs, 12.* Retrieved February 9, 2006, from http://www.colostate.edu/Depts/SAHE/JOURNAL2/2003/DiBritoChavez.htm

Chávez, A. F., Guido-DiBrito, F., & Mallory, S. (1996). *Learning to value the "other": A framework for diversity development.* Retrieved February 9, 2006, from http://www.sahe.colostate.edu/Journal_articles/Journal_2002_2003.vol12/Understanding%20the%20Ethnic%20Self.pdf

Coon, H. M., & Kemmelmeier, M. (2001). Cultural orientations in the United States (Re) Examining differences among ethnic groups. *Journal of Cross-Cultural Psychology, 32*, 348–364.

Council on American-Islamic Relations. (2004, June). *Survey: 44 percent of Americans would curtail muslim civil rights.* Retrieved February 13, 2006, from http://www.cair-net.org/default.asp?Page=articleView&id=1359&theType=NR

Council on American-Islamic Relations. (2003, October 31). *Florida Muslims students kicked off bus 5 miles from home.* Retrieved February 5, 2008, from http://www.cair-florida.org/ViewArticle.asp?Code=PR&ArticleID=154

Elias, M. (2006, August 10). USA's Muslims under a cloud. *USA Today.* Retrieved January 20, 2008, from http://www.usatoday.com/news/nation/2006-08-09-muslim-american-cover_x.htm

Freire, P. (1974). *Pedagogy of the oppressed*. New York: Continuum.

Frieden, T. (2004, March 31). *U.S. to defend Muslim girl wearing scarf in school: Federal position will oppose Oklahoma school district policy. CNN*. Retrieved February 12, 2008, from http://www.cnn.com/2004/LAW/03/30/us.school.headscarves/index.html

Guido-DeBrito, F., & Chavez, A. F. (2003). Understanding the ethnic self: Learning and teaching in a multicultural world. *Journal of Student Affairs, 12*. Retrieved February 16, 2003, from http://www.colostate.edu/Depts/SAHE/JOURNAL2/2003/DiBritoChavez.htm

Haynes, C. C., & Thomas, O. (Eds.). (1994, 1996). *Finding common ground: A first amendment guide to religion and public education*. Nashville, TN: First Amendment Center.

Jackson, M. L. (1995). Counseling youth of Arab ancestry. In C. C. Lee (Ed.), *Multicultural issues in counseling* (2nd ed., pp. 333–352). Alexandria: American Counseling Association.

Manning, M. L., & Baruth, L. G. (2004). *Multicultural education of children and adolescents* (4th ed.). Boston: Allyn and Bacon.

Marcus, H. R., & Kitayama, S. (1991). Culture and the self: Implication for cognition, emotion, and motivation. *Psychological Review, 98*, 224–253.

Muslim girl ejected from tournament for wearing hijab. (2007, February 25). *CBC News*. Retrieved February 12, 2008, from http://www.cbc.ca/canada/montreal/story/2007/02/25/hijab-soccer.html

Nord, W. A. (2000). Multiculturalism and religion. In C. J. Ovando & P. McLaren (Eds.), *The politics of multiculturalism and bilingual education: Students and teachers caught in the crossfire* (pp. 63–81). Boston: McGraw-Hill.

Nord, W., & Haynes, C. (1998). *Taking religion seriously across the curriculum*. Alexandria, VA: Association for Supervision and Curriculum Development.

Ouachita Parish: First in Freedom. (2006, December 4). *Red state rabble*. Retrieved February 4, 2008, from http://redstaterabble.blogspot.com/2006/12/ouachita-parish-first-in-freedom.html

Pang, V. O. (2005). *Multicultural education: A caring-centered reflective approach with internet guide*. (2nd ed.). Boston: McGraw Hill.

Pinar, W. F. (2003). Exile and estrangement in the internationalization of curriculum studies. *Journal of the American Association for the Achievement of Curriculum Studies* (JAAACS). Retrieved January 23, 2007, from http://www.uwstout.edu/soe/jaaacs/vol2/pinar.htm

Prothero, S. (2007). *Religious literacy: What every American needs to know – and doesn't*. San Francisco: Harper Collins Publishers, Inc.

Rogers, S. (2007). "Webber defends prayer tradition." *The Ouachita Citizen*. Retrieved February 21, 2008, from http://www.ouachitacitizen.com/news.php?id=884

Schwartz, W. (1999). *Arab American students in American public schools*. ERIC No. ED363531. Retrieved February 16, 2003, from ERIC database.

Suleiman, M. (2001). *Image making of Arab-Americans: Implications for teachers in diverse settings*. ERIC No. ED452310. Retrieved February 16, 2003, from ERIC database.

Tatum, B. D. (1997). *Why are all the black kids sitting together in the cafeteria? And other conversations about race*. New York: Basic Books.

Travis, S. (2004, April 13). Muslim girl complains of hate attack at Boynton Beach middle school. *The Muslim News*. Retrieved February 12, 2008, from http://www.muslimnews.co.uk/news/print_version.php?article=7181

Wolfe, M., & Beliefnet (2002). *Taking back islam: American muslims reclaim their faith*. Emmaus, PA: Rodale.

Nawell N. Mossalli
Educational Leadership
Louisiana Tech University

ÖZLEM SENSOY

WHERE THE HECK IS THE "MUSLIM WORLD" ANYWAYS?

The Orient has helped to define Europe (or the West) as its contrasting image, idea, personality, experience...Orientalism is a style of thought based upon an ontological and epistemological distinction made between "the Orient" and "the Occident"

Edward Said, *Orientalism*, p 2

INTRODUCTION

Where the heck is the "Muslim World" anyways? It is one of those questions that has floated in and out of my mind for years. It usually surfaces when I view the news, or read something in newspapers or magazines about *it*, or the people who live *there*. It must be near the "Arab World" because little seems to distinguish the two worlds from one another. I have also noticed that few other *worlds* outside the *regular* world, inhabited by the rest of *us*, seem to exist (Stonebanks, 2004).

This quasi-intergalactic discourse reminds me of another inter-planetary speech norm: you may have heard, *men are from Mars, women are from Venus* (John Gray, 1992). This distinction is meant to reflect more than biological differences between males and females as it aligns certain ideological attributes with men, and others (usually opposite ones) with women. For example, men are non-emotive, women only want to talk about feelings. Men like sports, women like *Oprah*. Watch any mainstream television program, and you'll get the idea.

Having this example as a reference, I began to wonder about the meaning and, more significantly, the *function* of the "Muslim World" discourse. What is the function of its planetary divide? At the very least, if we are to have the West represent freedom, democracy, and equality, then the East must in contrast represent oppression, autocracy, and inequality. If the West is a place of advancement and progress, the East is a place of backwardness and regress.

Men/women, Muslim/non-Muslim, East/West... these are the binaries that organize the social world. Scholars such as Edward Said (1979) and Stuart Hall (1992) have written about discourse as the institutionalization of particular kinds of sense-making about social life. Applied specifically, discourses about "East" (what Said calls the Orient) and "West" (the Occident) begin from but extend far beyond simple *geographical* referents. Contrary to such a distinction, these discursive

Ö. Sensoy and C.D. Stonebanks (eds.), Muslim Voices in School: Narratives of Identity and Pluralism, 71–85.

constructs encompass ideologies, and ways of thinking about, of representing, and *making sense of* ideas and people associated with the East and West. For instance, for the concepts East/West, we might organize ideas such as exotic/modern; third world/first world; autocracy/democracy, savage/civilized, etc. in particular ways. Similarly, this organization indicates that one half of the binary, the West (and the ideas associated with it), is preferable to the other. In this way, institutions (such as schools and media) that have the power to define, represent, and canonize these types of discursive organizations, of "sense-making" about those of the East, especially in mainstream Western institutions like schools, deserve close attention.

When I set out on this work, I was inspired by historian, Ronald Takaki. In a lecture he gave that I attended, he spoke about history, institutionalized knowledge, and ethnic stereotypes. In his talk, Takaki asked, it is not only important to ask *what* you know, but also *how* you know what you know? This simple question resonated with me, because as a Turkish Muslim who immigrated to Canada in 1980, I was bombarded with what I often describe as the Midnight Express phenomenon. I am, of course, referring to the popular film *Midnight Express* (Guber & Parker, 1978) about a U.S. man held and tortured in a Turkish prison in the 1970s. The film reinforced virtually every conceivable stereotype about the East/West divide: backward/advanced, barbarous/civilized, ancient/modern, and so on. Describing my experience this way helps me to understand not only *what* my teachers, my classmates' parents and others knew about me, but also the *sources* of that knowledge – specifically, the discourses of East/West, Muslim/non-Muslim – that organized their knowledge.

This essay is an examination of discursive sense-making about Islam and Muslims. It is organized around how the West represents information about who Muslims are, where they are, and what they do. My discussion draws on data collected from a content analysis study of the visual representation of Muslims in world history and social studies textbooks (Sensoy, 2004). The study coded visual images contained in textbooks published between 1996 and 1998, and that are widely used in a school district in a major urban centre on the west coast. The following questions guided my analysis: *Who* (according to textbooks) are Muslims? *Where* are they? *What* do they do? For the purposes of this essay, I explore how understanding discourses about "textbook Muslims" can help me better understand the discursive construct of the Muslim world.

WHO MUSLIMS ARE...

Just as definitions of the Muslim world and the Arab world in popular Western discourse about the Middle East and/or other predominantly Islamic societies and/or Islam are interchangeable, the terms "Arabs" and "Muslims" are also often interchangeable in mainstream discourse.[1]

But Muslims are not always Arabs. And Arabs are not always Muslims. *Arab* refers to an ethnic group, sharing a common Semitic linguistic history (Arabic) and/or whose ancestors lived in the region known historically as Arabia, or today as the Arabian peninsula – framed by the Red Sea on its west, the Arabian Sea to its south, and the Persian Gulf on its east. Prior to the seventh century, Arabia was home to mostly pagan, mostly fragmented, pastoral communities. The major empires in the Middle East at the time were the predominantly Christian Byzantine, and the predominantly Zoroastrian Sassanian empires (Hourani, 1992; Lapidus, 1988). Muslims believe that in the seventh century, the teachings of God were revealed to the prophet Muhammad through the angel Gabriel. Muhammad shared these revelations with the community. The recitations, believed to have been the direct word of God as heard by Muhammad, were recorded exactly as he uttered them in his native, 7th century, Arabic. These recitations are called the *Qur'an* (literally: the recitation), and this is the holy text of Islam.

Because the Qur'an is considered to be the actual revelation from God as heard by Muhammad, there is a great significance placed on all Muslims to learn to read the Qur'an in the originally-revealed classical Arabic. Thus in the early years of Islam, Arabs (and Arabic) played a central role in recording, canonizing, and spreading the word of God. However today (as in the early years) not all Arabs are Muslims. In fact, they comprise a small percentage of the global Muslim population. The top ten countries with the largest Muslim populations (in descending order) are: Indonesia, Pakistan, India, Bangladesh, Turkey, Iran, Egypt, Nigeria, Algeria, Morocco.[2] In this group, Egypt (in North Africa) is the highest ranked Arabic-speaking country with 58.6 million Muslim, which is about 30% of Indonesia's 182.6 million Muslims. For comparison and perspective, the U.S. is the country with the largest population of Christians, globally, at 190 million reported adherents.

So who are Arabs and who are Muslims? Consider the most popular figures of Arab descent you might know (perhaps Edward Said, Saddam Hussein, or Yasser Arafat), are they Muslims? All of them? Are you sure? Would you be surprised to learn that any of them were not? Your response to these questions reveals something about your familiarity with widely circulating social discourses related to people of Arab descent and their (real or presumed) relationship to Islam. It would be naïve to pretend that these expectations about who Muslims are and what a Muslim looks like were not mediated by race. If we consider how school textbooks are a part of this normalizing machinery, it may not be surprising to you that in textbooks most Muslims are presented as indistinguishable from Arabs. Here are some patterns that emerged in the textbooks. When considering who Muslims are, it was overwhelmingly the case that Muslims were ""Middle Easterners." The figure below shows how "textbook Muslims" were represented in this sample of 4 textbooks.

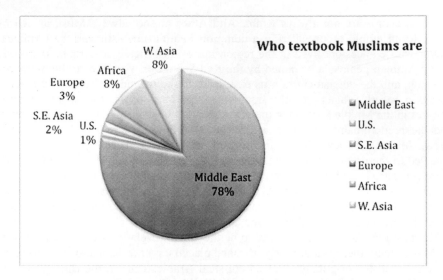

Figure 1. Distribution of Muslims in world settings in textbooks

As Figure 1 shows, the overwhelming number of textbook Muslims are located in the Middle East – 78%. Although many Middle Easterners *are* Muslim, the majority of Muslims, globally, are Southeast Asian. Only 2% of this sample represented Muslims in Southeast Asia.

Along with this geographical segregation is another compelling pattern relating to textbook organization. Of the ten textbooks initially surveyed, only four contained any images of Muslims. Three of those four texts had isolated a chapter called an "Islamic world," or a "Muslim South Asia" within a unit on Asia. No other region of the world presented in these textbooks has any other religious community isolated in a parallel manner, for instance, there is no chapter on the *Christian World*, no *Protestant North America*, no *Catholic Europe* etc. in these textbooks. If you are a classroom teacher, or work with teachers, administrators, or are involved in the publishing of textbooks – go ahead and have a look at how the chapters in your world history texts are organized. Are there chapters that isolate a Muslim or Islamic world or civilization? If so, what might the underlying discourses be that are invited by such an organization? Are you surprised to hear that most Muslims, globally, are not Middle Eastern? Do you think others would be surprised?

I would argue that repeatedly positioning Islam as outside of the "regular" world inhabited by the rest of us, and the virtual exclusion of Muslims from non-Middle Eastern contexts is significant. It is significant because such organizations (wittingly or unwittingly) uphold the norm that *Islam* (and the Middle East) and *the West* (and in particular, the United States, and democracy associated with the U.S.) are, in general, incompatible (Esposito & Voll, 1996). The partitioning of Islam into separate units and chapters of other "worlds" echoes in geographical discourse the perceived *ideological* incompatibility. Samuel Huntington famously wrote about a clash of civilizations between the rational, modern, West and the irrational, backwards, and immature East. It wasn't too long ago in human history that discourses about the inherent differences between groups of human beings were used to justify European activities to colonize and "help" the uncivilized savages of many parts of the world. This kind of logic of civilizational progress and decay is an old trope of Orientalism and (as has been well documented in postcolonial scholarship) functions in part to explanation and rationalize colonial expansions in to parts of the world (like the East) positioned as being "in need."

WHERE MUSLIMS ARE...

According to these textbooks, Muslims live in the past. At least their "best" is in the past. When examining the temporal era of the representations, these textbook Muslims were shown in contemporary settings (defined as post-1900) 74% of the time. This means, most representations in these textbooks are of post-1900 settings. However when we factor in the *type* of setting Muslims are in, Figure 2 shows the distribution of Muslims for the setting-type in this sample.

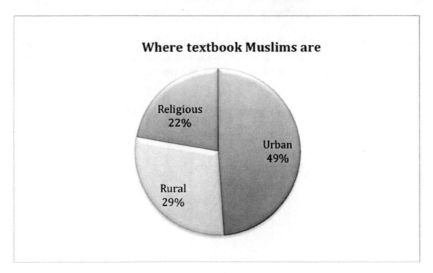

Figure 2. Representations of textbook Muslims in types of settings

Since the sample contained a substantive number of "religious" settings (mostly of mosques, but also multiple images of the Ka'ba as shown in Figure 3), religious settings were coded as a separate category. The category of "urban" setting meant settings that were non-religious but urban. And the category of "rural" referred to settings that were non-religious but rural.

Figure 3. Photograph taken by Muhammad Mahdi Karim[3]

This distribution reveals that in the majority of settings in which Muslims appear, those settings are non-religious, urban settings. However, when distributed according to the time period (post 1900 and pre 1900[4]), the pattern is as shown in Figure 4.

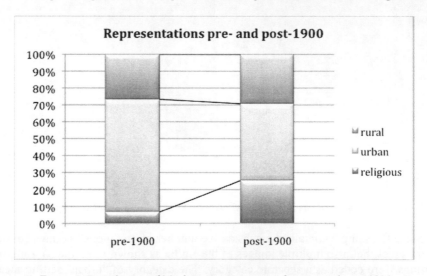

Figure 4. Distribution of Muslims in setting types for pre- and post-1900

Figure 4 shows the distribution of Muslims for images coded as pre-1900 (the past), and post-1900 (contemporary). From this organization, it is clear that contemporary Muslims are in *fewer* urban settings than Muslims of the past.

For example, in the images examined, an urban setting was identified by visible markers of urbanization such as: major city centres (Tehran, Damascus, Beirut), industry, resources, technologies, crowd size, and traffic. Based on this type of organization of the data, Muslims of the past were in *urban* settings 67% of the time, as compared to Muslims of the contemporary period at 45%. Muslims of the past were in *rural* settings 27% of the time, as compared with contemporary Muslim at 29%. And Muslims of the past were in *religious* settings in less than 1% of images as compared with post-1900 representations at 25%.

So according to this sample, since 1900, Muslims are in (22%) *fewer* urban settings, (2%) *more* rural settings, and (24%) a *greater number* of religious settings than Muslims of the past. Representations of Muslims in the past highlight their accomplishments during the "golden age" of Islam, the period up until the 9th century (CE), thus Muslims are frequently represented in libraries, centres of scientific inquiry, and long-established urban centres such as Baghdad, Beirut, Tehran, and Damascus. Comparatively, representations of contemporary Muslims are in greater numbers of religious settings. A much higher percentage of Muslims are shown in prayer, at mosques, and in Mecca. Although these activities are not new to Islam, it seems that the predominant activity of Muslims, in this sample, has shifted from scholarship (in the past) to religion (today).

When we examine the *quality* of the 45% of urban representations of contemporary Muslims, other patterns emerge. For example, familiar characteristics of contemporary urban environments (such as tall buildings, factories or industrial sectors, technologies, urban infrastructures and finance) were in only 32% of post-1900 images. Vehicles appear in 1% of textbook images. Industrial settings appear in 0.5% of textbook images. And only one image (0.3%) featured several of the most common codes of urban life: tall buildings, traffic, businesses, paved streets, and vehicles. This was a photograph of downtown Amman, Jordan. All other images coded as "urban" were identifiable by crowd size, and captions that identified the setting to be a major city, such as Tehran, Damascus, or Beirut.

This discourse of backwardness that is so evident in the textbook representations helps to explain my own "real world" experiences. I remember giving a talk to a class of preservice teachers, several of whom at one point confessed that they had *never* seen images of tall buildings or traffic in cities of the Middle East (such as Baghdad, Cairo, or Istanbul). In fact, few of them had any "mental image" of what these major urban centers might look like. The only mental images that came to mind when they thought about cities of the Middle East were camels and deserts. It also is not uncommon (still) for me to get raised eyebrows of surprise and "oh really!" when I mention *Skype*'ing with my friends and relatives in Turkey, or using bank machines and the metro system in Istanbul. People seem genuinely *surprised* that such familiar elements of modern life are a part of life "over there" too.

WHAT MUSLIMS DO...

So from textbook representations, I have learned that Muslims are Middle Easterners (often interchangeable with "Arabs"), they used to be intellectual and urban, but have regressed and are more religious and rural than in the past. And when I examine what textbook representations show me about what Muslims *do*, it isn't surprising perhaps that they seem to pray a lot.

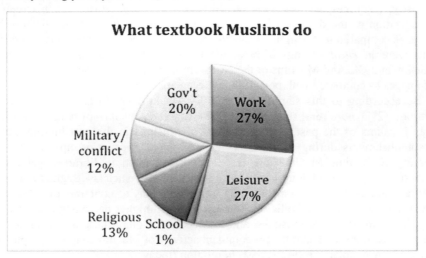

What textbook Muslims do

Gov't 20%

Work 27%

Military/ conflict 12%

Leisure 27%

Religious 13%

School 1%

Figure 5. Distribution of activities of textbook Muslims

Textbook Muslims were most frequently depicted in leisure and work activities. However the type of work Muslims do is traditional work: fishing, selling spices in the marketplace, leading camels, harvesting crops by hand, and carpet weaving (similar to Figure 6).

Figure 6. Photograph taken by Georges Jansoone[5]

The categories of "type of activity" (what Muslims do) were also coded for the degree of activity (no activity, sedentary, active, or high active/conflicted).

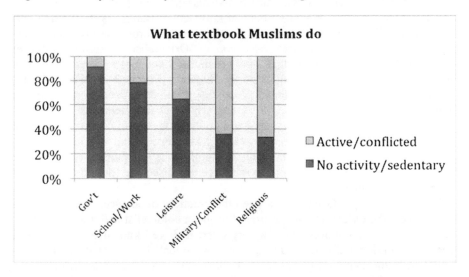

Figure 7. Distribution of degree of activity in activities of textbook Muslims

The images of textbook Muslims in this sample conveyed an overall sedentary nature of life among Muslims. This, in and of itself, may seem like a small point. However, I would argue that this type of depiction of sedentary-ness functions to uphold another familiar binary discourse in the West. "Rolling up one's sleeves" to "get down to work" and "hammer out agreements" are more than metaphors (Dyer, 1997). They are core elements to explaining mainstream Western experiences of advancement, progress, and modernity. The perceived absence of "hard work" among Muslims in domains of life that are arguably most valued (government, school and work) can contribute to an imbalanced view of who works hard and thus deserves the rewards of that labour. The sustained representations of Muslims in sedentary contexts across various domains of life reinforce popular knowledge[6] (Banks, 1996) that a majority of Muslims do not work hard and are, in general, lazy (Suleiman, 1977; Steet, 2000). Such representations simultaneously reinforce a discourse of meritocracy as they serve to be evidence of how a lack of hard work leads to an absence of advancement, modernity, and the personal reward of that hard work. I have been surprised to hear on more than a single occasion that Saudis and "Arabs" in general just watch the oil squirt out of the ground and sit back and shovel in the money (all, of course, at the expense of industrious and hard working families that need that oil to get to *their* jobs).

TEXTBOOK MUSLIMS & THE PRESERVATION OF THE EAST/WEST DIVIDE

Textbook Muslims serve to familiarize and stabilize particular ideas about the East/West discourse in mainstream popular knowledge (Banks, 1996). Said (1979) calls the invisible and pervasive network of (initially European) institutions that organize the world in this way, *Orientalism*. Orientalism describes a set of institutional practices that produce and normalize knowledge about the Orient (Arabia/Africa/Asia) often in contrast to the Occident (Europe/New World). These practices and knowledge developed *alongside* of nineteenth century European global colonialism and expansion. The (ancient) Orient was frequently recognized to be the *source* of European languages and civilization. But to concede the Orient as being this source was to simultaneously historicize *it* and the people *there*, setting it in this ancient (but no longer) significance, in perpetuity. Textbook Muslims seem to be representations to reinforce this discourse (or at the very least, they do not challenge it).

Discourses that produced and, through the practices of science, confirmed such "facts" about the Orient, in part, justified European colonialist activities (Jacobson, 1998). The eugenics movement is a very overt and well-known example of this type of institutional discourse and activity. As scientists dissected, studied and "confirmed" the genetic inferiority of the Oriental and African brain (see, e.g., Robert Knox, *The Races of Men* from 1850 or more recently Herrstein & Murray's 1994, *The Bell Curve*), colonization efforts into Africa, Asia, and North America were subtly justified based on the logic this type of formal school knowledge[7] established. Binaries such as civilization vs savagery, Christianity vs heathendom (Horsman, 1981; Jacobson, 1998).

This historical basis not only gains momentum as disciplines and practices are perfected, and norms of analysis are established. It also gains authority as a completely *normative* system of knowing, studying, and teaching about others. In this way, Orientalism is more than an explicit intent of any group to exert power or dominance over another group. Rather, it refers to accepted norms, and common-sense ideas about people and common-sense ways of organizing the world, and the people in it – such as *the Muslim World*.

The Islamic World is a current manifestation of this type of pervasive, invisible network of institutional practice that organizes our world, that tells us who lives where, and something about "our" identity in relation to theirs. But whether intended to isolate, or incidentally doing so, it is difficult to ignore that the relationship between those who have power (globally) and those who are made powerless depends on the *stability* of an East/West logic. The invisibility of that logic is in effect how those who have power stabilize and institutionalize that power, with the West as the beneficiary of the progress, and the site of contemporary modernity, advancement, and civilization. The construction of a normative discourse about "the world of Islam" is another manifestation of this logic that indicates where in the global order civilization and savagery reside, and where they are absent.

TEXTBOOK MUSLIMS & THE SIMPLIFICATION OF COMPLEX HISTORIES AND TENSIONS

Another result of the segregation of Islam and Muslims in particular (and Arabs and the Middle East in general) to other discursive worlds is the complexity that is diluted when trying to present, and make sense of very difficult *political* (not simply religious) histories, tensions, and social dynamics in the Middle East today. By isolating Islam and Muslims, textbook representations reproduce a cultural essentialism, creating the image of a community that is unified, homogenous, fixed, and consenting, while simultaneously positioning that entire community as opposite to all other religious traditions. Acknowledgement of a plurality or tensions *within* this Muslim world is avoided, and the perception of a homogenous Islamic world-view is cultivated. This not only supposes a unified location, experience, and Islamic community, but also misses an opportunity to reflect upon the significance and variety of Muslim work and scholarship, historically and today.

The effects of this segregation theme are considerable because while it isolates Muslims apart from all others, is also artificially isolates Islam from other Abrahamic religious traditions. The implications of this, given the attention needed to understand and resolve conflicts in important religious centres such as Jerusalem, are unavoidable. As prior research has shown (c.f. al-Qazzaz, 1983; Suleiman, 1977; NAAA, 1980), textbooks have historically emphasized a discontinuity between Judaism & Christianity, and Islam. Similarly, in popular culture and media, it is not uncommon to hear references to a "Judeo-Christian" heritage/culture/tradition, with no inclusion of Islam in partnership – although it would be just as reasonable to do so – *theologically speaking*. According to these detailed textbook studies, a discontinuity between Islam and Judaism & Christianity is consistently presented in textbook structures and narratives (c.f. Suleiman, 1977; Jarrar, 1976; NAAA, 1980; al-Qazzaz, 1983). When considered in tandem with the attention paid by both curricula and teachers to the Arab-Israeli conflicts in the Middle East (NAAA, 1980, Suleiman, 1977), the polarization of Islam and Judaism & Christianity can result in the organization of other binaries onto these artificial theological one. For example, how might binaries of savage/civilized, ancient/modern, backward/advanced, black/white, right/wrong, good/bad be organized within an Islam/Judeo-Christian binary?

This kind of discursive organization occurs despite the real opportunities that exist for *building* alliances across faith communities. For instance, Judaism, Christianity, and Islam are all monotheistic faiths of the Abrahamic tradition. Many of my students are surprised to hear that the Qur'an contains many of the same characters featured in the Old and New Testaments (including Abraham, Adam, Eve, Mary, Moses, Noah, and Jesus) and the same accounts about the creation of the world, the great flood, and the greatness of God's prophets. As Corrigan, Denny, Eire, & Jaffee (1998) explain, "all three of these traditions [Judaism, Christianity, and Islam] took shape within the network of cultures we call the 'West.' As Western religious traditions…they share a linear view of history, a belief that God created the world from nothing, and that creation is progressing toward its fulfilment" (p xi). So if there is such a strong continuity, why in textbook organization has that continuity not only been *avoided* – but, in fact, ruptured?

Perhaps the organization reveals more about the social context in which those textbooks are produced, than the accuracy or completeness of the information presented. al-Qazzaz (1983) offers a compelling case for the connection between contemporary social/political concerns, and the narratives about Islam that are presented in textbooks. As he explains about textbooks published during the 1950s, Islam was frequently referred to as "Mohammadism." However, by the 1970s, a shift had taken place in which the religion was correctly named "Islam," and some textbooks explained why it was important not to call the religion Mohammadism or its practitioners Mohammadens. This shift potentially reflects the social and political changes in the decades between the 1950s and 1970s. Shifts such as the heightened U.S. attention to the U.S.S.R. and the Cold War; the 1948 war in Palestine/Israel; the 1956 Suez War; and the 1967 Six Day War between Arab nations and the recently formed Israeli state. These events resulted in a shift of dominant U.S. political and social awareness of the U.S.S.R. and its power in predominantly Muslim regions of Central Asia, as well as of the Arab-Israeli conflict in the (predominantly Muslim) Middle East. Textbooks as products of a larger framework of social knowledge and practices thus reflect social ideologies.

CONCLUSION

So, what are we to make of this perceived "culture clash"? Is the East/West divide fundamentally a *religious* one? If it is, how do we reconcile this with the vast body of scholarship that strongly *aligns* the three Abrahamic faiths (Judaism, Christianity, and Islam)? Is it a *political* divide—places that "have" democracies versus those that do not? If so, why do Uzbekistan, Turkey, and Iran (all predominantly Islamic societies) regularly have a much higher voter turnout than Canada, the U.K., or the U.S.?[8] Does this higher degree of participation not make them *better* democracies, *more* democratic, and so, *Western*?

We are no longer (if we were ever) living in a world in which the role of social discourses in our organization of our ideas about human plurality can remain invisible. Young people must develop the language and skills with which to examine and respond to complex social, historical, and political dynamics within and beyond nation states. In this chapter, I have argued that textbook discourses reinforcing a Muslim world separate from "the rest" of the world, closely reflect broader social ideas circulating about Muslims. The representations of Muslims in textbooks contribute to the perceived ideological incompatibility between Islam and "the rest." I believe it is this perceived ideological incompatibility that, in part, drives popular discourses about the status of women, lack of modernity, and threat posed by Islam, Muslims, and the Middle East in general.

The images presented and re-presented in school textbooks have a productive – not simply reproductive – dimension. This means that images are not simply a reflection of some true three-dimensional thing out in the real world. Images (the contexts in which they are read, the means and motivations by which, and audiences for whom they are produced) are an integral aspect of understanding representation of groups (Hall, 1997; Sensoy, 2009).

The effect of these representations (whether they are true or false, real or fictionalized) is the essentializing and normalizing of these characteristics and associations exclusively with those who are, or are assumed to be, Muslims or from "over there."

DISCUSSION QUESTIONS AND EXTENSION ACTIVITIES

(1) Sensoy argues in this chapter that there is a strong relationship between school and broader societal discourses about Muslims. Under what conditions and by what means might textbooks also be used to *disrupt* stereotypical and essentialist representations of Muslims? How is your answer the same and different for the representations of other social groups?

(2) In this chapter, Sensoy argues that images matter, that what students see repeatedly presented in textbooks *produce* (not just reflect) how we think about social groups. As an activity to investigate this point, collect visual representations of a social group (Muslims, Arabs, women, persons with disabilities, or other) as found in the media, in textbooks, or in other sources. Have students return to class with their "data." In small groups, have students organize their findings in to the categories: *who they are* (are Muslims always shown alone, in groups, couples, friendship groups, same sex, mixed sex groups, etc); *where they are* (at home, school, work, urban, or rural settings, etc); and *what they do* (what activities are they shown engaged with shopping? sports? housework? on the computer? etc.). From these categories, students can practice connecting the representation of the group to broader social discourses about what it means: to have (for example) a good life? A productive family? To be free? Industrious? Friendly? Smart? Although persons are obviously never *simply* Muslims (they are simultaneously women, able-bodied, etc.), it is useful to focus on a single group for this activity. Part of the class discussion can include unravelling how the representation of the primary group identity intersects with other identities. For example, if you are collecting images representing women, how are Muslim women or women with disabilities, or lesbians, or working class women each as groups represented differently and similarly, and what are the implications of these types of differences?

IF YOU LIKED THIS CHAPTER, YOU MAY ALSO ENJOY:

Ali Khan, C. (2009). On being us and them: A voice from the edge. *In this book.*

al Houseini, D. (2009). The evolution of an identity crisis. *In this book.*

Kincheloe, J.L. (2008). *Knowledge and critical pedagogy: An introduction.* Dordrecht: Springer.

Marshall, E. & Sensoy, Ö. (2009). Save the Muslim girls! *Rethinking Schools*.

Sensoy, Ö. (2009). "Ickity ackity open sesame": Learning about the Middle East in Images. In B. Subedi (Ed.), *Rethinking Curricular Knowledge on Global Societies*. Information Age Publishing.

Steet, L. (2000). *Veils and daggers: A century of National Geographic's representation of the Arab world*. Philadelphia: Temple University Press.

Stonebanks, C.D. (2008). Spartan superhunks and Persian monsters: Responding to truth and identity as determined by Hollywood. *Studies in Symbolic Interaction*, 31, 207-221.

NOTES

[1] For an introductory discussion of Islam, see Christopher D. Stonebanks, Joe L. Kincheloe, & Shirley Steinberg (forthcoming). *Teaching Against Islamophobia*. New York: Peter Lang.

[2] Stats from aneki.com a nonprofit internet database operated from Montréal, Canada that compiles world statistics from sources such as the UN, and CIA *World Factbook*

[3] Distributed by Wikimedia Commons http://commons.wikimedia.org/wiki/Image:Kaaba_mirror_edit_jj.jpg

[4] data seemed to be distributed primarily as pre World War I and post World War I. So the coders agreed that "1900" would be an accurate reflection of how the images were divided in the sample.

[5] Distributed by Wikimedia Commons http://commons.wikimedia.org/wiki/File:Izmir010.jpg

[6] I use "popular knowledge" in the way James A. Banks (1996) describes it, as the concepts and explanations that one attains from mass media and popular culture.

[7] I use "school knowledge" in the way James A. Banks (1996) describes it, as the concepts and explanations presented in textbooks and other formal curricula.

[8] Stats from IDEA (International Institute for Democracy and Electoral Assistance) http://www.idea.int/

REFERENCES

Banks, J. A. (1996). The canon debate, knowledge construction, and multicultural education. In J. A. Banks (Ed.), *Multicultural education, transformative knowledge, and action* (pp. 3–29). New York: Teachers College press.

Corrigan, J., Denny, F. M., Eire, C., & Jaffee, M. S. (1998). *Jews, Christians, Muslims: A comparative introduction to monotheistic religions*. New Jersey, NJ: Prentice Hall.

Dyer, R. (1993). *The matter of images: Essays on representation*. New York: Routledge.

Esposito, J. L., & Voll, J. O. (1996). *Islam and democracy*. New York: Oxford University Press.

Guber, P. (Executive Producer), & Parker, A. (Director). (1978). *Midnight express* [Motion picture]. United States: Columbia Pictures.

Hall, S. (1997). *Representation: Cultural representations and signifying practices*. Thousand Oaks, CA: Sage.

Hall, S. (1992). The west and the rest: Discourse and power. In S. Hall & B. Gieben (Eds.), *Formations of modernity* (pp. 275–331). Cambridge, MA: Polity Press.

Horsman, R. (1981). *Race and manifest destiny: The origins of American racial Anglo-Saxonism*. Cambridge, MA: Harvard University Press.

Hourani, A. H. (1992). *A history of the Arab peoples*. New York: Warner Books.

Jacobson, M. F. (1998). *Whiteness of a different color: European immigrants and the alchemy of race.* Cambridge, MA: Harvard University Press.

Jarrar, S. A. (1976). *Images of the Arabs in the United States secondary schools social studies textbooks: A content analysis and unit development.* Unpublished Doctoral Dissertation, Florida State University.

Lapidus, I. M. (1988). *A history of Islamic societies.* New York: Cambridge University Press.

MESA. (1975).

National Association of Arab Americans. (1980). *Treatment of the Arab world and Islam in Washington metropolitan area junior and senior textbooks.* Washington, DC: Author.

al-Qazzaz, A. (1983). Image formation and textbooks. In E. Ghareeb (Ed.), *Split vision: The portrayal of Arabs in the American media* (pp. 369–380). Washington, DC: American-Arab Affairs Council.

Said, E. G. (1979). *Orientalism.* New York: Vintage.

Sensoy, Ö. (2004). *Popular knowledge and school knowledge: The relationship between newspaper and textbook images of Arabs and Muslims.* Unpublished Doctoral Dissertation, University of Washington.

Sensoy, Ö. (2009). "Ickity ackity open sesame": Learning about the middle east in images. In B. Subedi (Ed.), *Rethinking curricular knowledge on global societies.* Information Age Publishing.

Steet, L. (2000). *Veils and daggers: A century of national geographic's representation of the Arab world.* Philadelphia: Temple University Press.

Stonebanks, C. D. (2004). Consequences of perceived ethnic identities (reflection of an elementary school incident). In J. L. Kincheloe & S. R. Steinberg (Eds.), *The miseducation of the west: The hidden curriculum of Western-Muslim relations* (pp. 87–102). New York: Greenwood.

Suleiman, M. W. (1977). *American images of Middle East peoples: Impact of the high school.* New York: Middle East Studies Association of North America Inc.

Özlem Sensoy
Faculty of Education
Simon Fraser University

PART 2:

**VOICES & EXPERIENCES OF MUSLIM STUDENTS
IN THE UNIVERSITY YEARS**

DALIA AL HOUSEINI

THE EVOLUTION OF AN IDENTITY CRISIS

I am possessed with my nationalism. I am an Arab-Canadian who is Palestinian, and Muslim. My identity is in constant flux as I leap from one setting to another. Being born a Palestinian, a witness of media terror fabrication (which has heightened in the post 9/11 era), an Arab in North America, and a student of Communication, have all been factors in developing or suppressing, my identity.

I have been and still am going through many ups and downs in attempting to develop a strong, confident, and eloquent persona. Through four vignettes and four reflections, this essay describes the evolution of an identity crisis. An identity crisis that I believe many fellow Arab-Canadian, Middle-Eastern-Canadian and Muslim-Canadian individuals are also enduring.

To help construct this essay, I read Robert Mullaly's book, *Challenging Oppression* (2002), which discusses in depth the psychological consequences of being a member of an oppressed group. As I read the book, I connected with its themes of loss of identity, powerlessness, fear, suppression of anger, isolation, ambivalence, and a sense of inferiority. Reading about an internalized oppression nurtured from a sense of inferiority, with its patterns of "self-hatred, helplessness and despair, mutual distrust and hostility, feelings of inferiority, and psychological distress and madness" (p.123), I wondered, *is this me?*

Wondering lead me to search for answers for why I felt such a strong connection with the themes of the book, relating to the emotions expressed in it, and the way it painted identity and its various components. I had to dig into my memory box and put my 'identity-puzzle' together. Piece by piece, I chose the memories that stood out the strongest to me and reflected carefully on the impact they left on me. I really wanted to get to the root of what was causing my low self-esteem so I can immediately work on repairing the damage, rather than just being another witness to it dwindle day by day.

In great part, this chapter stems from the knowledge I acquired from course readings during my undergraduate studies at Simon Fraser University and the many courses that helped me in identifying and understanding the contributing causes for my low self-esteem. In small part, the class readings and course discussions began to give me a language with which to begin reflecting on possibilities to find solutions to my identity crisis. The next vignettes and subsequent reflections are my honest attempts to come to understand four noteworthy incidents out of many that have influenced my sense of self. I try not to over-edit my vignettes, instead exposing my own biases, nor to over-reference my reflections, citing work that

Ö. Sensoy and C.D. Stonebanks (eds.), *Muslim Voices in School: Narratives of Identity and Pluralism*, 89–98.
© 2009 Sense Publishers. All rights reserved.

does not speak directly to my experiences, hoping this will lead to a genuine, personal reflection.

VIGNETTE 1: HELLO.

I remember my first day at Alpha Secondary School, in my first year in Canada. It was the grade 12 orientation for school. I walked in to the classroom and I felt so cool, like I was in an episode of *Saved By the Bell*: big hallways, lockers, white boys, a lunch room, and no school uniforms. The student council was welcoming and friendly, I thought to myself, I can't be making a mistake, I shouldn't mind staying here. As I entered Chemistry in Block A, I found myself a seat in the back of the classroom, next to two East Indian boys. One of them asked me where I was from, and I said, "Palestine." He replied saying, "What? Pakistan?" I articulated, "Pa-les-tine." He had no clue where that was. He kept on calling me Iranian, even after we graduated. As I sat there, listened and observed, I had experienced my first five seconds of fame as the "other", Immersed in a flora of nationalities, the East Indian, Asian, Irish, Italian, Persian faces I was surrounded by, I was framed as an "other"; sometimes even by another "other." Everything was so different, everybody was aware of me, my accent, and my style. I began to tear up; I didn't know what to do. It was too late to leave and go back to Abu Dhabi.

Then came Block B, I was fortunate to sit next to a popular girl in the "white group" where I invited myself to have lunch with her and her friends as I frankly didn't want to be alone. Quickly, they took me in, questioning me about boyfriends, life as an Arab, and talking to me about what they will do on the weekend. I ultimately left the popular group, to befriend three East Indian girls who I stayed friends with until graduation.

Back in Abu Dhabi, I had been considered "cool" simply because I attended a private school which taught everything in English except for Arabic and Islamic classes. My classmates and I were considered cool to those who attended public schools because we spoke to each other in English and seemed "Americanized" (by that, I mean we dressed from shops like Zara and American Eagle and we would go out in groups of both males and females). That had been my first experience of social divisions.

I always assumed that North Americans were much better than we- the *Arabs-* were. Part of this assumption was due to the fact that the American students in my school, children of expatriates working in the U.A.E, were very popular; everybody wanted to be like them and everybody wanted to hang out with them. I was not cool enough to be accepted into their group, so I used to feel so flattered when people I'd run into on the street would speak to me in English thinking I was a foreigner. That gave me the satisfaction of feeling *almost* as cool as them. But as soon as I came to Vancouver, I began to wonder what had given me that false perception. Over the years, reflecting on that misconception, I realize that I had mostly received my information about North America from classmates, and the television.

To me, the media was the most influential in producing the illusion that North America is everyone's dream. With their fancy movies, their good-looking actors, and their dramatizations, the Americans seduced a democracy-deprived people into a fantasy of the perfect world. Not that the U.S. is a democracy in my opinion either, but by "democracy" I mean the *fantasy of freedom* to cross religious and cultural bounds without facing social complications.

A perfect example of the fantasy world American media created for people is Disney movies and television shows. They lured young viewers into assuming that the U.S. was a place of peace, love, happiness and a multicultural utopia. Disney was located in the U.S.; hence *it* must be the "happiest place on earth." This self-proclaimed image of Disney as a trademark of innocence is a diversion, protecting it from the questioning gaze of critics (Giroux, 2004). As a child, I always watched Disney movies with my parents fully promoting their viewing. It was not only an escape, but it basically sketched out my fantasies for me. I grew up thinking I was Snow White, wanting to be swept away by a tall handsome prince, and wishing I had a genie who would grant me three wishes. Because I was raised watching Showtime cable versus Arabic TV, I was quite familiar with this Western world and its fantasies.

As I was placed in the now-real setting of a North American city upon my arrival in Vancouver, and experienced first-hand being a character from an episode of *Saved by the Bell*, I quickly avoided the setting with the popular (White) group and resorted to becoming a character in the plot with the Brown group. When I was friendly with the popular grade 12 group, I was forced to listen to what I was taught to shy away from and avoid, both in my religion and tradition. There were constant conversations about sex and drinking and whatever happens in between. It was not something I could relate to and no matter how much it seemed cool on TV, I never got myself to accept that mentality, after actually experiencing it. In order to continue with that group and fit in, I would have had to conform to their wants, suggestions, behaviours, and norms. Although these friends knew I wasn't drinking because of my religious beliefs, whenever I was invited to a party I would be told things such as "We have to drink up" or "I will get you drunk." I felt so uncomfortable and pressured around them, despite the fact that they quickly accepted me in to their group. I do not recall feeling oppressed by my fellow classmates, the only way I can describe those feelings is – discomfort and insecurity. Discomfort that they were aware, as well as I was, of my accent; discomfort because we couldn't initiate or maintain conversations; discomfort and fear of being rejected because I do not conform to what they perceived as cool. I was insecure around them because I knew that although I did not want to be like them, with a little more pressure I *could* be like them.

As I befriended the brown group, I felt more welcomed. We had more in common. I remember one of the first things I was ever told by them was that I was *Brown*. Sometimes we would joke that I was *beige* because I looked White, but my ethnicity was not White. We would always discuss diversity issues such as foods we had in common, similar traditions and similarities in language. We all felt that we shared tradition and a common experience of oppression. We never outright said to each other that race was playing a major factor in our friendship, perhaps no one had taught us the language to express what we all knew, but we would find other ways to communicate our feelings. For example, we would confirm our differences from the privileged White group by calling them "snobby," even though they may have not necessarily been so.

VIGNETTE 2: MY NAME IS DALIA AL HOUSEINI.

In the beginning of the grade 12 school year, I once told my Biology teacher that I couldn't understand some of the things he said because I wasn't used to his accent yet. He immediately pointed his finger at me and said, "No, I, don't have an accent, YOU have an accent."

I sunk. Just because my accent was different than his didn't mean that he does not have an accent. Don't we all have accents? Who has the neutral and standard accent? He only began acknowledging me after I received the second highest grade in class. Worse was my English teacher. She seemed to specifically disregard my ideas and opinions in class. I approached her more than once about this after class, asking her why she treated me so differently, ignored my concerns, and sometimes even my existence. Why did I get a lower mark than others even though I'm fairly certain my writing was better than theirs? For a while, there was a brief change in the way she was towards me, but it wasn't long before I was once again ignored and made to feel invisible. The only teacher who would talk and joke with me was my Math teacher; he was Black, and we both recognized that we had accents.

I strongly believe that high school in Vancouver was my first experience of being racially discriminated against by most of my teachers. I was confronted by my teachers on matters of religion, race and intelligence far too often, rarely overt but hidden in their rhetoric. Although I was educated in the "British system" before arriving in Vancouver, the fact that I came from Abu Dhabi made my English seem inadequate by the school's standards. Other than my non-Canadian accent, I really thought my grammar and spelling was better than most of my classmates'. Yet still, I was made to feel inadequate by my teachers.

The teachers' behavior towards me can be described as "differential teacher expectations" (Mullaly, 2002) in which students from subordinate groups were usually regarded by their teachers as dull and hence fall below others students, usually those from the dominant group, who teachers perceive as bright. Because I came from a "third world country," had an accent, and couldn't articulate sentences properly, I was perceived as an unintelligent student, and had to work really hard to gain my teachers' positive attention. As Mullaly notes, the oppressor (in this case, the teacher) may not be aware of her own biases, yet imposes her ideologies on the oppressed because of her power advantage. As a 16 year-old immigrant Arab Muslim in Vancouver, new to everything, I did not feel like I was in a position to challenge my teachers on how their preconceived biases were affecting my self-esteem. Eventually, I forgave my teachers because I was able to prove to myself that I was capable of getting high grades. Even as a foreigner.

VIGNETTE 3: IT WAS A PLEASURE TO MEET YOU.

I didn't know how to react on my plane back from Abu Dhabi to Vancouver, during my school's Christmas break, four months after I had arrived in Vancouver. On the second leg of my KLM flight, from Amsterdam to Vancouver, there happened to be a change in seating on the plane. That's when an Israeli girl was moved to the seat next to mine. That was my first ever face-to-face encounter with an Israeli. I found out she was Israeli because she was loudly discussing her "amazing trip to Israel" with the people around her. She shared with everyone that she was a Jewish European who wanted to join the army. When she asked me where I was from, I answered, "We are neighbors. I am from Palestine." I can't recall her reaction exactly, but it was a mix of shock and, curiously, friendliness. I was extremely uncomfortable, fidgeting in my seat, not really listening to her, thinking about how to act, but furious as she talked about *my country* that she claimed was *hers*.

Ironically, she began talking about how uncomfortable and mad she was about the "German guy" she had initially been sitting next to and how *glad* she was to be seated next to me instead. She was livid about how she felt edgy about Germans because of their atrocities to "her people" in the Holocaust. I finally cooked up the courage to confess to her that I was highly uncomfortable with her being next to me as well, and we nervously laughed it off; actually, *I* nervously laughed it off. As we said our goodbyes, I felt really small and threatened while I watched her walk away, confident and strong.

In the United Arab Emirates, the country I lived in for the first 16 years of my life, I had never met a single Israeli or Jewish person for that matter. The only time in those 16 years in which I had met a Jewish person was during my trips to Palestine at the ages of 2 and 7, but I was too young to remember the whole trip. Whatever I had known about the Jewish religion and the Israeli culture came from what I had watched on TV and what I had heard people say. My plane experience was my first experience on a conversational level with an Israeli. Not only was I completely taken aback by it, but it also became a defining frame for any future interaction I had with Jewish people. I may have not been prepared for this first meeting, but it did give me much to consider for future interactions with fellow Jewish classmates, coworkers, and new acquaintances.

Although the plane experience was not a comfortable or happy experience, I did learn a few things from it. First thing I learned was that contrary to my expectations that I would be received by an Israeli in a hostile manner because I am a Muslim (and worse a Palestinian), she was kind of nice – especially given how awkward the situation was. Many of the assumptions I made came from Arabic mainstream television news and the predominant message was that Israelis were violently abusing the Palestinian people; I had never considered that perhaps some Israelis tolerated and even accepted Palestinians. My second lesson was that, we (she and I) had a shared mental state – the fear of oppression. I was unaware, and was completely taken off guard by her expressing that she was uncomfortable around Germans. This led me to use this phenomenon as a means of relating and understanding "my enemy," perhaps befriending her. *Her* innocent people had also undergone an oppression, which affected her and *my* innocent people were still undergoing oppression by her people. This shared experience may help us relate more to each other, and help me communicate more effectively with her.

Now reaching this conclusion on paper is way easier than overcoming a set of preconceived biases that have been snowballing for over 16 years. Coming up with a solution to the Palestinian/Israeli conflict is an altogether different challenge. In truth, I did not feel comfortable being around her; the fact that she appeared to me as confident, so powerful and so domineering greatly affected my self-efficacy and self-determination. I believe that the reason I felt incredibly uncomfortable, other than this being my "first contact," was that I was so used to freely hating my people's oppressors within my community in Abu Dhabi. Most of the community advocated for the Palestinian cause, and strongly opposed the apartheid regime, so I never had to think or act otherwise. I was free to get as angry as I wanted at the Israelis. Although I knew I had the full right to oppose the Israeli apartheid regime, I couldn't express that sitting in that airplane seat. I was unable to ask her, to challenge her, on how she could be *proud* to be an Israeli, given all I knew the Israeli army had done to my people. I felt like I had no backup whatsoever. Alone. I needed solidarity. I felt "oppressed," in my thoughts, my feelings and ideas. She probably would have felt similarly oppressed in the U.A.E., given that the overpowering majority would more that likely not welcome her ideas. She would have felt as threatened and weak as I did.

According to Mullaly (2002), oppression is the domination of subordinate groups in a society by a powerful (politically, economically, socially, and culturally) group. I felt exactly that being around her. Many thoughts were running through my head: If we gotten in to an argument, I had the feeling that I would have been proven wrong, and that everyone on the plane would have sided with her and against me. I felt vulnerable. I was not going to insult her, I knew I had to be careful, but I was worried that if I did say anything, I might reinforce stereotypes of Arabs as being hostile, stubborn and I was also fearful of being undermined because my knowledge of the history of Palestine was not absolute. In this context, her knowledge was *absolute* and unquestioned. Mine were "opinions" that could be completely disregarded. I risked being just another Arab Muslim who brings defamation to our reputation.

I admit, I do not know everything about my history and yet, I learn about the importance of knowing one's history and fully comprehending it in order to correctly depict the realities of oppression (Mullaly, 2002). This activity can assist an oppressed group in becoming more aware about all aspects of its oppression and in self-defining its identity to carry out what liberation theologian Martin-Baro calls the recovery of historical memory, "This activity undermines and challenges the ahistorical propaganda that the situation of oppression is a natural reality, and fosters a sense of solidarity and identity among oppressed persons" (as cited in Mullaly, 2002, p.176).

I was completely unprepared for my chance meeting on the airplane, because, quite simply, I had never met an Israeli. We both consider each other as the "other" and never had the opportunity to truly dialogue. Dialogue is a reciprocal form of participatory and committed communication. Therefore, dialogue, or at least my initial small step in dialogue that took place on the plane, helped in my understanding of the conflict and reshaped my understanding of my world. It did so first and foremost by challenging my biases as dialogue is a vehicle for uncovering people's subjective reality and opening it to critical reflection. It also opened up a whole world of communication for me that I never thought possible.

I realized that we both had a lot to learn about each other.

VIGNETTE 4: BY THE WAY, I AM A MUSLIM PALESTINIAN.

I took a Religion Studies course during my third year in university. I was an active participant in this class. With respect to Islam, I felt like I had to always present a truer image of what was being taught. I, along with my fellow Muslim classmates, was not convinced that the image of Islam being presented by the professor was accurate. We felt that it was subtly but unquestionable biased. In one of my tutorials, I recall expressing myself with my hands (which I do a lot) in order to explain a point. I had clasped my right hand vertically over my left hand, which was horizontal, while speaking; this hand gesture signifies the phrase "that is the point" in the Arab culture. Instantly, the professor said, "Calm down now." I remember perfectly the look of shock on my face and some of my fellow classmates' faces. *Calm down*?! I *was* calm!

As soon as I had left the classroom, I was surrounded by four girls, who were expressing regret on behalf of our professor for what she had said. They said that they understood I was not angry, they understood the messages I was trying to convey and said they always respected and appreciated what I contributed to the class. I eventually confronted my professor about the issue and she said she didn't even recall the incident, and that she hadn't meant it. No apology or regret for the misunderstanding was offered.

That class had been really exciting for me and I was always motivated to participate in its discussions. I felt like I, along with the very few other Muslims in class, were placed in that class for a reason, and that reason was to correct any misconceptions that may be taught to at least 75 students who are quite trusting in the credentials of the professor. Little did they know that that professor was not well educated on the subject of Islam, not only was it evident in her choice of curricula presented in class, but she openly admitted that to me as well. She said that was why she rushed through the subject matter so quickly.

For example, she presented Islam as a contradictory religion. She chose chapters of the Qur'an that were interpreted as advocating violence and hatred against Christians and Jews along with other chapters which did not portray Muslims in a good light. In post 9/11 circumstances, as a Professor, she should at least have chosen one of the 114 chapters of the Qur'an that are about peace. The only part of Islam that she "promoted" and elaborated on was Sufism. The issue here is that although that chapter was contradictory in its content, she neglected to offer the historical explanation for why the chapter may have been sent to the Prophet. By choosing to exclude the relevant *context*, the construction of meaning was obstructed.

Discourse frames the knowledge which is formulated from within it. As such, when language is manipulated in institutions, it can create misconceptions and form ideologies in the mainstream. That is exactly what Islam does not need right now. This incident gave me a live example of the concept of "hegemony." Gramsci's definition of hegemony states that "those in power maintain domination through cultural influence rather than force." This can be done through Ideological State Apparatuses (ISAs), or institutions that instil dominant ideologies in the population. In this case, the apparatus is an educational institution, my university in Canada. I was shocked to see how much power one holds because of the knowledge, or position, they carry, and I was appalled to experience how easy it is receive inaccurate information without questioning it. That is when I finally understood why most Americans supported the war on Iraq, believing that Bush's attack on Iraq was an innocent attempt at playing the role of a hero. Knowledge is power, and that is extremely dangerous.

In the end, I was very disappointed that she offended me in front of everyone because of her preconceived biases. Just because some Muslims on television may be irrational and aggressive in their delivery manner, that does not justify her assumptions about me, even if she had a personal experience with another Muslim who may have acted irrationally. I was being very normal, getting angry was not even in the context of what I was saying. In addition, I have had no record of ever being rude or offensive to anyone in any of my classes. As an authority figure she should at least have been careful when it comes to such a sensitive topic.

I also wondered, does she even believe Islam is a *real* religion?

CONCLUSION

Carlos Cortés (2000) states that outside the school curriculum there exists *another* curriculum known as the societal curriculum through which children learn about social diversity. This societal curriculum is subdivided into four intersecting categories: the immediate curriculum, the institutional curriculum, the serendipitous curriculum and the media curriculum. The immediate curriculum is the information center where we get most of our information from on a daily basis through our immediate social circle, such as family, friends and co-workers. The institutional curriculum is where we obtain our information through pupils who belong to institutions that we belong to that shape our perception of those around us; for example, churches, mosques, and synagogues. The media curriculum would include the information informally taught to us through our daily interaction with the media. The serendipitous curriculum includes random personal experiences, such as chance interactions with strangers or visits to foreign countries (Cortés, 2000).

This organized division of information centers segregates the sources through which humans in the 21st century shape their perception of the world and those in it. In the four vignettes, societal curriculum: the institutional curriculum -my

University and school experience; the media curriculum- Disney and the news; the serendipitous curriculum- my plane experience; and the immediate curriculum, my friends, were – and are – central to my experiences. The school curriculum in particular, was a major factor in influencing the process of meaning-making of the world around me. Thrown from one setting- the United Arab Emirates, to another, was difficult. Yet things could have been much worse if I had known no English. Attending Canadian educational institutes created many challenges, as staff and students critically viewed my heritage, but allowed little opportunity to critically examine their own dominance.

The reason I grew to love my university experience is because it helped me make sense of my world. Prior to it, my brain simply couldn't comprehend the existence of the seemingly insurmountable gap that separates the "Muslim East" from the "West". I also learned that I could not blame some North Americans for ignorance that when I consider my first real conversation with an Israeli, I found myself consumed in as well. Over time, I came to realize that since the school and societal curricula they are exposed to may not usually include a positive image of Arabs, I cannot expect them to search for the truth on their own if it doesn't immediately affect them. After all, if I did not meet the Israeli girl on the airplane, I would have kept avoiding contact with Jews in order to avoid confrontation, and I would have never pushed myself to learn more about Palestine. I also would have placed a barrier between myself and Jews/Israelis thereby blocking dialogue.

Writing this essay has acted as a catalyst to my understanding of my persona. I need to be able to learn from these experiences, now that I know why I am always fearful of confrontation. I need to be able to engage in dialogue within a multicultural setting to be able to clarify misconceptions and get over differences. I need to also advocate my cause and raise awareness without letting fear of oppression and making mistakes consume me to the extent that I become silenced. Finally, I need to continue to cast a critical eye on what I see think carefully about what I hear, and reflect.

DISCUSSION QUESTIONS AND EXTENSION ACTIVITIES:

(1) In several sections of this essay, al Houseini describes how the threat of being perceived in a particular way, influenced her actions. Claude Steele has described this phenomenon as "stereotype threat." What does this concept, and the author's experience reveal about educators' responsibilities to understand and respond to stereotype threat in productive ways that do not minimize students' fears and legitimate concerns?

(2) What "serendipitous" moments of learning have you had in the past? How can such moments be deliberately harnessed for the possibilities they offer for rich reflection of the kind al Houseini describes?

(3) In "Vignette 4: By the way, I am a Muslim Palestinian" al Houseini recounts a professor of religious studies who admitted that she was not well versed in Islam,

but who nonetheless portrayed the religion and its people in a stereotypical manner. What are your experiences with "learning" about Islam and Muslims within formal religion classes? What role could the other (non-Muslim) students in the class have played in order to be effective allies for both their Muslim classmates, as well as their own (mis)education?

IF YOU LIKE THIS CHAPTER, YOU MAY ALSO ENJOY:

Abo-Zena, M., Sahli, B., & Tobias-Nahi, C. (2009). Testing the courage of their convictions: Muslim youth respond to stereotyping, hostility, and discrimination. *In this book.*

Ali Khan, C. (2009). On being us and them: A voice from the edge. *In this book*

Bayoumi, M. (2008). *How Does it Feel to be a Problem?* Toronto: The Penguin Press.

Satrapi, M. (c2003). *Persepolis.* New York: Pantheon Books.

Steele, C.M. (1997). A threat in the air: How stereotypes shape the intellectual identities and performance of women and African Americans. *American Psychologist, 52,* 613–629.

Steinberg. S. (2004). Desert Minstrels: Hollywood's Vurriculum of Arabs and Muslims". In J.L. Kincheloe & S.R. Steinberg (Eds.). *The miseducation of the West: The hidden curriculum of Western-Muslim relations* (pp. 171–179). New York: Greenwood Press.

REFERENCES

Althusser, L. (1971). *Ideology and ideological state apparatuses. Lenin and philosophy and other essays.* New York: Monthly Review Press.

Cortés, C. (2002). *The children are watching.* New York: Amsterdam Avenue, Teachers College Press.

Giroux, H. A. (2004). Are disney movies good for your kids? In S. R. Steinberg & J. L. Kincheloe (Eds.), *Kinderculture: The corporate construction of childhood* (2nd ed., pp. 53–67). Boulder, CO: Westview Press.

Mullaly, R. (2002). *Challenging oppression.* Canada: Oxford University Press.

YOUNES MOURCHID

LEFT TO MY OWN DEVICES

Hybrid Identity Development of Religion and Sexual Orientation Among Muslim Students in the United States

INTRODUCTION AND BACKGROUND

The landscape of religious affiliations in the United States has been in perpetual metamorphosis for the past four decades. Adherents to Islam constitute an important part of this increasingly complex religious mosaic. While disagreements regarding the exact numbers of Muslims persist, the general consensus postulates that approximately six to seven million Muslims live in the United States (Smith, 1999). According to Leonard (2003), Islam is the fastest growing religion in the U.S., and is expected to surpass Judaism in the number of adherents, and become second only to Christianity. The Muslim community in the United States is increasingly diverse and includes many first-, second-, and third-generation immigrants of South Asian and Arab descent, as well as large percentages of African Americans. Furthermore, a small but sizeable number of Whites, Latinos, and Native Americans have converted to Islam over the past several decades (Smith, 1999). Accordingly, the adherents to the Muslim faith represent a broad range of ethnicities, cultures, nationalities, and sects.

While a substantial body of research exploring issues of identity exists, most reviews of identity theory and research have overlooked the role of religion in identity (c.f. Frable, 1997; Howard, 2000). At the same time, multiple studies by sociologists of religion have explored the role of religion in maintaining group identity and solidarity, especially among immigrant groups (Gibson, 1988; Hammond, 1988; Herberg, 1955; Williams, 1988). Rather than focusing on religion exclusively, many of these studies have examined the connection between religion and ethnic identity. According to Williams (1988), although religion is often deemed a significant part of ethnic culture, it is challenging to establish a correlation between the two. Some immigrant religious communities emphasize their members' religious identity more than their ethnicity, whereas others stress ethnic identity and rely on religious institutions primarily to preserve cultural traditions and ethnic boundaries.

A cocktail of theories has been put forward addressing why certain individuals and communities highlight and develop religious identities, as opposed to other forms of personal and social identity such as race, ethnicity, nationality, or sexual orientation. According to Smith (1978), immigration in itself can often be a

Ö. Sensoy and C.D. Stonebanks (eds.), Muslim Voices in School: Narratives of Identity and Pluralism, 99–115.

theologizing experience; immigrants frequently respond to the alienation and confusion that stem from their arrival in a new country by turning to religion. As a result, religion may assume greater significance in immigrants' definitions of self than may be relevant in their homelands, where religion may have had lesser salience. This is particularly the case when the immigrants come from a society where they were part of the religious majority and then relocate to a host society where they become a religious minority–for example, Indian Hindus, Pakistani Muslims, Arab Muslims, or Vietnamese Buddhists coming to the United States.

Various studies have examined differing aspects of personal and social identity among Muslim Americans, including gender role attitudes and identities of Muslim women (Bartkowski & Read, 2003); identity politics of Muslims (Khan, 2000); issues of religious identity transmission and retention (Abu-Laban, 1989). Additionally, other research projects have investigated the intersections of religious, racial, and ethnic identities among Arab American Muslims (Haddad, 1994; Naber, 2000). Haddad (2000) tackled the broader social contours that shape Islamic identity in North America, exploring the variable that affect various identities prior to emigration, the immigrant experience in America, and the options immigrants find as they struggle to make their home in a new, sometimes hostile, environment. Ajrouch (2004, 2000, 1999) has closely studied the identity development of young Muslim Arabs in Dearborn, Michigan. Although she does not specifically focus on religious identification, Ajrouch (2204, 200, 1999) does explore the intersection of ethnic and religious identity, the significance of gender relations, and how religious teachings and parental influence shape the identities of second-generation Arab American adolescents.

This inquiry sought to examine the process of integrating and expressing religious and sexual identity formation among Muslim students in U.S. colleges and universities and the emergence of religion as a salient source of personal and social identity for a group of lesbian and gay identifying second-generation Muslim in the U.S. Drawing on data gathered through interviews and focus groups with Muslim university students in New York and California, a three dimension religious and sexual orientation identity development are presented: 1) religion as ascribed identity; 2) religion as rejected identity; and 3) hybrid of religion and sexual orientation as declared identity. This chapter shows how religious identity emerges in socially and historically bound contexts, and demonstrates that in the context of a competing secular identity of sexual orientation, religious identity formation is more fluid than fixed. In addition, this chapter will discuss the influence of September 11 in invoking a religious (vs. sexual orientation) identity as more central to Muslims' concept of self. By the same token, this study will demonstrate that the choice of sexual orientation as a secondary personal identity served the participants in secularizing their primary identity as Muslims. This inquiry does not seek to compare or invoke discussions related to roads other religious groups have taken to negotiate their religious and sexual identities and thus will not reserve any space to the effect.

I begin by presenting the setting in which this inquiry was conducted, the research participants, and the qualitative methods employed. Next, I proceed to a discussion about the three dimensions of identity development, illustrating how sexual orientation identity emerges in concurrence with the religious identity and how the latter has gained saliency for the participants. I conclude by analyzing the individual and social factors that contributed to the dual identity of being Muslim and gay and at the same time discuss how this particular group of young Muslims understand, enact, and integrate their religious sexual identities.

SETTINGS AND METHODOLOGY

This inquiry was inspired by a multitude of conversations, which took place during the Arab Youth Symposium on September 20th of 2003 at the campus of the University of California at Berkeley. I was invited to the symposium as a one of the keynote speakers to talk about salient leadership qualities needed for community mobilization. The symposium's main theme was "challenges of being Arab-American Muslim in post 9/11 America." The symposium was interactive and focused on giving voice to youth experiences and perceptions around issues of religious, social, political, and sexual identities. The symposium participants voiced various identities: Arab-American, Muslim, Palestinian, Iranian, Muslim-American, and Muslim gay. These groups each related their experiences and perception around the challenges they face in living and asserting their respective identities in a society changed by the events of 9/11, where Islamophobia and anti-Arab racism are contending realities.

Accounts and stories told by the group identifying as Muslim gay were particularly striking. This group's representatives, in addition to the challenges of Islamophobia and anti-Arab racism, also expressed having to navigate the terrains blazed by homophobia not only in general society, but within their immediate Muslim community, which generally condemns any romantic form of same-sex relationships. In light of this background, the identity Muslim-gay invokes a great deal of curiosity. On a personal level, I could relate to the accounts shared by this group of symposium participants. As a 25-year-old Muslim immigrant to the United States pursuing graduate education, I experienced an identity crisis around my religious identity, especially in post 9/11 U.S. This crisis set me out on a journey of self-discovery, reconciliation of my religious identity with my other social identities. Energized by this kinship and the questions entailing from such curiosity, I set out to understand how the Muslim students in U.S. universities came to identify as Muslim-gays.

I made contact with the initial research participants through two important students association: the Muslim Student Associations (MSA) and the Lesbian, Gay, Bisexual, and Transsexual Association (LGBT) on their respective university campuses. I also located students identifying as Muslim-gay through key non-profit organization: Al Fatiha Foundation which promotes the Islamic notions of peace, equality and justice for Muslim who explore their sexual orientation or gender identity, and their allies, families and friends and the South West Asian and North African Bay Area Queers (SWANABAQ) which is a group and discussion forum for lesbian, gay, bisexual, trans-gendered, and inter-sexed (LGBTI) people who are

Afghan, Arab, Armenian, Assyrian, Azerbaijani, Berber (Amazigh), Chaldean, Copt, Cypriot, Greek, Iranian (Persian), Kazakh, Kurd, Kyrgyz, Maltese, Tajik, Turkmen, Turk, or Uzbek living in Northern California. Because of the need of anonymity relative to the subject, I relied on key contacts to help me recruit participants and arrange interviews, while also contacting interviewees through a referral snowball sample technique.

During the three years following the Arab Youth Symposium, I conducted seven focus groups, which ranged in size from three to eight participants and lasted between 60 to 90 minutes. I employed one-on-one, semi-structured interviews as the principle form of data collection. In sum, I conducted 32 individual interviews, each lasting between 45 to 90 minutes. Combining the focus groups and individual interviews conducted in New York and California, I carried out a total of 39 interviews, which were audio taped, transcribed, and coded for analysis. Many of the participants were interviewed two or three times during the two-year period of this inquiry. Twelve of the participants were women and 27 were men. The students ranged in age from 18 to 36 years old. Most were second-generation immigrants who were primarily raised in the United States and planned to stay. The interviewees reported a wide range of ethnic backgrounds: 45% of participants were of South or Southeast Asian descent, 40% of students identified as Arab or Arab American and 5% as other.

Most of the participants consider themselves moderately religious. Two out of three of the students reported praying five times a day, fasting during Ramadan, being active members of religious organizations, having Muslim first and last names, and abstaining from religiously prohibited activities (such as drinking alcohol or eating pork). The narratives provided by the interviewees suggest important insights about the experience of Muslim students as Muslim gay students, who through a process of introspection and social interaction consciously decided to identify first as Muslim and second as gay.

DATA PRESENTATION

The identity trajectories observed from the data show that Muslim gay students negotiate their religious identity in three separate dimensions: 1) religion as ascribed identity; 2) religion as rejected identity; and 3) hybrid of religion and sexual orientation as declared identity. This model implies that identity is shaped by a social and developmental process; that Muslim gay students' experiences in the three dimensions varies; and that this model applies to a particular group of individuals in a specific social and historical context and is not meant to serve as a universal model for all Muslim Americans.

Religion as Ascribed Identity

All 39 participants were born into Muslim families and a Muslim social milieu, and as such most deemed religion as an ascribed characteristic of their individual identity and social structures. In this first dimension of identity, study participants reported that they engaged in little introspection when they were children regarding the meaning of "being Muslim" because their religious identity permeated every aspect of their daily lives. Zainab[1], a female participant whose family immigrated to the United States from Egypt when she was 2 years old, elaborates on this point:

> Since I opened my eyes, I saw my parents and other family members pray and talk of Allah [God] and Islam as the way of life. I was told that attending to our duties toward Allah is what makes us who we are and that what we are here for. I never questioned these beliefs, until recently.

For some participants, not questioning religious identity and its entailing practices when they were younger did not mean that they necessarily understood what these practices meant in their everyday lives. Many remarked that simply being born into a certain religion did not mean that its belief system and practices were understood, appreciated, or integrated, particularly when they were children. Bahaar, a second-generation immigrant from Pakistan said:

> Yes, I was born into a Muslim conservative family. I had to pray five times a day and do all other things Muslims should do. But, I had no idea why praying five times as opposed to twice. I could not explain these things to my friends at school, so I just did not want to talk about it. When I asked my father questions about our religion, he would say we do not discuss matters of Allah, we just do what Allah and the prophet told us to do.

In general, individuals habitualized specific norms, values, and behaviors when they observed them exemplified by their parents, peers, and others before these were assimilated at an intellectual level. Although most participants lacked self-reflection about their religious background, their behavior and practices regulated by their parents in terms of normative Muslim dress code and attendance in religion classes at a mosque reflected a Muslim religious identity.

Because the majority of the students were the children of immigrants, they often identified according to their parents' national or ethnic backgrounds, at least when younger. Many of the participants reported that they were more likely to identify themselves in accordance with their family's nationality and/or ethnic background because of the external pressure in the United States to define oneself socially and at school according to race, nationality, or ethnicity rather than by religion. Most of the student interviewees who are identifiable as a Muslim or as an ethnic minority reported often being asked about their country of origin. Dhanesh related his experience on this point:

> Back where I grew up, people look at me sometimes and ask "you from around here?" I usually understand that to mean "where are you from?" After many episodes of being uncomfortable with answering these kinds of questions, I just decided to tell people "I'm from here, but my parents are from India." Sometimes people go on asking stupid questions about my origin, which annoy the hell out of me. I just learned to ignore them or just say: "this is America; everybody is from somewhere else..." I usually try to avoid getting to the part, "Are you a Hindu or a Muslim?"

Some of the participants felt stigmatized due to their minority religious, ethnic, and immigrant identities at school and in society at large. This stigmatization coupled with the pressure to assimilate often led the participants to ignore or conceal their Muslim identity. In the United States, the fact that religious affiliation is typically considered private made it easy for participants to shed their religious identity in order to be perceived as part of mainstream society. Hibaa, a female second-generation immigrant from Palestine discussed her fears of being singled out for wearing a hijab:

> When I turned 13, I had my first period and my mother said that I was about to become a grown woman that I needed to start covering my hair and my parts of my body in public and in front of strangers by wearing the hijab. I was terrified and I kept thinking about my classmates and friends and what they would say when they see me with my strange clothing. I pleaded with my mother and cried until my father said I could wait on the hijab until I go to high school. I just wanted to fit in and did not even ask the right questions then about the practice of wearing the hijab from a religious point of view.

The experiences related thus far by the participants of this study are diverse and point to the reality that for most of them Islam as a religion was an ascribed identity for them to adopt and adapt to. The data supports common theories that young children are typically not self-reflective about their identities and ascribed statuses (Adams and Marshall, 1996). However, as children mature, in response to the significant societal pressures to fit in, these children begin to employ identity management strategies. Among Muslim-gay participants, these pressures led to the rejection of religion as an identity and the adoption of a more secular identity, which reflects the negotiation of meaning around sexual orientation.

Religion as Rejected Identity

Prior research has documented that as children mature, they become more introspective and attuned to the values, symbolism, and beliefs of their mother religion (Parks, 1986). Many of the participants in this study voiced that as they matured into adulthood, they began to pose more important life questions relative to their religious backgrounds, and thus reconsidered the religious aspects of their identities against the large pictures of other identity positions. Raheem, a male participant of Afghani heritage, reflects on this point:

> You know, as a kid, I just did what was expected of me. As a teenager, I kept up with my religious duties and sought to understand it better by going to the mosque sometimes, attend lectures and ask questions. But later as other kids at school asked questions and commented about my faith and what it meant, I begun to think about my religion differently. I immediately realized I was really a minority in my high school and noticed that everyone treated me differently because of my religion. I began to think about what else defines me other than my religion. Soon I realized it did not matter how I defined

myself. What mattered was how people perceived my faith and my association with it. The 'shit' hit the fan with the events of 9/11 and my identity as a Muslim kid fossilized... I became associated with everything America was angry about. It was not fun; at first in the public sphere, I began to distance myself from my religious identity and the baggage that came with it... I asked my parents to move somewhere else where no one knew we were Muslim... I just wanted my faith to be a private matter and question for me.

As did 65% of the participants of this study, Raheem raised an important factor in the process of religious identity development: contact with mainstream identities in the public arena. This contact invited these participants into intense reflection about their religious minority identity and led to a redefinition of identity in the public sphere. As the events of 9/11 fueled unfavorable sentiments about Islam and Muslims, Raheem adopted the strategy of distancing himself from the identity he had assumed, and as a result, rejected his religious identity in public life.

The participants also spoke about having to make sense of their sexual orientation identity within the framework of existing narratives about being a gay in Islam. The growing need to reconcile their sexual identity with their religious one led to an intense questioning of the latter, and for the majority of participants, into an utter rejection of the religious identity not only in the public sphere, but in private as well. Jamal, a male participant sheds light on this development of his identity crisis:

There were these three voices I had to quiet at all times: the voice of my parents who preach about the importance of following the Qur'an and the teaching of the prophet, the voice of the outside world looking at Islam as a suspect and a violent religion, and the voice in my head that was the loudest of the three yelling, 'you are a fraud, how can you be gay and pray to Allah?' The talk of anything that had to do with religion reminded me of my shortcomings as a homosexual. Every time I faced Allah to pray, read or recited the Qur'an, or went with my father or brother to the mosque, I felt this intense feeling of shame, as if I have done a terrible thing. Mind you, at the time I had not explored my sexuality yet in the sense of being physical with another man. It was all in my head at the time. After a while as I went away to college, I felt the freedom to stop participating in any kind of activities that involved my religion. I decided to shut out any thoughts about religion and me being gay. It was too much pressure, so I went into hiding and denial for while, until I was a junior in college when falling in love with another man forced me to re-open the issue and deal with it.

The account presented by Jamal and echoed by many others brings to the surface the role of Islamic narratives about homosexuality and how such narratives impede Muslim gay individuals from embracing both their religious and sexual orientation identities. A review of these narratives is necessary to the understanding of the account presented above and the accounts to come. In conservative readings of Islam, homosexuals (called qaum Lut, the "people of Lot") are condemned in the story of Lot's people in the Qur'an (15:73; 26:165) and in the last address of the

Prophet Muhammad. According to a pamphlet produced by al-Fatiha, there is a consensus among Islamic scholars that all humans are naturally heterosexual. Homosexuality is viewed as sinful and a perverted deviation from the norm. The companions of the Prophet Muhammad held various views concerning punishment. The fatwa cited by IslamOnline.net states: "…this led to different views maintained by Muslim Jurists. For example: "In the Hanafi school of thought, the homosexual is punished through harsh beating, and if he/she repeats the act, death penalty is to be applied."

As for the Shafi`i school of thought, the homosexual receives the same punishment of adultery (if he/she is married) or fornication (if not married). This means, that if the homosexual is married, he/she is stoned to death, while if single, he/she is whipped 100 times.

The Hanbalite school of law is, the most conservative school of Islamic jurisprudence and widely followed in the Arab world, uniformly urged execution, usually by stoning.

Some minority liberal Muslims, such as the members of the al-Fatiha Foundation, accept and consider homosexuality as natural, regarding the Qur'an verses on homosexuality as either obsolete in the context of modern society, or pointing out that the Qur'an speaks out against homosexual lust devoid of love among non-equals, and is silent on homosexual love among equals.

It is against the background of this narrative that many participants negotiate their identity, re-examine their religious identity, and create space for their identity of being gay to take root. This identity development process for many of the interviewees was not simple or linear. Mona, a female of Moroccan background, attests to this complication in her identity development process:

> I grew up in a home where it was OK to discuss taboo topics, including sexuality. But although I came out to my sister as a gay woman, I could not do the same with my parents. I did not want to break their hearts. My parents don't have a strong sense of religiosity about Islam, yet as they are getting older, they are becoming more and more conservative in their outlook. Going away to college across the country created a distance that I needed to figure things out for myself. At first, I sought to find myself by associating myself with groups I thought I had things in common with. I had ambivalent feelings about my religion, Islam. So I decided to explore these feelings by joining the Muslim Student Association on campus. As a woman, who does not wear the Islamic attire hijab, I ran into many issues with members of the association who were more interested in principles and Islamic values than in getting to know me as a person. Being a feisty and strong-willed woman, I challenged these guys about the values they held about woman and sexuality. Few would engage me, but most just shunned me. No one took me seriously, because I did not take Islam seriously either by not wearing the hijab, as one female member told me once. I had hoped that by being on a large campus on the west coast, I would meet other progressive Muslim students who would give me space to have my own voice. I did not meet that many, so I stopped

attending MSA activities and my ambiguous feelings about my Muslim identity hardened.

Mona's account points to one of the strategies available on a university campus to students who experience the sort of identity crisis under discussion: the strategy of finding meaning of one's identity by associating with a related group. Here Mona took her ambivalence about her own religious identity from a private personal internal sphere to a public space, a group consciousness. Her experience and conclusion affirm that conservative values do no mix well with progressive ones within the confines of one group, like the Muslim Student Association. In this case, the search for a secular and unconventional identity within a religious discourse and narrative is like searching for a needle in a haystack.

This experience of not fitting in to a given group with a mixed identity of being Muslim and gay at the same time is also the experience of another participant of this study who, as a college student, joined the LGBT organization on his campus to make sense of his identity crisis. Wael, a male of Syrian heritage, elaborates:

When I was a freshman at Columbia away from home and friends, I felt alone and wanted to meet other Arab and Muslim students on campus. So, I thought it would benefit me to join the Muslim Student Association for this purpose. I did and was nice at first, but later I had questions about my sexuality and the fact that I was interested more in guys than girls. Most of the guys of the association were conservatives and kind of homophobic too, so I could not really discuss with any of them my issues around sexuality. I started drifting away from the MSA. I would spend more time online instead when I'm not studying. I then met this kid online who was Mormon and talked me into going with him to one of the LGBT events on campus. I did and I liked it at first. I made new friends who helped me explore my sexual identity and needs. But, I could not relate to the culture of LGBT folks. Most were white and had little issues with their religious identity except for the Mormon kid. Most were interested in gay rights and outreach, which really did not interest me. My problem was, how can be I be Muslim and gay? How can I live as a Muslim gay man in this world? I could not find the answers as a member of the Muslim Student Association and the LGBT Students Association. I could not fit in at home and talk about this with my family either. The Mormon kid suggested to me to go talk to a counselor on campus. I did after long hesitation and the guy had no clue about Islam and what it implied for my sexuality. He kept saying 'be yourself.' I had no idea what he was talking about. I was left to my own devices.

Wael's account about his experience with campus students' organizations in search of reconciling his religious identity with his sexual one is echoed by many of the subjects in this study. To begin with, there is no such organization on university campuses whose mission specifically is to help Muslim students explore and resolve these types of identity questions, as these students form a minority within a minority. The generic alternative available to all students on any campus is counseling. For Muslim students in this study, this alternative proved inefficient, as most counselors had little knowledge of Islam as a religion and as a culture and recommended generic, one-size fits all therapies. Although there are many outside options available to Muslim students who identify as gay or lesbian, in the end, these students are burdened with the task to take what works from the various available options and try to resolve on their own their identity questions. For many, as discussed in the testimonies above, a temporary repudiation of their religious identity allowed for space to explore the sexual identity. What is common to all the participants of this study in their process of identity formation is the question: "how can I be Muslim and gay in this world?" For one participant, this question proved, at times, crippling. Amer, a male of Egyptian decent and a graduate student sheds further light on this question:

> The question of choosing one identity over the other was a continuous struggle. If I choose to embrace my religious identity and the culture that came with it, I had to deny myself of my sexual identity of being gay. If I choose to honor my sexual identity, I felt that I had to reject my religious identity and native culture. I went through periods of choosing and rejecting one over the other. I have to say, it was easier to reject the religious identity as it was imposed and constructed from the outside. My sexual identity, as troubling as it has been for me, felt more like a part of me; the more I choose to ignore it, the more troubled and unhappy I became. In the end, I had to find my way around this conflict. I had to look at my religious and cultural backgrounds through new sets of eyes. Embracing my identity as a gay man first provided for me a new spiritual foundation which helped me much later in embracing my native religious and cultural identity... I have to say though. This is not quite as simple and definite as it sounds. Campus life allows for exploration and expression of identity if one is open to it. There is a great deal of tolerance and diversity on campus and you can identify as you wish with little consequences. You leave campus to the outer world and things become more gray and complicated. You cannot just identify as gay anywhere to anyone. Homophobia is a real threat to people like me. To add salt to injury, after 9/11, the identity of being Muslim is loaded. Islam-phobia is also a real threat out there in our world today. So, as people like me radiate to the larger world, the need to exercise judgment about which identity to express is real and changes with the change of my environment. Welcome to my world of being a chameleon!

Amer provides a summative account and answers to the question of how Muslim gay students may choose to reconcile their sexual identity against the background of their religion. In Amer's case, as is the case with many participants of this study, the rejection of the religious identity at first to make space and sense of the sexual identity of being gay took precedence and paid dividends in terms of resolving the identity crisis of the participants. This resolution, Amer's account elaborates, is a very fluid process which changes as the need to conform to certain situations and environments require. In a sense, this resolution of identity crisis is temporary in the way it plays out in the public sphere. However, Amer seems to have attained a resolution to the question "How can I be Muslim and gay" for himself at the internal level.

A Hybrid of Religion and Sexual Orientation as Declared Identity

The majority of participants of this inquiry attested to the tension between their sexual and religious identities, which for many was a struggle they resolved and for others a continuous conflict with no end in sight. Many of the interviewees reported that the need to explore their sexual identity compelled them to re-examine their religious identity, temporarily reject it, and later in the process of identity development, redefine their religious identity in spiritual terms. In this process of development, most participants have had to revisit the status of their religious identity and the cultures that come with it after the events of 9/11 took place and brought about a new discourse about Islam and Muslims in the West. Islamophobia became a new reality contending with homophobia in the lives of these Muslim gay students. Amina, a female student of Palestinian heritage, discusses how the events of 9/11 forced her to re-examine her religious identity as a Muslim woman, an identity she rejected to create space for her sexual orientation as a lesbian:

> When I came out as a lesbian, many of my family members and Muslim friends rejected me. After much thinking, I realized that the problem was not people per se, but it was Islam and its beliefs. I realized that being gay was not compatible with being Muslim. So I gave up organized religion all-together and distanced myself from family and Muslim friends. When the terrible events of 9/11 happened and people started talking of Muslims and Arabs as terrorists, I started getting defensive in my conversations with others about Islam and Arabs. I would go to events on campus and talk positively of Islam and the peaceful people who follow it and I would have arguments with others about this whole mess. I reconnected with friends from The Muslim Students Organization and The Palestinian Students Organization and became very active with them again. I realized that Islam was more than just a set of pillars and dogmas that one had to follow, it was a culture and set of values that connected me to my family, friends... I learned that I did not have to renounce my mother culture to have permission to recognize and live my sexual orientation. Being gay was a personal matter and a small part of me. Being Muslim was what connected me to the big picture, to my people, and ultimately to myself. My suffering lessened and the quality of my life improved. The upside of 9/11 for me is that I begun to identify as a Muslim gay woman; Muslim first and gay second. The downside of 9/11 is that I had two battles to fight: homophobia in and outside my immediate community and Islamophobia in the outside world.

Amina discussed how the events of 9/11 opened the door on her religious identity, which she had previously rejected to embrace the cultural aspect of Islam, and reconnected her with people that matter the most in her life. This process for

Amina led to a redefinition of her declared identity as a "Muslim gay woman." Several studies have noted that a real or perceived threat to a group leads to an increased group solidarity (Tajfel, 1981). To Amina, as to several of the interviewees, the events of September 11 brought Muslims closer together and reinforced their sense of belonging to a community of Muslims – defined in this sense more accurately as a cultural group than a religious one. The events also helped many of the interviewees to integrate their sexual identity with their religious/cultural one and identity as "Muslim Gay." Ayman, as a male student of Lebanese heritage, said:

> When I was a sophomore, I was feeling depressed most of the time because of my sexual orientation that I had to cover from my family. I started seeing a counselor on campus and decided to come out to my parents. I had hopes that their high level of education and long years in America will help them cope with it. I came out to them and sure enough my mother had a nervous break down and my father asked me to leave the house and never come back or call. I got out on my own and life was never the same. I did find a community and a sense of belonging though with other gay Arab men and women in the Bay area. I was never religious and neither were my parents, so Islam as a religion was not part of this drama for me. But, when 9/11 hit, and Muslims and Arabs came under attack in the media and so on, I began to look at things differently. I became conscience of my association with Islam and Arabs because of my name, my skin color, and my family of origin. I entered this period of self-reflection and I noticed that most things I do have Muslim or Arab cultural meaning: The way I speak, the kind of food I prefer, the music I listen to, what makes me laugh, my views on relationships, integrity, and honor, the kind of people I hang out. I realized that I was more Arab and Muslim than gay. The only gay thing about me was my preference for same sex love. Shortly after this period, I caught myself describing myself to others as "Arab Muslim gay man"...

Despite being disowned by his parents for revealing his sexual identity, Ayman has found community and meaning with other gay men and women. Post 9/11, Ayman developed a new awareness of his cultural identity as an Arab and as a Muslim, although Islam as a religion did not play a part in his new identification. This account describes the process of integration that takes place between different self-identities; in this case the sexual and religious/cultural identities; a process that seemed necessary for the participants of this study to attain some sort of understanding of themselves and a way to show up for their lives. Other participants have arrived to this reconciliation without the interference of the events of 9/11. Kareem, a male student of Algerian heritage, said:

> My mother raised me as single parent and sacrificed so much to put me and my sister through school. My mother is conservative and would be heartbroken and done in if I were to come out to her and say I'm gay, meet my Jewish boyfriend, deal with it. So I had to find a way to be ok with the cards I was dealt. Since I was in high school, I took interest in other religions

and spiritual philosophies and rediscovered Islam through Sufism. I also took a deep interest in Buddhism when I met my current partner. My spiritual quests and practices helped me embrace my sexuality, maintain a Muslim identity, and develop enough compassion for myself and my mother to protect her from a sexual identity and a lifestyle which her conservative mind and upbringing is incapable of grasping and tolerating. When my mom bugs me about marriage and women, I just tell her I'm not ready yet to settle down.

Kareem is not the only Muslim gay student in this study who has reconciled his religious and sexual identities outside the framework of the 9/11 events and who decided to conceal his sexual identity from his immediate family. Fifty percent of participants have made the same choice to protect their parents from the truth of their sexual identity more out of compassion than fear and lest their parent suffer the consequences of their conservative boundaries being stretched out by their ignorance of alternative sexual identities and life styles.

On the other hand, 25% of interviewees made a different choice than what other participants revealed above. These participants have not yet come to reconcile their religious identity with their sexual one and managed to keep these two identities separate. These participants usually identify themselves in social setting as "Muslim American." Farid, a male student of Iranian decent, offers a perspective on his choice:

> I cannot say that I ever accepted my identity as a gay man. I go back and forth about it. The thing is that my relationship with Allah and my family is important to me. I don't think I can disappoint them. So, I pray that Allah lifts this desire I have for other men off of me. That's where I'm now. Allah will show me the way.

The task to reconcile a sexual identity with a religion and culture that reserves little space for understanding this sexual identity, proved quite daunting and crippling for many of the participants in this study. The connection that these participants have to their faith and culture through their families prohibits them from exploring the meaning and future of their sexual orientation and integrate it into other parts of their overall identity.

CONCLUSION

In this chapter, I have presented three dimensions of identity development among Muslim university students who also identify as gay or lesbian. The accounts featured in this study illustrate the continued importance of Islam as a basis of personal and social identity for many participants and explicates how Muslim students religious identities develop in relation to other forms of personal and social identity. The accounts also illustrate that saliency of religious identity can create tremendous tensions and at times a crisis to the point where the participants began to explore the meaning of their sexuality identities. The dominant Islamic narrative about homosexuality is conservative, and condemns any alternative sexual orientations and practices outside of the traditional relationship between a man and a woman in wedlock. This perspective did not encourage the participants to explore their identity questions in a public sphere occupied by immediate family members and related community members. The exploration instead took place for some of these participants in a private space where no one else was involved, and for others in a public space outside of the Muslim community on the university campus in dialogue with peers from students' organizations of interest and with non-Muslim friends and peers.

The events of 9/11 opened the debate about Islam and its adherents outside of Muslim communities and brought about a great deal of self-reflection about Islam as a religious identity. For many participants, this debate opened their consciousness to the fact that Islam has been for them more than a set of dogmas, *do's* and *don'ts*; it has been a culture, a way of life, a spiritual source, and the cement that bonds them to their families and communities. This realization paved the way for many participants to begin to integrate and reconcile their sexual identities as lesbian or gay with their cultural and social identity as Muslims. In the process, the participants have separated their sexual and cultural identity from the theology of Islam and the orthodox views associated with such theology. One can argue that the struggle to embrace the sexual identity of being lesbian or gay has secularized and spiritualized the religious identity of these Muslim students and created a third space or discourse where tensions of the sexual and the religious identities have been renegotiated, re-examined, and redefined.

The model of a hybrid identity development among Muslim gay and lesbian students presented here is by no means a universal one and does not apply to every Muslim student. While many other Muslim students have not emphasized their sexual identity or sought to reconcile and secularize their religious identity of being a Muslim to the same extent that other interviewees have, this inquiry nonetheless uncovers how religious identities can be reconstructed and enacted, particularly by Muslim gay students in their attempt to reconcile their multiple, sometimes conflicting, forms of identity.

DISCUSSION QUESTIONS AND EXTENSION ACTIVITIES

(1) What potential benefits can the mechanism of ijtihad (or, informed inter-pretation, comes from same root as jihad, "to struggle") and constructive debate among moderate Muslims bring to Muslim members of the GLBT community, who struggle to reconcile their religious identity with their sexual counterpart?

(2) What similarities and differences are observable between the identity development trajectory of Muslim GLBT students and GLBT students of other faiths? What can academic institutions do to effectively reach out to Muslim GLBT students?

IF YOU LIKED THIS CHAPTER, YOU MAY ALSO ENJOY:

Ali Khan, C. (2009). On being us and them: A voice from the edge. *In this book.*

DuBowski, S.S. & Sharma, P. (Producers), Sharma, P. (Director). (2007). *A jihad for love* [Documentary]. United States: First Run Features.
http://www.ajihadforlove.com/

Grace, A.P. & Wells, K. (2005). The Marc Hall prom predicament: Queer individual rights v. institutional church rights in Canadian public education. *Canadian Journal of Education* 28(3), 237-270.

Jivraj, S. & de Jong, A. (2005). Muslim moral instruction on homosexuality. In J.T. Sears (Ed.), *Youth, Education, and Sexualities: An International Encyclopedia* (pp. 574–579). Westport, CT: Greenwood.

Tooms, A. & Lugg, C.A. (2008). Oh, we've got trouble! Right here in Ravenna City: It starts with "g," and has an "s," and ends in "a" (with apologies to Meredith Wilson). Journal of Cases in Educational Leadership 11(1), 111-128.

Walton, G. (2006). "Fag church": Men who integrate gay and Christian identities. *Journal of Homosexuality* 51(2), 1-17.

Al Fatiha Foundation
http://www.al-fatiha.org

The International Gay and Lesbian Human Rights Commission (IGLHRC)
http://www.iglhrc.org

Equality for Gays and Lesbians Everywhere (EGALE).
http://www.egale.ca

Gay Lesbian and Straight Education Network (GLSEN)
http://www.glsen.org

NOTES

[1] all names as pseudonymns

REFERENCES

Abu-Laban, S. M. (1989). The coexistence of cohorts: Identity and adaptation among Arab-American muslims. *Arab Studies Quarterly, 11*(2), 45–63.
Adams, G. R., & Marshall, S. K. (1996). A developmental social psychology of identity: Understanding the person-in-context. *Journal of Adolescence, 19*, 429–442.

Ajrouch, K. J. (2004). Gender, race, and symbolic boundaries: Contested spaces of identity among Arab-American adolescents. *Sociological Perspectives, 47*(4), 371–391.

Ajrouch, K. J. (2000). Place, age, and culture: Community living and ethnic identity among Lebanese American adolescents. *Small Group Research, 31*(4), 447–469.

Ajrouch, K. J. (1999). Family and ethnic identity in an Arab-American community. In M. W. Suleiman (Ed.), *Arabs in America: Building a new future* (pp. 129–139). Philadelphia: Temple University Press.

American-Arab Anti-Discrimination Committee. (2003). *Report on hate crimes and discrimination against Arab Americans: The post-September 11 backlash.* Washington, DC: American-Arab Anti-Discrimination Committee Research Institute.

Arab American Institute. (2002). *Healing the nation: The Arab American experience after September 11.* Washington, DC: Arab American Institute.

Bartkowski, J. P., & Read, J. G. (2003). Veiled submission: Gender, power, and identity among evangelical and muslim women in the United States. *Qualitative Sociology, 26*(1), 71–92.

Council on American-Islamic Relations. (2002). *American muslims: One year after 9–11.* Washington, DC: Council on American-Islamic Relations Research Center.

Frable, D. E. S. (1997). Gender, racial, ethnic, sexual, and class identities. *Annual Review of Psychology, 48,* 139–162.

Gibson, M. A. (1988). *Accommodation without assimilation: Sikh immigrants in an American high school.* Ithaca, NY: Cornell University Press.

Haddad, Y. Y. (2004). *Not quite American? The shaping of Arab and Muslim identity in the United States.* Waco, TX: Baylor University Press.

Haddad, Y. Y. (2000). The dynamics of Islamic identity in North America. In Y. Y. Haddad & J. L. Esposito (Eds.), *Muslims on the Americanization path?* (pp. 19–46). New York: Oxford University Press.

Haddad, Y. Y. (1994). Maintaining the faith of the fathers: Dilemmas of religious identity in the Christian and Muslim Arab-American communities. In E. McCarus (Ed.), *The development of Arab-American identity* (pp. 61–84). Ann Arbor: The University of Michigan Press.

Hammond, P. E. (1988). Religion and the persistence of identity. *Journal for the Scientific Study of Religion, 27*(1), 1–11.

Herberg, W. (1955). *Protestant-Catholic-Jew: An essay in American religious sociology.* Garden City, NY: Doubleday and Company.

Howard, J. A. (2000). Social psychology of identities. *Annual Review of Sociology, 26,* 367–393.

Jivraj, S., & de Jong, A. (2005). Muslim moral instruction on homosexuality. In J. T. Sears (Ed.), *Youth, education, and sexualities: An international encyclopedia* (pp. 574–579). Westport, CT: Greenwood.

Khan, M. A. M. (2000). Muslims and identity politics in America. In Y. Y. Haddad & J. L. Esposito (Eds.), *Muslims on the Americanization path?* (pp. 87–101). New York: Oxford University Press.

Leonard, K. I. (2003). *Muslims in the United States: The state of research.* New York: Russell Sage Foundation.

Naber, N. (2000). Ambiguous insiders: An investigation of Arab American invisibility. *Ethnic and Racial Studies, 23,* 37–61.

Parks, S. (1986). *The critical years: Young adults and the search for meaning, faith, and commitment.* New York: HarperCollins Publishers.

Read, J. G. (2003). The sources of gender role attitudes among Christian and Muslim Arab-American women. *Sociology of Religion, 64*(2), 207–222.

Read, J. G., & Bartkowski, J. P. (2000). To veil or not to veil? A case study of identity negotiation among Muslim women in Austin, Texas. *Gender & Society, 14*(3), 395–417.

Smith, J. I. (1999). *Islam in America.* New York: Columbia University Press.

Smith, T. L. (1978). Religion and ethnicity in America. *American Historical Review, 83,* 1155–1185.

Tajfel, H. (1981). Social stereotypes and social groups. In J. C. Turner & H. Giles (Eds.), *Intergroup behaviour* (pp. 144–167). Oxford: Blackwell.

United States Department of State, Bureau of International Information Programs. (2004). *Muslim life in America*. Retrieved from http://usinfo.state.gov/products/pubs/muslimlife/demograp.htm

Williams, R. B. (1988). *Religions of immigrants from India and Pakistan: New threads in the American tapestry*. New York: Cambridge University Press.

Younes Mourchid
International Studies
Cogswell College, California

SHABANA MIR

DIVERSITY, SELF, FAITH AND FRIENDS

Muslim Undergraduates on Campus

INTRODUCTION

What if I [had] met the wrong people [at college]? What if there was no
MSA[Muslim Students Association] at this school? ... When I think of it, I'm
always thinking of myself sort of just attending a school ... that's non-
Muslim, having friends that are non-Muslim, so I don't know what I'd have done
... What if other people [had] influenced me the other way? – Intisar

Diasporic Western Muslim parents often worry about the impact of peer culture in
public schools. But the impact of peer culture is a major source of anxiety not just
for adult gatekeepers but also for some second-generation American Muslim youth,
who work in a space of tension between religious identity and assimilation. American
Muslim youth grapple daily with the problem of how to engage with diverse peers,
Muslim and non-Muslim, in social spaces including school. In this chapter, I focus
on the struggles of Muslim undergraduate women to be American, Muslim *and*
friendly, within White majority secular, liberal, as well as within Muslim community
spaces and peer culture on campus. When I discuss Muslim women's "friendliness,"
I refer to their delicate negotiation between the differing expectations – majority
and minority – regarding friendship in college.

Peers are "the single most potent source of influence" on college students
(Astin, 1993, p. 398). Many theorists on diversity in higher education highlight the
importance of increasing interaction among different student communities (Astin,
1993; Hurtado, Dey, & Treviño, 1994; Chang, 1996). Many academics believe that
such interaction among students of different backgrounds is the best preparation for
democracy. Indeed, for many White students, college may be the first opportunity
to encounter non-White and non-Christian peers, and encounters with diverse
students have resulted in positive outcomes for many students. Still, as for the
nature of interracial (and intercultural) interaction, little is known (Antonio, 2001,
pp. 66–67). Indeed, for many White students, college may be the first opportunity
to encounter non-White (and often non-Christian) peers, and encounters with
diverse students have resulted in positive outcomes for many students. On the flip
side, minoritized students can often become "used" as default diversity educators
for their majority peers, with little regard as to the impact of this exchange upon
minority students. As universities seek to foster increased diversity, it is important

Ö. Sensoy and C.D. Stonebanks (eds.), Muslim Voices in School: Narratives of Identity
and Pluralism, 117–133.

to heed the power dynamic inherent in the social exchange between minority and majority students, between minority groups and majority peer culture.

Dominant models of integration have presumed that minorities will eventually become "less different" and ultimately adopt dominant college culture (Hurtado and Carter, 1997, p. 327), just as they may have adapted to White-majority schools before college. When minority students seek out the oases of supportive groups (such as religious communities) on unsupportive campuses, majority peers (and academics) become uncomfortable with "racial segregation" and "balkanization" (Loo and Rolison, 1986, p. 72). But many minority students criticize such "segregation" too, and perform "good" minorities by studiously seeking out diverse (i.e. White) friends rather than "sticking to" their religious, cultural and/or racial communities.

Though, as Tinto (1993) argues, many campuses still hold that "[i]n order to become fully incorporated in the life of the college, [students] have to physically as well as socially dissociate themselves from the communities of the past" (p. 96), home communities actually facilitate students' adjustment to college (Hurtado and Carter, 1997). Students' roots in prior experiences, their homes and their ethnic and religious communities may provide them with the security and support they need in the midst of the potentially corrosive work of dominant peer culture. In other words, the neoliberal multicultural assumption that *more* encounters with others are necessarily *better* than isolating oneself within one's chosen "home" community, does not account for power and hegemony in the encounter. What is "good" for majority students is not necessarily so for minority students. For minority students, often, the safety of some nesting within the home community is important for "healthy" identity work. I use "healthy" for identity work to mean identity construction that takes place with relatively less obstruction and interruption by dominant groups and individuals (c.f. Tatum, 2003).

Driven by a discourse to heighten diversity, universities superficially recruit "diverse" students (including Muslims) as poster children, demonstrating the inclusiveness and welcoming climate of the campus. But the "menu," both academic and social, remains overwhelmingly White, and minority students must retain only a splash of color (religion, culture, etc.) to remain palatable. The range of difference permitted to be displayed on campus is relatively limited. Muslim community spaces and organizations work as sub-cultures on campuses in ways similar to those of religious schools, providing "sites of resistance" (Zine, 2000, p. 297) for Muslim students.

In the context of Canadian Muslims, Jasmin Zine explores young Muslim students' efforts to maintain an Islamic lifestyle despite racism and the pressure to conform to the dominant culture (2000, 2001). She shows how "negative peer pressure, drugs, alcohol use, dating and violence in schools pose many challenges for Muslim students attempting to maintain an Islamic lifestyle and identity while at school" (Zine, 2007, p. 72). While many neoliberal scholars feel that religious schools create "ghettos," she argues that minority schools in White-dominated societies "seek to move the realities and experiences of their students from the margins to the centre of the educational focus" (p. 74). Zine found that being in an

Islamic school gave Canadian Muslim students a basis of strength from which to engage with pluralistic society, while still maintaining their identities (2007, p. 82). In many "diverse" educational spaces, the hegemony of Anglo knowledge and culture affects the identities and experiences of non-White students (Zine, 2007).

Apart from academic knowledge, youth cultural norms and unofficial peer leisure rituals are even more effective, powerful and unquestioned in establishing the dominance of Anglo culture. I contend that peer leisure culture in social spaces is a powerful medium that constructs marginality for other (e.g. Muslim) ways of being (Mir, 2006).

BACKGROUND OF THE STUDY

In 2002-03, I conducted ethnographic research with U.S. Muslim undergraduate women at Georgetown and George Washington Universities, in Washington, D.C., focusing on issues of identity and campus climate. Of the 26 participants with whom I conducted in-depth interviews over a period of about one year, I selected three women – Intisar, Tahira and Haseena[1] – and through their accounts I tried to convey some sense of the multiple worlds they navigate. My focus was on Muslim women undergraduates' struggles to be, and the role played by their friends, both Muslim and non-Muslim, in their navigation of dominant cultural spaces. Through my research on American Muslim undergraduate women's identity work, I hope to shed light on the gaps in North American pluralism as it occurs in the leisure spaces of educational contexts.

Intisar, Tahira, and Haseena were all undergraduate women in Washington, DC. In very different ways, they exemplify the urge to seek self within community and without, inwardly and outwardly, and they also exemplify the compromises that this urge entails.

A key dimension in my participants' identity work was the pull towards community. Acutely aware of the power of college culture, many of my participants tried to "limit" themselves to ethnic and religious "sites of resistance;" groups such as Muslim organizations helped mediate the alienation and minimize the marginality Muslims generally experienced in dominant educational culture (Zine, 2000, p. 307). Some avoided dominant groups because they reduced the minority participant through the gaze of power. Almost all my participants sought out Muslim friends: some of them had *only* Muslims as their close friends and even secularized Muslims tended to maintain close friendships with other Muslims. The reasons for this were more profound than xenophobia of White dominant culture, of far graver import than "mere" comfort: it was about finding home and rest from oppressive White society, finding acceptance in the midst of stereotyping and incomprehension; *and* protecting one's religious and ethnic identity. Though not free of difficulties, Muslim student sub-cultures can provide "safe harbors" (Tinto, 1993: 123) to religiously-observant students (Mir, 2006), and are an important resource for spiritually struggling students.

As an immigrant, a Muslim, and a woman of color, I had faced many of the same struggles as my participants. As a Muslim feminist, I wrestled with Muslim and non-Muslim static conceptions of Muslim gendered behavior and identity work. I had alternated between spending most of my time within the Muslim community, and then pulling my hair out over the religious politics of this same community and withdrawing to secular academic circles. I came to relative "rest" within a small community of like-minded Muslim religious-but-progressive-types. Still, like many other diasporic Muslims, I remain in search of community, whether it be "diverse" (open-minded non-Muslims of shared humane values) or Muslim (progressive, reflexive, and culturally somewhat mixed). I share, therefore, my research participants' search for belonging, and the chaos, compromise, and unstable tension of this quest. In my research, I sought to allow Muslim women to speak, in their own voices, without having Others—Muslim or non-Muslim—tell them what they should say, think, or be, and what kind of social worlds they should occupy and construct.

INTISAR

Intisar was a sophomore, a vibrant, outgoing, intelligent young woman who was involved in Muslim Student Association work as a non-officer. She was the youngest of many children in a Somali family headed by a widow who had fled Somalia's civil war. Intisar had seen conflict, flight, racism, prejudice, loss, trials, and barely experienced childhood nor stability. The trauma of war and her father's death seemed to have blocked all her memories of her life in Somalia. Though she often felt alienated in her family, loyalty to her family also centered her, but as she grew older, she found that an emotional and spiritual home with friends and faith superseded family and ethnic culture. As she made her place in her new "home," she found herself making social choices that would strengthen her faith. Her family and home culture, however, slowly lost their place in her life.

Due to tumultuous family events, including a sibling's death, Intisar's family was forced to move from the west coast to Washington, DC. In her hometown, she had gradually *worked* to gain a cultural foothold and a peer group. Had she stayed in her west coast hometown, she would have attended the school of her choice and moved away from her family. Moving to Washington DC and attending college here meant she had to live with her family, and give up the prospect of freedom from them. Her frustration with the change of plans was combined with a spiritual-philosophical acceptance and filial loyalty:

> I had my doubts but now I know I was supposed to be here, in some spiritual sense. I'm glad...I can do what I please, but still – you've got to take care of your family...I didn't want to be here...The decision to come to this school was already made for me. I had other plans.

Intisar resented the move because it meant that her life continued to revolve around family. At her college – predominantly White and upper middle class – this Somali refugee felt out of place. Even with the (mostly South Asian) Muslim friends with whom Intisar felt an intense spiritual fellowship, race still created an invisible barrier. She also struggled with racist stereotypes of Somalis as "deadbeats." She said:

> [Recently] my focus was a Somali get-together...across campuses, across DC...Because no one even knows there's Somalian kids going to [this college]. Everyone hears Somalian and thinks, oh—deadbeats, or they're going to [the community college]...But I mean, yeah, I just want to sort of meet everyone, see what we can do as Somalis, to help our community. Because you know, not a lot of people speak Somali, and you know, there's really no like, lawyers, and there's no help out there for Somalians, in terms of immigration, INS, in terms of politics or other things.

At college, Intisar experienced emotional growth with her Muslim friends as never before. "The type of family I wanted, I get it here [at college]," she said. "Emotionally I've opened up to these girls and it's amazing. I smile a lot." But as one of the few Somalis she knew at her college, Intisar had a strong sense of responsibility to mobilize and represent her community. It was about helping her people, a shared racial-cultural background and a shared sense of being:

> But in general I wouldn't share my emotions...with someone else other than my Somali friends: someone else just might not understand...Because I know someone else, they'd probably say, if I might be feeling bad about doing something, they're just going to...say, "Well, do what you're happy with." You know, to some extent, that's just not honesty...But to some extent, you want someone, if you are on the wrong path, someone who can correct you...[While growing up] most of my friends weren't Muslim...They were friends and they feel comfortable opening up to you, but I can't do the same thing myself because I *know* they don't understand. If...you just share something you feel, they're just going to be amazed, they're going to almost tell you, "Oh, you know you're such a great person for handling this" because they're not quite understanding what you're struggling with. They just say, "Oh wow, you have a big family."...There *is* no connection really. As opposed to if you share with someone who's already been there, who knows how it is...You can grow with that person because you have something to share already from the get-go. You don't have to spend time building up something and then opening up...No one likes to be so pitiful they feel sorry for you.

Intisar poignantly described the nature of shared ethnic-cultural community, and how non-Somalis simply failed to "own" her trials and to "struggle with" her. Non-Somali friends were on the outside, disconnected and even patronizing. Their gaze was sympathetic, not empathetic; pitying and admiring, not accepting. For all her struggles, she did not need her friends turning the othering gaze upon her family – the same family that could not nurture her emotionally.

Her mother disapproved of her sociability, so Intisar kept it private, like a guilty secret. As the only child who had grown up in the U.S., culturally, Intisar was different from her family. She saw no reason to practice traditional Somali roles, and had little sense of cultural ownership. Abandoning them was inevitable, simply a matter of time for her. She likened family pressure to practice traditional cultural roles to force-feeding, "You know your body's not going to digest [it]: at some point you *are* going to let it go."

Islam helped mediate her friends' religious influence, her bicultural identity, and her family's Somali expectations. She did not work towards a grand resolution to these matters. Instead, she focused on a day-to-day balancing act between her roles. She explained:

> The tension is coming from my mom, the tension is coming from my friends here. Because I constantly have to choose…I'm not really resolving it, but it depends on whatever that day is: how do I deal with it?…Trying to learn about Islam and how I'm really supposed to be courteous to my mother even if her approaches I don't agree with…The part of me that's really embracing Islam – because I know there are other parts of me that don't, but I want to suppress those – but the part that does is the one that keeps me balanced… Because those things are both extremes so – the free and the restricted, constrained Somali…The Muslim part of me is what keeps me balanced from rejecting either extremes or accepting the other one.

Intisar's faith helped balance her desire for independence, mobility, social connection and self-discovery with partial acceptance of maternal authority. Intisar did not rebel outright: she let off steam by taking small liberties such as staying at college late, playing basketball, and socializing with friends. These activities helped her breathe just enough to make it from day to day. With great skill, Intisar deconstructed her own identity into the Islam-embracing, the rebelling, the Somali, and the American components. She did not pretend that she had control over each component at all times. She used her religiosity to help her maintain her bicultural identities. At home, she continued to be respectful and obedient to her mother for Islam and because it gave her mother stability and confidence. In terms of wearing the hijab, her older sisters refused to obey their mother, "Just being me, and being the youngest, I took the responsibility, for my mother, because they didn't, so at least she had *someone* who listened to her." But gradually, Intisar's close ties with her friends and her gradual loss of Somalian language skills affected her relationship with her mother. Religion alone sustained this strong but tenuous and tense relationship:

> I've become so out of touch with my family that…any free time I'd rather be outside the house than in it…If I see someone here [at college], we can chat about nothing and – I'm losing my Somalian, so that's another aspect. And there's a lot of conflict, a lot of difficulty that comes for me, when I speak to my mom. Because we'd just rather be quiet than try to struggle, try to translate and explain what this means or what I'm trying to say…There's just no common ground…There's just nothing to talk about…Other than religion.

The lack of common ground with her family was in sharp contrast to the shared American Muslim youth experience of college camaraderie with her friends. Intisar derived a great deal of strength from her faith, strength that she had independently developed outside of cultural conformity or filial obedience. Its externality to filial or cultural conformity, in fact, turned it into another force that distanced her from her family and Somali culture:

> It was harder for me, because here I am born into this family, which is Muslim, from a country which is 99.9% Muslim and you just kind of conform to whatever situation you're given…But then the biggest change was the past two years. I've grown on my own, and I've learned about Islam and I've developed this spiritual relationship with God. That has taught me a lot, because I did it on my own and I wasn't conforming to anything.

The urge to be "free" and *non*-conforming linked up with religiosity, while she represented her cultural and filial ties as a matter of conformity and subordination. Her relationship with God became something she did on her own, just as she played basketball in secret from her family. Religion became one of those enjoyable, independent activities that she engaged in for herself.

The rhetoric of pluralism and diversity implicitly places the burden of educating White peers upon people of diverse background. Intisar flipped the standard, and chose to protect her own spirituality, while still extending support and friendship to non-Muslim peers. She "controlled" these friendships by defining "good fences." In the delicate areas that affected her religiosity, the connection ended. While most other students interviewed for this study described accepting the need (almost the civic obligation) to transcend their communities, Intisar focused on her own religious and social needs, keeping potentially anti-religious influences at a safe distance, outside her selfhood:

> Intisar: I tend to hang out with the people that have the best influence on me…I can still keep the other ones around, but just so long as I know the scale is tipped the other way, to the good side, I'm okay…Less time with them, and…try to have a little bit of distance so you don't get too deep…But try to just stay focused on my priorities is what I'm concerned with.
>
> Shabana: Your first duty -
>
> Intisar: Is to me.

Intisar's choices were leavened by the self-awareness that she had been a cultural "conformist" in high school. In college, for the first time she had close Muslim friends and an MSA. These were her lifeline, protecting her from the many possibilities of an irreligious life. She did not want to risk losing the religiosity she had achieved:

> The thing is, I'm glad to have Muslim friends and to be so close with almost all of them and to have more of them surrounding me than anyone else…I'm glad because most of my life, junior high, high school, I had no Muslim friends, not *one*…No matter what, you have to keep going back to the center…Just so you don't go off the cliff and kill yourself. I know that's kind

of extreme but honest to God, I really wouldn't know what I'd do if I didn't have these people, or if I didn't feel this connection with them enough so that they'd have this big influence on me. What if I [had] met the wrong people? What if there was no MSA at this school?...When I think of it, I'm always thinking of myself sort of just attending a school...that's non-Muslim, having friends that are non-Muslim, so I don't know what I'd have done...What if other people [had] influenced me the other way?

Intisar sought refuge from the influence of majority friends with religious Muslim friends. And as she put it, she did not want the "consequences" of making "mistakes." Intisar was terrified of becoming influenced "the other way," in the face of the overwhelming pressure to conform, assimilate, and disappear into the White American melting pot – to party, to drink, to date, to do drugs. The loss of identity, the loss of a way of life, the loss of community, the loss of that selfhood that she had been raised with, were high prices to pay for "belonging" to a majority peer group. The price for belonging was social, spiritual, religious, and personal, and the process was via "mistakes." In Tahira, we can see discussion of some such regret for "mistakes."

TAHIRA

Tahira is a Pakistani-American and, by her own accounts, was a "party girl." Tahira's family was the only Pakistani and the only Muslim family in her overwhelmingly White town. At the time of our interviews, she was an undergraduate who sought a career in health services so she could help troubled children. She often relived the angst about her social failure at school. "I was a dork," she said. "I was a loser."

After she graduated from high school suddenly Tahira became "cool," popular and outgoing. From being a fairly conservative, naïve young woman who did not drink, she veered in to casual dating, drinking, and "really partying." She explained:

Well, it was who I thought I wanted to be. I was a dork in high school and I didn't drink, you know...I went to [a beach resort] for senior week after I graduated, with a friend. And I drank some there, and I was really popular...It was like, 'I'm popular, I'm attractive!' I had a lot of attractive issues. Nobody *looked* at me in high school...It was partly the fact that you're at the beach, everyone's hooking up with everyone; it's a hormonal free for all...[I] drank here, I was popular, I had boys. I had whatever I wanted.

At college, drinking for popularity became normal for her, as well as a cause for very frequent casual sexual encounters. But Tahira was not a one-dimensional party-girl. In her search for religious community, she had joined a university that had a well-established Muslim Student Association, and she had also taken a course on Sufism. She wanted to be spiritual, she said, but "I don't think I'm very successful at it." With clear-eyed honesty, Tahira knew where she stood socially vis-à-vis the Muslim community: it was not their approval she sought. At the

Muslim student group, Tahira's lifestyle stood out as different. The community she desired became another space where she was unpopular and did not belong:

[At the prayer hall last] year I got some looks. One time I wore a baseball cap backwards [instead of a scarf]…In the long run, okay, so you didn't have your *wudu* [ablutions for prayer], okay, fine…You weren't facing the right direction. In the end, what's more important? The fact that you did all those things or that you're remembering God?... "Ohmygod, I saw you wearing a skirt, or shorts, or a short sleeved shirt," – stupid stuff like that aggravates me. I'm like, it's more important to me to be a little bit God-conscious and to be at peace with Allah rather than to be worried about [exoteric details].

Because Tahira had been raised mostly among non-Muslim Whites, she was not used to socializing with Muslims and South Asians. *They*, and not Whites, made her feel out of place:

My closest friends here are White. I feel more comfortable with them, but that's how I was raised…I'm not really used to having [brown people around]…I don't allow myself to hang out with them too much, because – I drink, you know what I mean …I don't have to worry about anything [around White people], I'm uninhibited. And then I'm hanging out with my desi friends and it's like, [demurely] "Yes, I didn't do anything last night."

Tahira had had to "earn" her White friends by giving up her former lifestyle; but now that she was popular with them, she came to the conclusion that she could not have and/or keep her brown Muslim friends. She could not have both. In relative terms, one always had to choose between one's religious/cultural community and majority-group friends. Tahira preferred to keep her religious identity private during forays into nightlife to avoid becoming a representative of Islam, and her "party" life private from Muslim friends:

Islam is such a beautiful thing. I feel like my actions reflect negatively on Islam. It's why I don't want people to know I'm Muslim. It's not like I'm ashamed to be Muslim…[I] don't want people to be like, "Oh, she's the Muslim chick…she's taken another three shots."

Tahira kept her religious life private. Islam, she claimed, was too good to be publicly associated with her person. By junior year, she was trying to achieve a balance between her religious aspirations, her sexuality, and her desire for emotional health:

I was very conservative in high school and so you lose that and [I] kind of went to the other extreme. And now I'm kind of trying to come back to the center which is difficult for me.

In many respects, she was negotiating her way through intense relationships, a fast lifestyle and an incongruent social circle:

[My] crowd right now is very macho party crowd -..."let's hook up with a random guy."...That's what college is about, you know – having fun, having a good time. But you know, I have my own reservations about it, and I'm working to be a better person, in my own opinion. It *is* difficult because you want to be cool and you want to hang out, and you want to be part of that group.

Tahira was coming to a reflective understanding about her lifestyle. The fun, "normal," party lifestyle of college, so intensely celebrated by mainstream youth culture, is revealed in Tahira's experience to be an empty performance that is draining on multiple levels. It is what is "expected" in college, and participation in that culture may have gained her popularity with others, but it also alienated her from herself:

And once I lost [my virginity], I kind of, as a psychological protector, really had to devalue sex and make it okay. And that's why there's so many random guys...So it's not satisfying to me, doesn't make me happy. It makes me feel worse, and...it continues the cycle...[I'm] moving away from the physical validation from guys and focusing on emotional validation from myself... Because I haven't been healthy and I haven't been happy in such a long time.

It is possible that Tahira faced these kinds of challenges because she had not had the benefit of a "site of resistance" (Zine, 2000) in primary and secondary schooling (i.e. a community of other young people like her, racially and in terms of religious acculturation). She yearned to belong, yet the only community/friendship circle that had been available to her in her White town and White school were White peers. By the time she got to college, she was a figurative exile from "Brown"/Muslim community circles as she did not (in many ways) have the cultural capital to belong there. Her sexuality and her unorthodox religiosity made her an outcast in Muslim circles. She had worked hard to belong in White-majority circles, by giving up (by her own account) an emotional tranquility. Now, she was faced with the challenge of relocating this emotional tranquility.

HASEENA

Haseena is a Pakistani-American sophomore from a fairly religious and protective family. She had lived in a larger, more diverse urban environment than Tahira, but she had had a predominantly White schooling like Tahira's. Now, she was relieved to have South Asian and Muslim friends who understood her religion and culture. Haseena wanted a wide variety of friends at college, but, she said, Muslims and South Asians "are the people that really understand you." Though the two groups intersected, South Asians and Muslims served somewhat different purposes in Haseena's life. There was a time to party with the (liberal) South Asians (many of whom drank), and a time to be with the (religious) Muslims (c.f. Hall, 2002, p. 171 who discusses British Sikhs' adjustments across peer groups). Like Intisar, Haseena valued her Muslim friends as a religious influence:

I figured I'd have to have a double life: like, with my Muslim friends I would be really *good,* and other friends I could go out and party and have fun with...Because if you don't associate yourself with Muslims, then you're not really going to have that pull to go to *jum'ah*...[or] *Iftar*...Because it's hard in college, because it's the first time you're on your own and you're surrounded by so many different [kinds of people]. And you just get so busy. It's really hard to remember your religion unless you make a conscious effort in order to do it.

The powerful magnetic orbit of college life could change a person by drawing her into an almost regimented academic and social schedule, and Haseena felt she needed to attach herself to her Muslim friends to preserve her religiosity. But the norms of college sociability functioned to distance people from their own protective communities. By sophomore year, Haseena felt guilty for not having "more diverse"–more White – friends:

I do have American friends – White friends – but not as many as I think I should...I think it's bad to have only one type of friend...because I think it's having to do with being in America...You can't just be like, I'm going to only deal with people that are like me...And I kind of see that that's something my parents did wrong...[My mom] just felt like [the mothers of other children at school] weren't very friendly to her...And I'm sure that was the case. But I was just like, "Mom you have to be more assertive and make them *see* what kind of person you are."

The onus is on the nonwhite person to establish her personhood. Unlike her mother, Haseena worked to establish her American-ness and normalcy in college culture, and did not limit her interactions to her ethnic or religious community. She felt strongly that at college, one "ought" to transcend one's comfortable ethnic community, even in the choice of freshman roommates. Haseena was surprised that she got away with a Muslim roommate. "And I don't know how that happened, because I would think they'd try to force you to be with people that are different. Because that's what college is all about." The orthodox college experience *should* be about abandoning "your own people" and seeking a "diverse" social circle. Haseena represented Muslim and South Asian friends as a guilty pleasure, a "non-diverse" clique—even though this circle comprised Indians, Pakistanis, Bangladeshis, Arabs, White and Black converts, and others. Because they shared a common culture and religious culture, they ought to look outward and not rest with each other. They should move outward, to new experiences and different friends. In Haseena's case, one of these new experiences was a boyfriend:

I knew I wouldn't be as strict as I was at home...I know this is kind of wrong, but sometimes being more strict within yourself kind of holds you back from different experiences. For example, if I had followed the rules at home I would never have gotten involved with Zafar. I mean, that's debatable, whether or not that was a good idea, but I'd never have that experience...I was like, "Don't hold yourself back from experiences."

127

Despite her eagerness to seek experiences, Haseena went back and forth between guilt ("I still feel like I've gone against myself") and arguing with herself to establish her own religiosity ("I feel like the decisions I make here are still in line with my religion. You know—like—I—I go to a party but I don't drink.") She had to go against herself to seek experiences: "experiences" would take her outside herself and her community, beyond her comfort zone and beyond the familiar. This was what college was all about: it was the required cultural curriculum, and Haseena diligently pursued it.

Haseena enjoyed participating in a collective Muslim life, such as the MSA. At the same time, as she pursued diverse experiences, she was surprised by the changes in herself. In high school, she was the girl who never disobeyed her parents and had never seen herself having a boyfriend nor attending nightclubs. At college, she was thrust into a world of relativism and moral pluralism:

> And that's how I became more liberal when I came to college, because when I was in high school and at home, I was more like, "No. This is how it has to be"…And now it's more like, "People have different ways of practicing, you know"…And now I'm like, "They can do whatever they want, and I can do whatever I want."

Ironically, whatever she wanted was not necessarily what she did. In many ways, she did what majority college culture wanted her to do, and ultimately went against "herself." This powerful new life in college led her into the long-term romantic and sexual relationship with Zafar:

> I wasn't like, "what are the consequences going to be of this?" It was definitely college. You don't have someone looking over your shoulder, [asking] "What are you doing?" At home, I have my brother and my cousins, and they'd be like, "What are you *doing*?!"…Here, who's looking?

Haseena was in a complicated situation vis-à-vis Zafar. They had a long-term commitment, but as a Pakistani Muslim woman (from a conservative family), Haseena wanted a public engagement as soon as possible. According to Haseena, her boyfriend would not approach his family about an engagement: preoccupied with other family matters, they did not want her disrupting their son's academic career. She struggled with religious guilt, fear of disrepute, fear of her own family, fears for their future, Zafar's desire to appease his family, Pakistani Muslim norms, and the norms of American youth culture:

> I do [want to be engaged] but then it would be weird to be engaged at this point because I'm only nineteen…If my [American] friends knew we're planning on getting married they'd be like, "You don't know what you're doing." And that's not really my mindset or his mindset. Yeah, because you think of that right away whenever you meet someone, "Oh, is this the person I can marry?"…Yeah, I'm stuck. And it kind of makes me mad because I'm not the one that can [change anything]…I have the whole struggle in my mind, he really doesn't. Because he's a boy, and boys just don't worry that much about…what their parents think.

Haseena and Zafar felt trapped within American youth cultural norms about the appropriate age for commitment. Zafar's sexuality was not monitored by his parents, but Haseena was terrified of her parents discovering that she was in a relationship at college. She also had a stronger sense of guilt vis-à-vis the sexual relationship:

> But when I got involved in this relationship, I ignored the aspect of, the fact that it made me [religiously] uncomfortable…Even though I knew – I mean *I know!* I *know* I'm not right, but so I've ignored it though…Once you start down that road on a relationship like that, it's really hard to go back…[I] was just a freshman kid, and I was like "Oh, look at this guy," you know…[My friend] Mohamed was actually the only one that was like, "what are you doing?"…All my other friends were like, "Oh, that's so cool!"

Haseena followed the norms of undergraduate college culture by entering into a romantic and sexual relationship, and in her words, "ignoring" her background, her family's expectations, and her own religiosity. She justified ignoring these factors by arguing that this was long-term relationship, but her personal guilt seemed to surface. Her desire to "make it right" by getting engaged was disrupted by Zafar and his family's discomfort with an early engagement. As a man, Zafar did not have the same degree of urgency about correcting a wrong. His relative comfort with premarital sex and his family's control of the timing of a marriage proposal, all combined to disempower her:

> We try not to discuss how we're wrong…If religion's important to you, you shouldn't ignore it…That's been my mistake since I came to college: ignoring that it made me uncomfortable. Because when I tried to tell him, he'd just be like, "I understand, but I can't do it, because of all the reasons I gave you." And he just didn't seem excited about [engagement/marriage]… [He] just didn't seem excited about the timing…I was just like, "Well, I don't want to be badgering you."… It's a limbo stage and I don't want to be in that limbo stage.

With Zafar's lack of enthusiasm about an "early" engagement, Haseena was deprived of any power over the situation.

CONCLUSION

The rhetoric of pluralism and diversity assumes that a variety of friends is always and for everyone a "good thing," that it is always good to seek friendships with cultural and religious others. For Intisar, Tahira and Haseena this was not always the case. Students like them struggle to find a foothold in faith and racial community as they navigate the, at times, lonely intersections of race, religion, culture, and gender. At times, they try to replace memories of adolescent rejection with happier ones of being "normal" and popular with their peers. Muslim students may struggle and flounder in working towards a sense of belonging and community via dominant majority social networks (Mir, 2006).

Muslim students struggle to preserve identities and they struggle with racism, at times retreating to religious and cultural enclaves for protection. All three young women yearned for belonging. Deprived of her own ethnic-religious community in her upbringing, Tahira threw herself into mainstream White peer culture, and into a party lifestyle that practically broke her. The dominant discourse of what college is about forced her to publicly distance herself from her religious life, and did not give her happiness. Ultimately, her religiosity was not about conformity to a community, and she was trying to break her conformity to majority culture as well. But she was engaged in these struggles alone. No one was helping her, whether Muslim or non-Muslim, and every peer group simply "wanted a piece of her."

Intisar had many majority acquaintances but she reserved her inner circle of friendship for Muslim friends and the innermost circle for Somali friends. If one is to achieve belonging in majority peer groups, the price is high in regret and loss, Intisar found as a new refugee arrival. Her growing American-ness alienated her from her Somali family, and her growing religiosity allowed for her to keep feet in both worlds, even if superficially, with an emotional home in Muslim peer friendships that served to further alienate her from her mother.

Haseena was torn between desiring South Asian and Muslim friends, and the "obligation" to sustain White friendships, but she struggled to keep herself under the influence of Muslim friends. This led to a "double life" which was actually a triple one, divided between Muslim, South Asian and White peers. She "used" Muslim peers to protect her religion, since religiosity was difficult to guard without support. But a "diverse" (read: White) friendship group was a civic and cultural obligation, and one for which White peers' reluctance had to be overcome, and they had to be won over. Haseena worked to follow the college curriculum of "new experiences." But then she discovered how she was torn among each of Muslim, immigrant, and American norms.

These Muslim women had their own private personal, religious, spiritual and cultural goals, beyond White universities' agendas to establish their institutional multicultural profiles. They all had a variety of friends, but they all saw how friends who did not share their religious-spiritual heritage could at times be unhelpful influences at this tender age that combined tumultuous social lives with heady spiritual quest. Oftentimes, it seemed safer to rest with fellow Muslims, and to engage in conscious personal growth within one's own framework. But at times, as Haseena argued, it did not seem "right" to seek out only one's own type – because, after all, wasn't "America" about a "multicultural" ideal? The onus was on the "diverse" individual to conform to mainstream normative ideals. It is them that ought to make themselves available as diversity education for the mainstream population, for the good of the body politic, whatever the costs and however much it may put them personally at risk. For students who have experienced struggles between cultures, even the dislocations of war and trauma, often forced to choose between family and being American, breaking has meanings beyond the "broadening of cultural horizons" that White students seek in study abroad programs.

People like Haseena, Intisar and Tahira, who have in many ways been deprived of their own ethnic/cultural circles for their entire schooling, are in college also immediately shunted into diversity mode. The official culture of a university treats all students the same: yet many non-White students have scarcely had sufficient opportunity to be shaped by or to "nest" within their home communities, while many White students haven't had non-White friends. Because White society urges non-Whites to assimilate, and uses non-Whites to diversify mainstream spaces, Muslim students like other minority groups must join in the White-monitored development of the "proper" body politic, which in mainstream neoliberal circles entails White-majority-with-White-influenced-minorities. Minority students such as Muslims engage in social encounters with majority students within the broader cultural context of White-dominant, Christian-majority society. Individual and collective encounters cannot fail to be infected by the power dynamic inherent in these encounters. As students of higher education, it is essential for us to grapple with the difficult question of how minority students may preserve identities, while we seek to promote diversity and inter-racial and inter-cultural exchange on campuses.

DISCUSSION QUESTIONS AND EXTENSION ACTIVITIES

(1) Mir argues that certain social worlds can complicate Muslim students' religious and cultural identity construction. What creates the circumstances that put minority students' identities at risk?

(2) What might be the ideal circumstances under which students of various faith and cultural backgrounds socialize without such danger? Design the charter or mission statement for a school– or community-based organization that would support students of various faith and culture in ways that affirm all of their backgrounds.

(3) How central is your religious belief system to your "culture"? Consider norms of family get-togethers, celebrations, mournings, transitions in life (childhood to adolescence, marriage, old age). How visible or invisible is the role your religious acculturation plays in your cultural practices and value beliefs? What are the implications of this in/visibility?

IF YOU LIKED THIS CHAPTER, YOU MAY ALSO ENJOY:

Abdurraqib, S. (2009). On being Black and Muslim: Eclipsed identities in the classroom. *In this book*.

Mourchid, Y. (2009). Left to my own devices: Hybrid identity development of religion and sexual orientation among Muslim students in the United States. *In this book*.

Abdul-Ghafur, S. (Ed.) (2005). *Living Islam out loud: American Muslim women speak*. Boston, MA: Beacon Press.

Hasna M., M. (2008) "Forbidden Love." Finalist in the One Nation Many Voices Contest. At http://www.linktv.org/onenation2007/films/view/235

Karim, J. (2008) *American Muslim women: Negotiating race, class, and gender within the ummah*. New York: New York University Press.

Fine, M. & Selcuk, S. (2008) *Muslim American youth: Understanding hyphenated identities through multiple methods*. New York: New York University Press.

Magolda, P. (2000). The campus tour: Ritual and community in higher education. *Anthropology & Education Quarterly*, 31(1), 24–46.

Bryant, A.N. & Astin, H.S. (2008) The correlates of spiritual struggle during the college years. *The Journal of Higher Education*, 79(1), January/February 2008.

Seifert, T. (2007). Understanding Christian privilege: Managing the tensions of spiritual plurality. About Campus, May-June, 10–17.

Zaal, M., et al. (2007) The weight of the hyphen: Freedom, fusion and responsibility embodied by young Muslim-American women during a time of surveillance. *Applied Developmental Science*, 2007, 11(3), 164–177.

NOTES

[1] All names are psedonymns

REFERENCES

Antonio, A. L. (2001, Fall). Diversity and the influence of friendship groups in college. *The Review of Higher Education*, 25(1), 63–89.

Astin, A. W. (1993). *What matters in college?* San Francisco: Jossey-Bass.

Chang, M. J. (1996). *Racial diversity in higher education: Does a racially mixed student population affect educational outcomes?* Unpublished Doctoral Dissertation, University of California, Los Angeles.

Fine, M., Weis, L., & Powell, L. C. (1997). Communities of difference: A critical look at desegregated spaces created for and by youth. *Harvard Educational Review*, 67(2), 247–284.

Hall, K. D. (2002). *Lives in translation: Sikh youth as British citizens*. Philadelphia: University of Pennsylvania Press.

Hurtado, S., & Carter, D. F. (1997). Effects of college transition and perceptions of the campus racial climate on Latino college students' sense of belonging. *Sociology of Education*, 70(4), 24–345.

Hurtado, S., Dey, E. L., & Treviño, J. G. (1994). *Exclusion or self-segregation? Interaction across racial/ethnic groups on college campuses*. Paper presented at the annual meeting of the American Educational Research Association, New Orleans.

Loo, C. M., & Rolison, G. (1986). Alienation of ethnic minority students at a predominantly white university. *Journal of Higher Education, 57*(1), 58–77.

Mir, S. (2006). *Constructing third spaces: American Muslim undergraduate women's hybrid identity construction.* Unpublished PhD Dissertation, Indiana University, Bloomington.

Shaffir, W. (1979). *Life in a religious community: The Lubavitcher chassidim in montreal.* Toronto: Holt, Rinehart and Winston.

Tatum, B. D. (2003). *Why are all the black kids sitting together in the cafeteria? and other conversations about race.* New York: Basic Books.

Tinto, V. (1993). *Leaving college: Rethinking the causes and cures of student attrition.* Chicago: University of Chicago Press.

Zine, J. (2007). Safe havens or religious 'ghettos'? Narratives of Islamic schooling in Canada. *Race Ethnicity and Education, 10*(1), 71–92.

Zine, J. (2004). *Staying on the 'straight path': A critical ethnography of Islamic schooling in Ontario.* Unpublished PhD Dissertation, University of Toronto.

Zine, J. (2001). Muslim youth in Canadian schools: Education and the politics of religious identity. *Anthropology & Education Quarterly, 32*(4), 399–423.

Zine, J. (2000). Redefining resistance: Towards an Islamic subculture in schools. *Race Ethnicity and Education, 3*(3), 293–316.

Shabana Mir
Qualitative Inquiry & Social Foundations
Oklahoma State University

SAMAA ABDURRAQIB

ON BEING BLACK AND MUSLIM

Eclipsed Identities in the Classroom

INTRODUCTION

In his article "Arab America's September 11," Moustafa Bayoumi (2006) begins
with an interview with a Palestinian-American who laments the fact that a close
friend was actually an undercover police detective who was spying on him and his
friends. When asked what life post-9/11 is like for Arab-Americans, the man states,
"We're the new blacks [sic]…[.]You know that, right" (p. 1)?

There are, of course, many ways in which this idea is true. But if Arab-
Americans are the new Blacks, where does that leave American Muslims who also
happen to be Black? As an African American Muslim-born and raised woman who
wears a hijab, I find that I am particularly troubled by this idea. Conflating race
with religion has the potential to overshadow the many different racial lives of
Muslims. This is detrimental because it concretizes certain images of Muslims that
are currently available in the U.S. social imaginary while simultaneously
invalidating the centuries-long connections that the African American community
has had with Islam. This invalidation affects me as a teacher and a student who is
African American and Muslim because it erases certain knowledge that I may have
through my experiences as a Muslim.

What the comments by the Palestinian-American in Bayoumi's article bring up
for me is the ways that Muslim identity is generally equated solely with
Arab/Middle Eastern identity. This alignment then leads to a conflation between
religion and race that constrains the potential connections between other racial
identities and Islam. What I mean to say is, in the U.S., if you are Muslim, you are
(at least in terms of the national imaginary) most likely Arab.[1] In both graduate and
undergraduate classrooms I experience this alignment in others' assumptions of
"authority." As either a student or as an instructor, I find that my Muslim identity is
often eclipsed by my African American identity. Generally speaking, this eclipsing
is not terribly troubling, but it does translate into assumptions about my
experiences and knowledge of Islam. When Islam is discussed in the classroom,
the assumption is that I am not necessarily speaking from a position of knowledge
or authority, and thus my experience of being Muslim and the knowledge that
stems from that experience are not perceived as valid. On the other hand when race
and Black-ness is discussed, I am immediately afforded a position of authority.
This does not necessarily mean that students and colleagues ask me about my

Ö. Sensoy and C.D. Stonebanks (eds.), Muslim Voices in School: Narratives of Identity
and Pluralism, 135–150.

opinion specifically (i.e. "how do you feel about this since you're Black"?), but it does mean that my arguments are less contested and people assume they know and understand my position on certain issues.

What the comments by the man from Bayoumi's article also reveal is the hierarchy of identity categories that have structured U.S. society for centuries. Previously, these hierarchies tended to be structured primarily around race, ethnicity, and country of origin. The Palestinian-American's comment envokes a historical legacy of immigrants and other U.S. minorities defining themselves in proximity to Blackness. Sometimes, Black struggles are like their struggles – to assimilate, to belong. Other times, a distance between the immigrant group and African Americans is sought in order to make the case for their assimilation and belonging in mainstream society. Muslim identity is a newer category and, because it sits across various racial and ethnic lines, it is always more complicated to position along this spectrum. When someone expresses anti-Muslim/Islamic sentiment, they are clearly expressing bigotry, but are they also expressing racist sentiments? Are they xenophobic? I think the problematic nature of Islamophobia causes Muslims and others to view Muslims as fitting into either a racial and/or immigrant category. In post-9/11 U.S., the Muslim identity is transformed into primarily a "visible" identity, rather than an identity based on religious/spiritual affiliation. If one "looks like" a Muslim (read: brown or veiled), the particularities of one's identity – nation of origin, ethnicity, actual religious affiliation – are easily overlooked.

Linda Alcoff (2006) states that visible identities tend to be organized into two main categories. In *Visible Identities*, she writes:

> Race and gender operate as our penultimate visible identities...[.]Social, cultural, and political affiliations, from orthodoxy to anarchism, must be marked by some form of visible dress code: a veil, a cross, *payos* (the side curls of the Hasidim), a tattoo, a particular hairstyle or hair treatment, or a strategically placed body piercing" (p. 7).

For me, this means that my racial identity takes precedence over my religious identity – despite the fact that I wear the hijab, a marker that ought to immediately signal my identity as a Muslim. In most contexts, I am identifiable as African American first and foremost, and in many of these contexts (the classroom included) my African American identity eclipses my Muslim identity. I would argue that this is because my racial identity, at least as it is perceived, is bodily; while my Muslim identity, at least insofar as it is symbolized by my hijab, is considered an accoutrement – something that can be taken on or off at will, like changing a blouse or pair of earrings.

In many cases, my hijab does not even signal as religious garb. Instead people assume that it is an expression of some kind of African culture-ness or heritage. Alcoff (2006) nicely states the way in which, in our minds, race is a bodily marker and is often divested of its ability to hold any other identities: "But the social identities of race and gender operate ineluctably through their bodily markers; they do not transcend their physical manifestation because they *are* their physical manifestation, despite the fact that the same features can support variable identities" (p.102). Because my racial identity looms large in people's minds, my Muslim identity is, for the most part, obscured. I cannot count how many times strangers have asked me where I was from. Then, after my explanation that I'm from the U.S., they gesture towards my scarf or to their own heads as though they were wearing a scarf and explain, "Oh, I thought you might be African because of the head covering." There have been other occasions when I have explained that my name is Arabic and that I am Muslim, and have had people respond with surprise, "Oh, that's why you cover your head. I thought it was just a head wrap."

I am currently a PhD student studying English literature. The school I work at and conduct my research in is a large, research-intensive university in Wisconsin. The fact that I teach in a predominately White university (and city) in the northern Midwest means that I fairly frequently vacillate between these two identity categories– more often than not, I am the only African American *and* the only Muslim in class. Living, teaching, and researching in an environment that is not accustomed to a great deal of diversity (let alone intersecting diversities) has made me more conscious of the ways in which my multiple identities are interpreted. I organize my classroom/campus experience into two categories: the graduate classroom and the undergraduate classroom. I separate these two experiences because, in the undergraduate classroom, as the instructor, I am already endowed with a certain level of authority I am frequently denied in the graduate classroom. In both environments, it has been difficult for my students and colleagues to overlook my African American identity, yet they disregard my Muslim identity with ease. This means that my experiences being Muslim are never translated into knowledge and in turn are not afforded any authority. In the remainder of this chapter, I will explore how my intersecting identities as an African American Muslim operate in these domains.

AS AN INSTRUCTOR: IN THE CLASSROOM

I teach in a city that is, for the most part, White. Students see my name on the roster, hear the supervising professor introduce me, see my hijab, and my brown skin and immediately classify me as being something other than American. However, once they talk to me, recognize my mannerisms, and hear my American accent, they reclassify me as American. This means that they see me as sharing an identity closer to theirs and this, I imagine, comforts them in some ways. Although recognizing my American accent does not always help. I humorously recall a well-intentioned, fresh-faced freshman classmate in a Spanish language class turning around and asking me, "Where are you from?" And, after I surprised her with my answer, "Ohio," she responded, "Oh, I thought maybe you were a foreign exchange student or something…"

When racial issues arise, which they often do in my literature classes, my students either take me as an authority figure or they begin to generate certain expectations about my responses to their comments and to the texts we study. My racial identity obscures all other aspects of my identity. My students then assume that I understand Blackness, Black life, racism, etc. because I have experienced all of these things. And they are able to pull from culturally available ideas about how African Americans respond to racial issues to predict how I will respond and react to what we are discussing. But because I generally teach American literature, and because Muslim American literature has not made its way onto our university course syllabi, my Muslim identity tends to remain irrelevant to them. Yet, when Islam *does* emerge as a topic, the students react to me as if I have the same amount of knowledge they have. For example, when I was a teaching assistant for a *Women in Literature* class, we read and discussed Marjane Satrapi's *Persepolis I* and Fatima Mernissi's *Dreams of Trespass: Tales of a Harem Girlhood.* One session, I gave a lecture on Mernissi's text. When lecturing on the two texts, the professor and I spent time talking about veiling and about how it is problematic to think about veiling as inherently oppressive. Nevertheless, during discussion sections and in their papers, my students were reluctant to hear what both the course professor and I were trying to explain. For them, the fact that I cover did not imbue me with any more or less experience and knowledge base from which "to know" than the lecturing professor. In many ways, I was no more an authority on Islam, veiling, or discourses about women's oppression in Islam than they were.

AS AN INSTRUCTOR: AT THE WRITING CENTER

One specific example of a student stripping me of whatever personal knowledge I might have occurred just recently at the university's Writing Center where I am an instructor. A young White man brought in a short paper for his *Western Religions* class;[2] the paper was about misogynistic interpretations of the Qur'an. Now, to be fair to this student, I was left with the impression that the course instructors did not do a satisfactory job contextualizing Qur'anic verses – I got the sense the students were just presented verses with a minimal amount of historical background and then were left to generate their own interpretations of extremely complex and historically- and culturally-dependent theological texts (in translation no less!).

This student was attempting to temper his preconceptions of Islam, but instead of challenging his cultural assumptions about Muslim/Middle Eastern culture, his superficial interpretation simply solidified common assumptions: Islamic cultures are backwards, stalwartly patriarchal, uneducated, and misogynist. As he began, I braced myself for the moment of recognition that generally occurs when White students bring in their papers about race: they hesitate, become visibly uncomfortable, and are often quick to accept whatever suggestions I may have about their language and tone.

Despite the fact that students often misread my veiling, I hoped that he would recognize that I was a Muslim and would then go through the same process White students tend to undergo when they bring in papers dealing with race. With this student, such a moment of recognition never occurred. The style I chose to wear my hijab that day was a bit ambiguous and, I can imagine, could have easily been interpreted as simply some sort of "ethnic" (or ethnic-inspired) expression. However, the resistance I describe with this student is not an anomaly in the

Writing Center. Once we began talking about his paper his lack of recognition was obvious as he referred to Muslims as "they" and Westerners as "we," thus implicating me in what he deemed Western interpretations of Islam as misogynist (as evidenced by these Qur'anic verses). His association also presumed that we, as non-Muslim Americans, shared similar opinions about "them." So, when I reacted to his xenophobic and over-statements about the ways these verses are interpreted in Islamic countries by stating that these interpretations stem from a lack of education and/or a "radical" education, misogynist culture, and patriarchal societies, he was taken aback. But I want to argue that his inability to read me as Muslim did not influence his response. What I mean to say is, when I challenged his assumptions, my experiential knowledge did not come in to play. I was re-interpreted in relation to my (divergent from his) political leanings and ideologies rather than the knowledge I may have about Islam stemming from my experience as a Muslim. As our conversation continued, he persisted to bundle me in with Westerners rather than questioning whether or not I was actually from a country "over there."

During parts of our conversation in which we discussed specific aspects of Islam, he pushed against my recommendations, attempting to drown me out with the knowledge he had acquired from his religion class over the past seven weeks (during which Islam was already the second religion they were "covering'). The first example of this occurred when I made the move to correct his terminology. Throughout the paper, the student was conflating Qur'anic *suar* (chapters) with Qur'anic *ayat* (verses) – he referred to the singular ayah as a Surah. I waited (wanting to establish some rapport) then corrected this error. However, when I corrected him, he cut me off and said, "Yeah, a Surah is the line," as if he was explaining to a person who just did not understand the terminology. When I spoke again, to correct him, he reiterated, but this time in defense: "No, a Surah is just the line." I restated my correction, this time using the terminology of ayah and he was finally able to remember what he had been taught in class: "Oh yeah, a verse is that 'a' word. Right." He corrected his use accordingly.

The second, slightly more disturbing moment occurred at the close of his paper where he was analyzing a verse about property and inheritance. After he read this section, he began to talk about another ayah he could bring in that referred to the distribution of wealth and property between the sexes. He had written something to the affect, "issues of owning property are new and contentious in Islam countries." Before I had a chance to ask him what he meant, he began to talk about a verse in which division of property was discussed. He claimed that the verse said that for every one item a woman has, a man should have two. I tried to engage him in terms of argument by asking him what he was trying to assert. He pointed to the sentence about owning property being contentious and I informed him that people in Islamic countries actually do own property. When I tried to ask him what he meant by this statement, he talked over me in a rush stating: "Well, you know, in those countries women are not allowed to have anything, and they're treated…". I interrupted and explained that, by law, women were allowed to inherit property. He argued with me, stating again that women were not allowed to own anything. I reiterated what I had said about Islamic law, but with a bit more firmness. I decided not to go into the details about how this inheritance works and how these laws are used in different predominantly Islamic countries because I thought it was important for him to understand how his absolute statement was problematic. He was silent for a moment and then he acquiesced by saying "Oh, I guess I didn't know that. I just thought they weren't allowed to own anything." When I tried to ask him where he had gotten that idea from, he said he wasn't sure. But yet he was so sure he was *right*, and simultaneously so sure that I did was wrong.

Ultimately, I am not sure that this student ever actually recognized that I was a Muslim. He did, perhaps, see where his knowledge was sparse – at the end of the appointment he said that he just wanted to stop being ignorant. I commend him for that comment, yet that was not the same standpoint he held when he entered into debate about Islamic law (for example) after seven or less weeks of study of Islam. My goal in my interaction with this student was not to teach him the correct way to think about nor talk about Islam, or the correct way to understand the Qur'an. My goal was to help him understand that his knowledge wasn't exactly extensive and/or absolute. I cannot say with certainty that I was successful.

IN THE GRADUATE CLASSROOM

In the graduate classroom, the ways my colleagues interact with me as a Muslim is not much different. In classrooms and/or learning environments where I am a figure of authority, students I interact with can perhaps associate my knowledge of Islam with a research interest rather than as personal experience. But in the graduate classroom, my research becomes more personal to me because much of my research interests are related to my experiences. So when my Muslim identity is eclipsed in these environments, and when my colleagues dismiss my knowledge and experience, I tend to take it more personally.

In both types of classrooms "issues of 'essence, identity, and experience' erupt in the classroom primarily because of the critical input from marginalized groups" (Fuss, 1989, p. 113). I tend to feel this more when I am situated as a student in the graduate classroom because I see it as a place where I can allow my experience to contribute to the generation of scholarly knowledge, as opposed to when I am an instructor and am more concerned with the ways in which my students generate knowledge. I feel that my experience and the knowledge it produces is particularly important in my present university setting because the graduate student body in the English department is fairly homogenous; I think the diversity of experiences I embody can bring new perspectives and new knowledge.

Diana Fuss (1989) writes that "'Experience' emerges as the essential truth of the individual subject, and personal 'identity' metamorphoses into knowledge. Who we are becomes what we know; ontology shades into epistemology" (p.113). For Fuss, the notion of lived experience as truth emerges in the classroom when we put aside theoretical and "experiment-based fact" in order to privilege empirical evidence. This impulse comes from a well-intentioned place; it is the impulse to privilege people's experience of oppression, for example, when discussion the impact of racism, sexism, heterosexism, xenophobia, and so on. Fuss complicates the authenticity of experience by acknowledging that, though well-intentioned, *solely* relying on experience may result in essentializing identity categories. She writes, "the problem with positing the category of experience as the basis of a feminist pedagogy is that the very object of our inquiry, 'female experience,' is never as unified, as knowable, as universal, and as stable as we presume it to be" (Fuss, 1989, p. 114).

In *Teaching to Transgress*, bell hooks (1994) takes this complication a bit further by pointing out how using experience as authoritative knowledge can easily be coopted by dominant groups in order to foist their experiences onto marginalized groups – thus further silencing them. My Writing Center student, for example, somehow assumed that his seven-week experience with Islam and selected verses from the Qur'an necessarily trumped my unspecified experience and knowledge as a Black woman. I would argue these claims hold true when there is a lack of diversity in a classroom because these experiences that stem from a persons identity represents a certain degree of authority – Fuss (1989) calls this the "authority of experience." But, in the graduate classroom, this authority is contingent upon the *type* of experience that is being presented. Perception of authority depends upon the visible and recognizable locations from which that experience comes.

As an African American, I am primarily situated by my skin color, and because "only what is visible can generally achieve the status of accepted truth" (Alcoff, 2006, p. 7), the authority of my experience is only relevant in discussions about race. Race is what dominates my colleagues' perceptions of me – despite the fact that I wear a hijab. While I am criticizing the fact that my voice is silenced when it comes to intellectual discourses about Islam, I am still aware of Fuss (1989) and hooks' (1994) cautions, and recognize the ways in which asking marginalized people to "testify" to their experiences is problematic in any setting, especially the classroom. In response to challenges such as these, hooks (1994) writes that "systems of domination already at work in the academy and the classroom silence the voices of individuals from marginalized groups and give space only when on the basis of experience it is demanded" because the "'authority of experience' [has] already been determined by a politics of race, sex, and class domination" (p. 81). Ultimately, she argues, the idea that marginalized groups should have space to speak of their experience(s) as a site of knowledge is an idea that is easily co-opted by dominant groups who are obsessed with ideas of essentialism.

When Islam is being discussed in the classroom, Islam moves into the realm of "intellectual property" – it becomes an idea that can be discussed, rather than a part of identity that an individual experiences or embodies. In these moments, experience is only relevant if one can claim to have "intellectual ownership of Islam." This is not to say that simply claiming rights to the intellectual property of a subject matter will mean one's experiences will be validated in the classroom. Dealing with experience in the graduate classroom (as far as my department goes) is in general, fairly taboo. In the current U.S. cultural imaginary, being Muslim is equated with being Arab, which (if we follow this logic) gives Arabs the right to this intellectual property.[3] A perfect example of this conflation occurred during the recent campaign for the U.S. presidential nominations. At a rally, Presidential hopeful Senator John McCain spoke with a woman who, in her attempt to explain her distrust of McCain's rival, claimed that Senator Barack Obama was "an Arab." She of course was referring to the rumors that he was a Muslim, but for her, these two identity categories were one in the same. When experience-based authority enters the discussion of Islam, my experiences being a Muslim, and the knowledges that arise from those experiences, are easily dismissed because Islam's longstanding connection with the African American community has been erased in the cultural imaginary. My *true* history and experience, in other words, lies with my experience as an African American, and that's it. My input and "speech" is de-authorized (Fuss, 1989, p. 113) because mainstream Eurocentric conceptions essentialize Islam in a way that inherently (and exclusively) connects it to Arab-ness. And since I am not assigned any intellectual ownership of Islam, my opinions, ideas, arguments, etc. cannot be grounded in any *experiential* knowledge – the discussion about Islam's realities, and the experience of being Muslim become intellectually up for grabs in the classroom.

DISCUSSIONS OF VEILING IN THE GRADUATE CLASSROOM

To discuss this situation, I'd like to move from Fuss's notion of "authority of experience" and take up bell hooks's revised notion, "passion of experience." hooks (1994) states that the difference between this terminology and Fuss's is that "passion of experience" – or "passion of remembrance" as she also calls it – is specifically generated from a place of suffering (p. 91). I am interpreting this suffering to mean, generally speaking, an experience of oppression. hooks (1994) writes:,

> When I use the phrase 'passion of experience,' it encompasses many feeling but particularly suffering, for there is a particular knowledge that comes from suffering. It is a way of knowing that is often expressed through the body, what it knows, what has been deeply inscribed on it through experience (p. 91).

By changing the terminology, the focus shifts from abstract ideas of experience to knowledge that is grounded in concrete bodily experience of oppression. I move to this slightly different concept when I present my experience because hooks's call on *passion* helps to explain a) my *emotional* connection to the experience of wearing a hijab in the U.S.; and b) how the lack of attention to my experience and the knowledge it provides resonates with me, emotionally.

Nowhere is this issue more painfully apparent to me than in *Women's Studies* or women's studies focused classrooms when the issue of veiling in Islam is studied. The hijab, as many scholars, women and men alike, have stated is a complicated intellectual and spiritual issue. In the women's studies classroom these discussions become especially charged because of Western perceptions of what constitutes freedom and restriction. Sherene Razack (1998) captures this problem when she writes, "when we in the North [or West] see a veiled woman, we can only retrieve from our store of information that she is a victim of her patriarchal culture or religion. Few alternative images or more complex evaluations are possible" (p. 7). These discussions tend to construct and reproduce certain binary notions of Muslim women that are founded on dichotomy of East vs. West. In accordance with this dichotomy, Muslim women are inherently "third world" or "from over there" and are oppressed and affected by the "underdevelopment, oppressive traditions, high illiteracy, rural and urban poverty, religious fanaticism, and 'overpopulation' of particular Asian, African, Middle Eastern" countries (Mohanty, 1991, p. 5). Transnational feminism has done a great deal of work attempting to contest these types reductive and binary analyses that "freeze third world women in time, space, and history" (Mohanty, 1991, p. 6).

Here again, I am contending with an essentialized idea of what a veiled Muslim woman is; she falls on the other side of the binary of a Western woman and all that she represents. The fact that I am American, and more specifically African American, and still wear hijab does not translate in terms that are intelligible to this binary. So instead of attempting to incorporate my physical existence and proximity into their perceptions of veiling, many of my colleagues disregard my Muslim identity all together, and talk about veiling as if they, in their understanding of women's oppressions, know more about hijab, Islam, and Muslim women than I could possibly know. In the more "ideal" situations, I remain silent and observe as the conversations vacillate between cultural relativism ("they" have a different culture "over there," who are "we" to say it's oppressive) to simply reductive (veiling is oppressive, period).

The more painful moments for me are the moments when I make efforts to interject my thoughts, informed by my knowledge of Islam and my experiences with veiling. And here is where I want to return to hooks's phrase "passion of experience." I have worn some form of scarf and/or hijab my entire life; it is an integral part of my identity as a woman. I have experienced varying degrees of ostracism because of my choice to cover – most of the ostracism I experienced was when I moved away from African American communities. This is not to say that the Muslim communities I have lived in are havens of gender equality, of course they are not. This is just to say that I have never felt pressure to cover coming from inside these communities. All of the oppression I have felt has come from outside Muslim and African American communities.

Islam is a religion that has important connections and history in the African American community. While in the African American community, my Muslim identity existed in tandem with my African American identity. This meant that being a Muslim and being African American made sense (Jackson, 2005; Curtis, 2002, 2006; Dannin, 2002; Diouf, 1999). This essay is not the place to catalog all of the ways in which I have been discriminated against or treated with hostility because of my hijab or because I am presumed to be a foreigner, but I will say that my experiences range from ridiculously funny to ridiculously infuriating. The ridiculously funny: being complimented by medical practitioners on my command of the English language and ability to speak without an accent. The ridiculously infuriating: being yelled at by drivers to "go home" and "get back on my camel;" or a neighbor accosting my roommate about the "fact" that I "probably didn't even speak English." Regardless of these incidents, I embrace wearing a hijab (for reasons that are profound and real, and not necessary to explain here) and I passionately defend my choice and my right to wear it. But all of this – the richness of my experiences, the nuanced ways that context and environment contribute to people's perceptions of my hijab, the fact that I am clearly not an "oppressed Muslim woman from the East" – become irrelevant when I attempt to voice the particularities of my experience as an African American Muslim woman who has worn hijab all of her life.

MINI-CONFERENCE EXAMPLE

In order to make my explanation concrete, I'd like to share an incident that occurred during my first year as a PhD student. At this point in my graduate career, I began working on a paper that dealt with immigrant women who wear the hijab in the post-9/11 U.S. The paper started as a seminar paper, and in this seminar, we had to present our research as part of a "mini-conference." While this was not a Women's Studies class, it was a women's studies focused course – the professor holds a joint appointment in both the *Women's Studies* and the *English* departments; the vast majority of the students were women; several of the women in the class focused on women's studies issues.

At the opening of my presentation, I explained how veiling is a highly contested aspect of Muslim womanhood and that it is problematic to understand it in a monolithic manner – namely, oppression. I presented my points in what I thought was a well-supported way; I quoted Islamic scholars, feminist scholars, and provided (very briefly) my personal reasons for being interested in this issue. The only response and feedback that I received was from a woman who was curious about why I did not find veiling oppressive. She talked about the oppression of veiling in "here vs. over there" terms. For a while, I tried to rearticulate what I had presented by restating how veiling is complicated and cannot be understood within an "either/or" framework. This did not work. She essentially retorted, "Yeah, ok, but how is it not oppressive"? At this point, I was flabbergasted. How could she, looking at me, seeing that I wear the hijab, seeing that I am clearly invested in my work, not understand the position I might be coming from?

This situation, unlike the Writing Center situation, felt like a failed moment. After going back and forth with this classmate I found myself at a loss for words. Because she was convinced that I did not know what I meant when I said that wearing the hijab was not inherently oppressive, she was unable to even hear the rest of the arguments in my paper. Again, this opening to my presentation was merely a preamble; my focus was on immigration and assimilation. This colleague, armed with whatever bits of knowledge she may have had (she does not study Islam, Muslim women, veiling, or anything similar) was able to disturb me so much by questioning my authority that I was unable to continue on to present my research/writing. I did not receive any other questions or comments. Her question was the first and our exchange went on so long that we had to move onto the next presentation. I felt defeated, deflated, and offended because I felt as if I was not able to convince her that my experience provided me with a certain degree of authority.

THE GREATER UNIVERSITY COMMUNITY

While these issues affect me a great deal on a personal level, I can easily see how it may not seem to necessarily speak to a greater concern in terms of the academic environment. My experiences, while particular to *me*, are perhaps indicative of larger social concerns as they play out in university setting. I believe that what happens in the classroom is representative of ideas that are being produced and circulated in broader university settings.

The problem that this conflation of race and religion produces is an inability to connect Islam with an identity that is *not* foreign. This means that there's no recognition of *American* Muslims in general, and *African American* Muslims in particular. This lack of recognition has heightened since 9/11 and has virtually erased the previous long-standing connection the U.S. has had with Islam stemming from the African American community. This erasure is particularly problematic in the U.S.'s current civil rights/liberties battles and the ways that Islamophobia constantly places Muslims in the U.S. in a position of having to explain and defend our identities. This erasure means that Muslims constantly have to prove that we are and can be a part of American society. And (to return to the quote from the beginning of this essay) this means that Muslims often rely on the racial discourses available to compare ourselves to mainstream (read: White) U.S. society.

This comparison ranges from simple assessments of various struggle types, to more active distancing from whatever Black-ness is meant to represent in broader social discourses. The man's comments (quoted at the beginning of this essay) are complicated, but not outright objectionable. I say this because sometimes the comparisons between struggles can lead to fruitful cross-cultural coalitions. Despite the fact that the comment overlooks the existence of African American Muslims, it at least presents a certain degree of understanding and awareness that comes from racial oppression and discrimination. I would like to hope that this could lead to a solidarity – that this man would protest racial profiling against African Americans in the same way he protests the racial profiling spawned by 9/11 and the USA Patriot Act. Distancing, on the other hand, creates a rift between African Americans and Muslims. First of all, it overlooks the fact that large portions of the Muslims in the U.S. are both. According to a Zogby Internal survey conducted in August of 2000, 24% of Muslims in the U.S. are African American; South Asians (Pakistani, Afghani, Bangladeshi, Indian) and Arabs make up 26% each (http://www.allied-media.com/AM/). Second of all this position looks to actively define Muslim as something other than Black. This same tactic has been used by immigrants to the U.S. over the last few centuries. In order to assimilate and become "American," White immigrants defined themselves in opposition to whatever racial/ethnic groups occupied the lower rungs of the U.S. racial hierarchy. More often than not, this meant defining oneself in opposition to Blackness (Roedigger, 1991, 2006; López, 1997; Jacobson, 1999).

I am reminded of a moment in which this dilemma was perfectly crystallized – it was an uncomfortable moment for me because it was infuriating, yet understandable, and I found that I was at a loss as to how exactly to respond. The incident took place in October of 2005, roughly a month after the infamous Danish cartoons of the Prophet Muhammad [PBUH] were published. After the violence erupted in predominantly Muslim countries around the world, one of our more conservative campus newspapers took it upon themselves to reprint the cartoons in the name of free press and in defense of the First Amendment. Both Muslims and allies of Muslims were appalled and responded as such. Flurries of letters were written to editor; comments were posted on blogs; students demanded that the newspaper and its editor apologize for the offense. Islamophobes and proponents of "free speech" – sometimes occupying both categories – also responded. Some wrote letters, but some responded with hatred: Islamophobic slurs were shouted at hijab wearing women (some were told to "go back home"); violence was threatened; one woman was spat upon. The campus community immediately put together a forum in which there were a panel of speakers: two professors, two graduate students, one newspaper editor (from a national newspaper), one undergraduate, and the editor of the campus newspaper. The panel was fairly diverse; one of the professors was even an African American Muslim[4].

One of the brief talks was given by one of the graduate students on the panel, a Muslim man who was an international student studying Islamic history. I cannot remember the specifics of his talk, but his emphasis was on making/helping the audience understand that Muslims were "just like them." He focused on the "middle class" aspirations of Muslims, mentioning that they were (and aspired to be) "doctors, lawyers, and professors." He painted Muslims as productive members of society, aspiring citizens who work to keep this country going rather than looking for handouts. As he continued, I became more and more disgruntled because I realized that he was defining himself and Muslims in opposition to both a racial category and a national category that I occupy. When I heard "productive members of society" who aspire to be "doctors, lawyers, and professors" I understood him to be saying that Muslims are not what African Americans have been historically stereotyped as being – lazy, unproductive, a burden on society, and so on. I also heard him distancing himself from other U.S.-born Muslims who did not follow the same "American dream" trajectory, who, perhaps, were not privileged with the wherewithal or even certain motivators to aspire to this middle class. I heard him separating himself from a whole community of U.S.-born Black Muslims who have lived in this country since slavery and who have continually contributed to society. In his talk, I understood "being like you" to mean Muslims (clearly immigrant Muslims) are just like upper/middle class White Americans.

In my mind, this graduate student's speech was more detrimental than the comment about Arabs being the "new Blacks." The graduate student's comments placed Muslims in opposition to Americans in general, and African Americans in particular. They reinforced and perpetuated the idea that being Muslim is inherently something different from being American by pointing to the ways in which Muslims (as a specific category of immigrants) "aspire" to be mainstream. It also placed a rift between African Americans and Muslims by rejecting the commonalities of our experiences. His speech calcified notions of what a Muslim is and is not – leaving no room for African American Muslims who have been living in the U.S. for centuries. Also, because this speaker fit nicely into the stereotypical idea of what a Muslim is (based on his definition and the definition in the U.S. social imaginary), he is understood to be one who is an authority on what Muslims in the U.S. are like; he is seen as being representative of the Muslim community.

This precipitates into divisions among student organizations who should, in my estimation, have similar goals in mind. This particular forum was sponsored by several multicultural student organizations on campus (Muslim Student Association, Multicultural Student Center, MultiCultural Student Coalition, Black Student Union, to name a few), and many of the undergraduate members of these groups were present at the forum to show support and to educate themselves on the events surrounding the published cartoons. The graduate student's talk, in essence, worked against this particular coalition initiative by essentializing Muslim identity and experience.

I am not arguing that this student's remarks single-handedly undermined all of the coalition efforts that had been burgeoning on campus; I am arguing that by reinforcing the separation between African Americans and Muslims, the "knowledge" disseminated in his talk made it more difficult for people to work across that divide. As evidence of this, I recall another similar forum that was staged approximately two years later to discuss David Horowitz's upcoming visit[5]. The conservative and controversial Horowitz is not a friend to most marginalized groups – African Americans and Muslims included. His current campaigns spread Islamophobia and hatred, but he has, in the past, focused his attentions on African Americans. This, to me, signaled a crucial opportunity for coalition, understanding, and a time to look at the ways in which our lives as African Americans and/or American Muslims may overlap. The forum was disappointing for me because the exact opposite happened: the protest against Horowitz was constructed as a "Muslim issue" rather than an issue that addressed both the Muslim and African American community. The agreed upon response to Horowitz reflected this split – African Americans (and allies) wanted to respond one way, the Muslim Student Association members wanted to respond a different way. The only consensus the group could reach was to have two different and separated responses.

CONCLUSION

As a person who occupies both Black and Muslim identity categories, this inability to speak across divides troubles me. It is troubling to me because I sometimes have to bounce between identities and the experiences I have as a member of both are not always aligned. However, as a person who occupies multiple oppressed identity categories (along race, gender, and religion), I find that this is bound to happen in some contexts. What is really troubling is the perceived incommensurability of these experiences and the knowledge these identity categories afford me. In a post 9/11 climate, I witness how African Americans and Muslims are widening a gap between them, neither group wanting to be stigmatized by the other. What are the implications of these for me, and many like me who embody both places? The U.S. administration will potentially be embroiled in this "war on terror" for many years to come. This means that Islam and Muslims will continue to be an oft-discussed topic, and these discussions will inevitably continue to find their way into the classroom. The incommensurability of experiences compromises my ability to help my students and colleagues understand, first of all, that Muslim identity is not only synonymous with immigrant identity. And second of all, compromises my classroom experience because it obscures the fact that there is an experience of Islam that is rooted in the Muslim community and that this experience generates a unique kind of knowledge. I ardently believe that this unique knowledge and these unique experiences can be used to help bring both communities together in this racist and increasingly Islamophobic time. I believe that the experience of oppression – different types of oppression – is perfect fodder for coalition building both inside the campus community and in the broader U.S. social context. However, if there is an inability to connect the African American and Muslim histories and experiences, then these coalitions will fail.

DISCUSSION QUESTIONS AND EXTENSION ACTIVITIES

(1) Abdurraqib argues that her racial identity (as African American) often trumped her religious identity (as Muslim). Do a field study by observing people in an public environment. Record what aspects of their identities do you notice first? For example, many of us often notice disabilities (for instance we notice if someone is using a cane or support for walking), but we do not notice *ability*. Similarly, we may not notice gender (i.e. women as an identity) but notice "Muslim women." Pay attention to these patterns. Consider which identity categories often (or under what conditions) "eclipse" others.

(2) How do you think the idea of converts to Islam affects perceptions of Muslims in the U.S.?

(3) In the past, censuses have conflated people of Arab descent with White. This was most often because the early wave of Arab immigrants were Christians from Syria/Lebanon. How do you think that the events of 9/11 have changed mainstream ideas about who is (or who is presumed to be) Arab, Muslim, and Christian?

(4) Abdurraqib hints at the long history of Islam in the African American community. While many of us could name (or at least recognize) the Nation of Islam and Malcolm X as contributors to that history, what (else) do you know about the history of Islam in the African American community? What is the

relationship between this history and mainstream perceptions (or stereotypes) about African American Muslims?

IF YOU LIKED THIS CHAPTER, YOU MAY ALSO ENJOY:

Mogra, I. (2009). Being a Muslim and a headteacher: Insights from a life history approach towards accessing leadership. *In this book.*

Ali Khan, C. (2009). On being us and them: A voice from the edge. *In this book.*

Esack, F. (1999). *On being a Muslim.* London: OneWorld Publications.

Haley, A. (1965). *The autobiography of Malcolm X.* New York: Grove Press.

Imam Zaid Shakir (2005). *Scattered pictures: Reflections of an American Muslim.* Hayward, CA: Zaytuna Institute.

Kahf, M. (2003). *Emails from Scheherazad.* Gainesville: University Press of Florida.

Kahf, M. (2006). *The girl in the tangerine scarf.* New York: PublicAffairs.

Schlosser, L.Z. (2003). Christian privilege: Breaking a sacred taboo. *Journal of Multicultural Counselling and Development,* 31, 44–51.

Turner, R.B. (2003). *Islam in the African-American experience.* Bloomington: Indiana University Press.

Tate, S. (1997). *Little X: Growing up in the nation of Islam.* New York: HarperCollins.

NOTES

[1]   And also most likely an immigrant.
[2]   As a side note, I must say that I was intrigued and impressed that an introduction to Western religions class would include Islam on its syllabus, especially considering the view that Islam is strictly an "Eastern" religion.
[3]   I must attribute the idea of intellectual ownership to Dr. Sherman Jackson who, during a talk on February 29, 2008, presented this idea when discussing the history of Islam in the Black community. His use of the term really helped me crystallize what I'd been trying to articulate about how people interact with me as an African-American Muslim.
[4]   This particular professor did not, however, initially reveal his Muslim identity, and his brief talk focused on issues of human decency and understanding. I imagine that these two things made it difficult for people to initially perceive him as Muslim. I believe he ended his brief talk with a verse from the Qur'an and he gave salaams as he left the podium. I vaguely recall confused/interested murmuring after he closed in this manner.

[5] Again, this event was sponsored by a bevy of Multicultural student organizations. The main speakers at the event were a member from the Black Student Union, the president of the Muslim Students Association, and a member of the International Socialist Organization.

REFERENCES

Alcoff, L. M. (2006). *Visible identities: Race, gender, and the self.* New York: Oxford University Press.

Bayoumi, M. (2006). Arab America's September 11. *The Nation, 283*(9).

Curits, E. E. (2002). *Islam in black America: Identity, liberation, and difference in African American Islamic thought.* New York: State University of New York Press.

Curtis, E. E. (2006). *Black muslim religion in the nation of Islam, 1960–1975.* Chapel Hill, NC: University of North Carolina Press.

Dannin, R. (2002). *Black pilgrimage to Islam.* New York: Oxford University Press.

Diouf, S. (1989). *Servants of Allah: African muslims enslaved in the Americas.* New York: New York University Press.

Fuss, D. (1989). *Essentially speaking.* New York: Routledge.

hooks, b. (1994). *Teaching to transgress: Education as the practice of freedom.* New York: Routledge.

Jackson, S. (2005). *Islam and the black American: Looking toward the third resurrection.* New York: Oxford University Press.

Jackson, S. (Lecture). (2008, February 29). *The history of the black muslim movement in America.* University of Wisconsin-Madison.

Jacobson, M. F. (1998). *Whiteness of a different color: European immigrants and the alchemy of race.* Cambridge, MA: Harvard University Press.

López, I. H. (1996). *White by law: The legal construction of race.* New York: New York University Press.

Mohanty, C. (1991). Cartographies of struggle: Third world women and the politics of feminism. In C. Mohanty, A. Russo, & L. Torres (Eds.), *Third world women and the politics of feminism* (pp. 1–47). Bloomington, IN: Indiana University Press.

Razack, S. (1998). *Looking white people in the eye: Gender, race, culture in courtrooms and classrooms.* Toronto: University of Toronto Press.

Roediger, D. (1991). *The wages of whiteness: Race and the making of the American working class.* New York: Verso.

Roediger, D. (2005). *Working towards whiteness: How America's immigrants became white: The strange journey from Ellis Island to the suburbs.* New York: Basic Books.

Samaa Abdurraqib
Department of English
University of Wisconsin-Madison

PART 3:

VOICES & EXPERIENCES OF MUSLIM TEACHERS, SCHOLARS, AND ADMINISTRATORS

CAROLYNE ALI KHAN

ON BEING US *AND* THEM

A Voice from the Edge

Creation happens more than once. In our lifetimes, we are re-created over and over again.

Cynthia Chambers – Creating a curriculum of Metissage

REALITY

"Nigger!" the word was hissed at me. I was surrounded by a small group of girls. I was seven years old and the rain was lightly falling. Hemmed in by the walls of gardens on one side and traffic on the other, on a south London street, running seemed like a bad idea. "Nigger!" the leader of the group of girl schoolmates who surrounded me spat the word at me again, raising her fists menacingly. Then she spat at me. Literally. Somehow I managed the reflex to dodge her spittle by catching it on my dangling umbrella. I was so pleased with myself for this moment of quick thinking, and so mortified at the idea of bodily fluids flying towards me, that for a moment I forgot my terror. I had avoided being spat on. Ha! I had won. But victory promised to be fleeting. Before they left, the girls hissed more insults and although apparently satisfied for that moment, promised they would "get me later." Walking home, hoping that the rain would wash off the spit, I wondered if they would...

REALITY JUST GETS IN THE WAY.

"Nigger" was a slur of choice that was used against me when I was young even though I am not Black. I am half Pakistani and half German, and olive skinned – but nuanced distinctions have never mattered much to prejudice. As the child of a Muslim/Catholic marriage, throughout my K-12 school years I became accustomed to being assigned an identity over which I had little control. I was not white so I was one of "Them," a "Nigger," and a "Paki," (it was all the same). The message to me was clear, I did not belong; I was not welcome; I needed to "Go Home" to some dark place that Niggers and Pakis belonged. The fact that I was born and raised in London meant nothing to my tormentors. As I did not know anyone (aside from my Dad) who was of Pakistani ethnicity, those who taunted me about it were the ones who defined what it meant to be a "Pakistani." I was one of "them" – "dirty", "stupid", leeching, etc, and of course, deeply unwelcome.

Times have changed. Now in schools, the terms I hear against children perceived to be from the East are "Sand-Nigger" "Towel-head" and of course, "Terrorist." Anti-Muslim sentiments seem to have become commonplace in a post 9/11 world. They are reinforced by Western news-screens perpetually flood with menacing images of a Middle Eastern "them." The oppositional positioning of "Islam against The West" is not new (Said, 1978, 2001). But in recent years, as the United States and its allies wage wars against several predominantly Muslim nations, the restrictive conception of an Islamic "other" appears to have resurfaced with a vengeance. As the world divides into "us or them" individuals are assigned belonging to one or the other category. The question of identity looms, invariably to be answered by those in power: "Are you *us* or *them*?" Westernized Muslims and/or culturally hybrid children who are caught in the crossfire of this ideological battle, are (as I was as a child) forced into a polarized, and externally-defined ethnicity. The details of their real lives don't matter; perceived identity is all that counts. Christopher Stonebanks (2004) speaks powerfully of the absurdity and injustice of (anyone) being forced into a category of a Muslim/Arab *them* who are perceived as *being all the same*. But complexity is not a friend of prejudice.

I write this in the United States, where Muslim communities and individuals are repeatedly presented in the media as monolithic. Mark Zuss (1999) reminds us that, "binary oppositions and logic" have "confined and set limits to human relation, identity and ethics" (p. 10). Nuances and differentiations appear to be the luxury of power-holders, ("we" get to have many different faces), whereas the lines of Muslim identity are crudely drawn, ("they" are all the same). "They" (unlike "us") do not negotiate multiple worlds/selves in contested and conflicting ways. Many theorists (Kincheloe, 2004; Said, 1978, 2001; Steinberg, 2004) join those who argue against the flattening and misrepresentation of Muslims. Yet, everywhere I go, I am cautioned by public notices that my civic duty is to "be alert" and to "be suspicious," presumably of "them", *Muslims, the potential danger*. Linda Alcoff's (2006) point that, "strongly held identities *in reality* do not uniformly lead to the disasters critics portend because identities *in reality* are not what critics understand them to be" (p. 41) appears unheeded in the current discourse about Muslims.

YOU SCARE ME.

I spend my summers in Pakistan, where my parents *chose* to retire. When I share this in America it is almost always greeted with incomprehension. Maybe it's because my mother is European. Maybe it's because Pakistan as a nation and its people have been so relentlessly demonized in the mainstream media (well before current political upheavals), that it is impossible to think of it as a place anyone, compos mentis, would *choose* to live. (Or maybe it's because I don't look like a terrorist or I don't look that tough?) Meanwhile I travel home every year, and see friends and family whom I love dearly and who are sane, kind, normal people. With each visit, they again tell me that, in this political climate, they will not come to New York to visit me because they don't want to visit a country that views them uniformly as criminals. Most importantly they (justifiably) fear the ramifications of being positioned, collectively, as a danger.

Such mainstream and deeply negative views have crept in to official formal institutional teaching machines. Here are a few examples of recent anti-Muslim curriculum that contributes to public perception of "The Dangerous Muslim." Eight years after the Oklahoma bombing,[1] journalist, Jayna Davis published a book claiming Muslim connections behind McVeigh's actions (AOL, Jayna Davis interview). This book has been celebrated by Fox News and other right wing media as *uncovering the truth*. The truth of a demonized identity in a prejudiced world perhaps? As another example, recently the educational resource company "Performance Education," who claim to have a teacher readership of "10K" (personal correspondence with the publishers), published a free current events lesson called, "Pakistan: On the Brink." The lesson package consists of 31 pages centered around why "we" need to be afraid of Pakistan. Several lessons note that the United States already (justifiably in their view) is at war with two of Pakistan's neighbours. The chilling hint, evident through this classroom lesson plan, is that Pakistan is next on the list of forthcoming wars with the United States. One lesson is called, "Forget the War on Terror. Think of World War III." Apparently we have curriculum on World War III. The site links to video that begins with images of Pakistani missiles and then goes on to *show,* in full technicolor, a spectacular nuclear annihilation. Meanwhile, The American Textbook council (historytextbooks.org) has published a report entitled, "Islam in the classroom, what the textbooks tell us." It argues that portrayals of militant Islam are *not enough* a part of classroom textbooks.

The bias and fear mongering about predominantly Muslim nations and Islam are not limited to K-12 school curricula. Somewhat behind the scenes, The Foundation for Individual Rights in Education (thefire.org), works to *defend* anti-Islamic hate speech in university settings. Concurrently in the broader public world, anti-Muslim prejudice is reinforced in the media through endless spectacles of unruly, victim or victimizing, and rabidly violent Muslims. Some well-meaning solutions to this inadvertently compound the issue. Amartya Sen (2006) illuminates the dangers of a "ham-handed" response to terrorism through which "respect for other people is shown by praising their religious books" rather than fostering understandings of real, complex and interactive people (p. 12). Respect for other people, is also missing in the U.S. media *silence* over the escalating hundreds of thousands of Iraqi and Afghani deaths.[2] The underlying message in all of these examples is an insistence that there is a clear divide between Americans, and "the West" on the one side, and Muslims/Arabs/"people from over there," on the other; a natural irreconcilable gulf between *them,* and *us.*

I would like to think that this "us/them" thinking is just the tentacles of the political right, structural not individual, and that it does not in fact reach into our classrooms to touch us all as students and teachers. But it does. I teach courses to pre-service teachers at a New York university. Whenever I have asked my students about their prior knowledge about Islam and of Muslims, they overwhelmingly state that they remember having formally learned either nothing or only negative

ALI KHAN

things. I also work as a high school teacher, and my adolescent students echo these views. My students have spoken about learning in classrooms only (if anything) a smattering of information about the Qur'an, while learning from the world around them that Muslims are, "terrorists" "they don't respect women" and "starve themselves to get to heaven." The research of Sirin & Fine (2008) found Muslim college students to be all too aware of often being perceived negatively and of the danger that this prejudice can place them in. They cite research from Cornell University that reports most Americans are quite comfortable with the idea of curtailing civil liberties for Muslims (p. 22). The findings of the Council on American Islamic Relations confirm that disparaging views of Muslims are common in America, and notes, "Approximately one-in-four Americans believes that Islam is a religion of hatred and violence" (CAIR, American public opinion, 2006). My experiences in multiple layers of schools and higher education are that educational and societal curricula do little to confront deeply seated and normalized prejudices in anti-Arab/Muslim/"people from over there" sentiments. Meanwhile, those who reside on the numerous edges of a Muslim identity (real or perceived) are repeatedly faced with both the injustice and the absurdity of the "us/them" divide. Perhaps one strategy for teachers to confront all of this is to examine instances where the essentialist narrative of a Muslim "them" simply falls apart.

PURE THEM.

The mixed blood person was once "theorized in social science as a problem" (Squires, 2006, p. 33), but that was before interraciality found its new position as the (biologically deterministic) solution to America's race problems (pp. 170–175). The rhetoric of interracial/interethnic harmony, however, does not extend to include Muslims. Perhaps the numbers of interfaith Muslims and Arabs are considered too small, or the differences too great. The silence here is misleading. According to a recent survey from the Council on American-Islamic relations (American Muslim Voter Survey, 2006) 8% of Muslims are in an interfaith marriage. As estimates of the Muslim population vary widely between 1.5 and 5 million, the numbers here are not insignificant. If, to be conservative, we assume there are 2 million Muslims, and we calculate that 5% of these are interfaith/ interracial; that means in the U.S. alone, there are at least 100,000 people who are either the spouse of a mixed marriage or the child of one. Are these people "us" or "them"? Adding to the numbers, according to the U.S. Census (2005) "1,190,000 people reported at least one Arab ancestry." My intention in citing these figures is not to be definitive, but to shed light on those who reside in the spaces *between* Muslim and non-Muslim. For these people, the irreconcilability of Muslim versus non-Muslim is simply not an option.

My history is one of the "us *and* them" stories, which challenge the myth of irreconcilable difference. My mother is a German Catholic who moved to England in her twenties and fell in love. She fell in love with a man, not with his culture (that she knew next to nothing of), nor with his religion, (which she knew even less about), but with a person, who loved to joke, was kind, and was from Pakistan. For almost half a century, my parents have been fiercely loyal to each other; during this time each continued to practice their separate religions. Neither saw the need to educate each other on their religious practices and beliefs, so the religion of each has remained rather a mystery to the other. Yet my father would accompany his wife to Christmas and Easter mass, and my mother would wake in the predawn hours to sit with my father as he breakfasted in the years that he chose to fast in the holy month of Ramadan. Both my parents were deeply aware of a striving for lovingness and tolerance as core teachings of their respective faiths.[3] Like the millions of believers of all faiths who support the notion of tolerance, neither parent felt God required them to convert anyone.

I FOUND "THEM" (AND THEY WERE HAVING LUNCH).

One of my earliest memories (of a repeating event) is of sitting at the kitchen table with my mother, my father and their best friends (who are Jewish) and eating bacon sandwiches. The smells of frying eggs, bacon, warm toast and butter, were, for me, the smells of love. Over the years I have shared meals with Jews who eat pork, Catholics who eat meat on Fridays, and Muslims who believe that at inception of Islam pigs were unclean and the source of much disease, but who feel that in the twenty-first century such concerns are no longer relevant. Other Muslims I know drink alcohol, and have spoken to me of believing in a God who still welcomes them. In 2005, a Danish newspaper famously published an insensitive and inflammatory cartoon that ridiculed the prophet Muhammad. Responding to a question about the cartoon from Bill Moyers, the iconoclastic Muslim author Salman Rushdie answered, "What kind of a God is it, that's upset by a cartoon, in Danish?" Some of my Muslim friends and family align themselves with those who believe in a God that will not condemn them for a fondness for a nice scotch or breakfasting on bacon and eggs. I am sure that some Muslims reading this may frown at the behaviour and beliefs I mention here, and at my mentioning them, but there are others who will nod in recognition. My point is not to highlight or advocate for Muslims who do not follow all of the ideals advocated by some in their faith, but rather to illuminate that there are contested definitions and interpretations involved in being a member of *any* religion, including Islam.

Turkey provides numerous illustrations of diversity in Islamic practice. As one example, the Alevis are Muslims in Turkey who constitute 15-25% of the population, their numbers are widely estimated as between 10-15 *million* people (Erdemir, 2005), and they are a visible and flourishing minority. Their rituals traditionally follow patterns very different from mainstream Islam. They do not prostrate themselves during prayer, they do not go to mosques, they do not pray five times a day, and they do not segregate women. Their celebration of religious occasions includes a ritual alcoholic drink and dancing (Öztürkmen, 2005). I wonder where they fall in the Western categorization of "us and them." Where is the line between us and them when the lines are multiple? Within the category of "them" lie diverse peoples who are not bound to the simple definition of what it means to be Muslim. Kincheloe & Steinberg (1997) note, "identity formation is socially constructed, it is constantly shifting in relation to unstable and discursive ideological forces" (p. 19). Not only are Muslims not a single identity category but they also shift and change within different regional and political contexts. Alcoff (2006) notes that although identity is often perceived as such it is never, "coherent, uniform and essentially singular" (p. 45). The Western notion of a uniform Muslim "them" is a misconception. In a complex reality, identity (religious or otherwise) is connected to culture, context and interpretation, and the scope of variation is vast indeed.

OWNING LIFE

"What is that in your hand?" "Nothing Dad...just some leaves, from the bush." *"Why?" "I dunno." "Let me see." I opened my small hand. "Ahh," (my father sighed, shaking his head gently) "Look at how perfect even this tiny leaf is. Beautiful. That little plant in your hands was growing outside peacefully. It is one of God's creations, just like you. And you pulled those leaves off, and now you will just throw them away. (He paused). You know Jani, ('my love' in Urdu, the language of Pakistan) the Qur'an says that God put even the smallest thing on this earth for a reason." Clearly I was not the reason for this plant. I hung my head...*

Positive connections between Muslims and the physical sensual world have been silenced in the dominant Western narrative about the Muslim "other". As the child introduced to the East through books, I spent many hours with a beautifully illustrated version of "The Rubaiyat of Omar Khayyam" (1120/1952), which had been given to me by my father. Khayyam was an eleventh/twelfth century Muslim Persian scholar, a mathematician, astronomer and poet of Renaissance proportions. His poetry (The Rubaiyat) addresses the importance of each moment, and calls for celebrating the wonder of God, the sensuality of the world, (including a love of wine), and the all too brief joy of being alive. Khayyam was far from alone. Tariq Ali, using research of Medieval Islam, speaks of the erasure of the sensual and the erotic from Islamic history (Tariq Ali, interview, 2007). It is not uncommon to open a Muslim newspaper (in Pakistan, Jordan and Egypt where I have lived) and find an article or photograph that expressly illustrates the connection between God and nature. In keeping with this, the Islam that I learned from my father, regards the sensual, (with the joys of food/drink, music, and love of nature), as a way to be respectful of God's perfection as it is mirrored in a rich world. I have yet to see a representation of Muslims as embodied and sensual beings in the news or in school curriculum in the U.S. What concerns me about the silence around Muslims and the sensual is not just the way in which this silencing plays into the notion of "us and them." I also worry that the image of less embodied Muslims implicitly allows for the idea that "they" inherently are less physically connected to (and therefore less deserving of) life itself.

CONTAINING MULTITUDES.

Since adolescence I have loved Walt Whitman's line, "Do I contradict myself? Very well then, I contradict myself, (I am large, I contain multitudes)" (1892/2004, p. 76). In high school in Pakistan, as an awkward teenager, I struggled with a biculturalism and racism that left me feeling that I belonged nowhere. The Whitman quote validated *my* belonging in the world, my adolescent yearning for the acceptance of a self (however difficult that self might be to define). I was both proud and ashamed of having an ethnicity that always made me an outsider. These feelings were accentuated by travelling back and forth between the West and the East; like many teenagers I was afraid of being boxed into someone else's definitions and someone else's dream. Many years later, as a high school teacher, I found Whitman's words applicable to the fight against standardization and high stakes testing. But in recent years the Whitman quote has taken on a whole different meaning. I have grown to the awareness that identity can be fluid and political, complex and contested (Sen, 2004), within a single life. But more importantly, that contradictions can be imposed. We may not contradict ourselves as much or as often as the world contradicts, shapes, reshapes and defines us. Whitman's metaphor of multitudes has (for me) rung ironically true, not so much in the internal vagrancies and the idiosyncrasies of a complex being, but rather, as the difficulties contained in external power positionings and imposed essentialist identities. As a person of Muslim heritage, I have not always had a say in my multitudes.

MOVING AMONG US.

Travelling back and forth from America to Europe as a young adult I used to wonder where on the journey I switched race. In the United States, before 9/11, I was usually perceived as White but alternatively I was sometimes "exotic." When I first came to the U.S. I found it confusing to be labelled "White" and a member of the dominant majority. White people had not always look fondly on my kind. My parents lived in England, and there I was definitely *not* White. I was a minority, usually labeled with the slur of "Paki" or "Nigger", and the recipient of disdain and racism. On the long flights from New York to London, I would imagine myself slowly turning brown as I neared the U.K. Or I would wonder where the halfway point was, fantasizing a moment somewhere over the Atlantic Ocean where I miraculously switched ethnicity. Confusingly, my skin color/ethnicity was somehow both fixed and variable; both an inescapable absolute and one completely defined by my geographic place.

Then I grew up. As I acquired the cultural capital of sexuality, middle-class, money and re/productive age, my ethnicity became a secondary issue. Unexpectedly, I was no longer "one of them," even in England. My visible identity became fluid and contingent. My father however, was still perceived as a "Paki." His experiences, and those of Muslim family and friends, dispelled any hope I might have had that my new entrance into a full-fledged humanity was a sign that times had changed. I began to realize that *my* experiences had changed, but the bigotry I grew up with remained alive and well. I started to reflect on how racism, in my case anti-Asian/Muslim prejudice, preys on the members of the group least able to defend themselves and least empowered to speak out. Children are at the forefront of this category. Henry Giroux (2000) notes, "Historically poor kids and children of color have been considered to be beyond the boundaries of both childhood and innocence" (p. 9). As Islamic cultures (Steinberg 2004a) and children (Kincheloe, 2004) are demonized in the media, children of Muslim descent living in the West are twice maligned, and like black and brown children they must search to find positive images of themselves. Perhaps they struggle to grow into a place where they can experience acceptance without prejudice. Sirin and Fine (2008) studied the "weight of the hyphen" of Muslim-American young women who found themselves negotiating home and public worlds with different demands and identities, "keenly aware of the weight of living "between" and "within" multiple cultures/selves (Sarroub, 2001, 2005; Wiley, Perkins, & Deaux, 2006)" (p. 17). The women in Sirin and Fine's study were in college and could express some degree of agency. Younger children perceived as Muslim may have few options to defend themselves from either being moored to, or removed from the right to belong to, identities crafted by political agendas and cultural stereotypes.

ONE OF US.

Stonebanks (2004) relates an experience of racism against a Sikh who was perceived as a Muslim/Arab/one of them/terrorist, "My heart sank" he writes, " 'it' had returned" (p. 95). The "it" he is referring to is the racism against Arabs and Muslims, (he does not claim that it had ever left, but that at times it is more clearly expressed). "It" is the structural as well as the personal impact of Islamophobia, ranging from the violations of basic human rights, to the stripping of the right to be nuanced. "It" writ small, is remembering my abject shame as a child when I would lie awake rehearsing the White name I planned to one day use as an adult (although later, ashamed at my self hatred, I abandoned this idea). But as a young child, the name "Acorn" worked in my little girl head, "Acorn" was close enough to Ali Khan that I would not forget it was me. I would, I told myself over an over, learn to turn around when it was called in a list of names. I would "pass" as White. I bit back my guilt at giving up my father's name. Growing-up and symbolically distancing myself from parents I loved seemed, for a brief moment, a reasonable desire, in my child quest for safety from "it".

I am safe from racism now, generally, until I point out my heritage. That is not to say that I have escaped it, or that I am never intimidated. For those of us who can be perceived as Muslim there is always cause for alarm as the racism against Muslims/Arabs/"people from over there," is rampant, systemic, expected (Sirin & Fine, 2008), publicized, and accepted. For example, when I show identification, I am stopped at security checkpoints when no one else is. I whisper jokes about not looking good in orange[4] to friends to hide the fact that being stopped by people in uniform, in this political moment, with a Muslim name, is frightening. However, most often I am perceived as one of "us" not "them," and now must often work to reassert my identity and heritage. When I tell my high school students in New York the origin of my last name, invariably there is a child who immediately bursts out "Oh, so you're a terrorist! I'm scared of you." In the class I teach to pre-service teachers on diversity, I speak of my heritage and one of the topics we study is Islamophobia. Over and over again my students confirm that they have *never* been asked to consider the prejudicial way they have been taught (both in and out of schools) to think negatively about Muslims. One of my students confessed that post 9/11 she found herself afraid of sitting on a plane next to "someone with a turban, you know, a Middle Easterner, one of *those people*." "That would be *me*," I responded. We all laughed.

A few years ago, I felt prompted to ask a black teacher colleague about her definition of my ethnicity. "Oh" she said, "You're Black. You're one of us." Us: not power-holders in opposition to them. It was meant as a compliment, a sign of the trust that she had in me, that aligned me with her and removed me from the possibility of being "one of them." But I cannot find this a place of comfort. Ethnicity, as I keep living it, is a position of someone else's doing. Us and them. Us versus them. Us: comprehensible and reasonable, them: not. The traditional binary oppositions of early anthropology and colonialism: rational/irrational, fanatic/reasonable, civilized/barbaric and so forth (Kincheloe, 2004; Smith, 2002; Sturken & Cartwright, 2001) persist in identity perception today. "In a system of representation meaning is established through difference" (Sturken & Cartwright, p. 103). In his foundational work *Orientalism* (1978) Edward Said explicates out how a Eurocentric ideology of difference positioned the good or bad dichotomy as West or Other (Arab, Muslim). Underlying the acceptance of me is a logic that suggests that if I am not bad enough to be them, I must be one of us.

I am reminded of the words of Kincheloe and Steinberg (2007), "In this world other people's children are screwing up our schools, immigrants are ruining our society and the poor and the non-white just don't have the same values as 'we' do" (p. 16). Implicitly, "they" do not have much *right* to power and to ownership of the world as "we" do, (even if some of them are ok, and "just like us really"). bell hooks (1994), Kincheloe (1998, 2004, 2008), Giroux (1997) and other educational theorists challenge this, urging teachers to destabilize traditional power structures and to create non-essentializing classrooms that are cognizant of the harm done to those on the bottom of power structures. Perhaps this can only happen when "we" can figure out how in solidarity to refuse to be "us"?

LOOKING LIKE US.

As I left childhood, I gained an embodied membership in "us" in a way I could not have anticipated. My skin color lessened in meaning next to my adult gender, as the signifier of my place in the hierarchies of identity. As a woman of reproductive age, who generally is most comfortable in western clothing, I have gradually become aware that my participation in capitalism as an object that consumes and is consumed, sexualized and commodified, can outweigh my ethnic status. When I entered adulthood the fact that I have a woman's body was more significant to how

I was treated than my ethnicity. Gender, apparently, can outweigh color. Steinberg (1997/2004) notes how multicolored Barbie dolls are emblematic of capitalist logic. Benetton advertisements capitalize on using models of a variety of ethnicities to reduce both politics and identity to fashion. In both Benetton and Barbie, differently hued female models with identical body types, carry a message that strikes me as screaming, "We will forgive your race/ethnicity as long as you participate in the logic of women who aspire to be frail, sexy, and buy things." I cannot help but wonder if some part of the demonizing impulse in Islamophobia lies in a Western incomprehension of its rejection of commodified sexuality and its public refusal to offer women (and everyone else) as objects for public consumption. My father, recently suffering from dementia, insisted on going to an emergency room in Pakistan in his shorts. Although he was treated by the medical staff, he was also advised that he would not be treated in the future if he arrived, able-bodied and in such disrespectful attire. Attire and the public Muslim body is framed as a gender issue in the United States, whereas in reality it is a broader concept. Meanwhile there are plenty of fashion magazines and beauty salons in the Muslim world. Reality is a complex and contested affair.

Nonetheless, the Islamic female body is frequently represented in the media in the United States as repressed, oppressed and silenced. Skalli (2004) writes powerfully of Muslim women's bodies as the site of power struggles between the fundamentalists and the west. Susan Smith (2007) notes how the currently popular memoirs of Muslim women that present them as *victims* have enjoyed more success than stories of Muslim women who are feminists or present the voice of secular Islam. Akhavan, Bashi, Kia & Shakhsari (2007) note the popularity of Muslim women's memoirs which pit them against their men and their cultures, and play into the imperialist projects for regime change. The Muslim female body as I have witnessed it, through the sharing by Muslim women friends and family, is *not* a body denied pleasure, but a body that does not generally partake in the media spectacle of being rendered as an object for the pleasure of others. Abukhattala (2004) points out how Muslim female attire is a statement of cultural identity that has been used as a political tool (pp. 161–163). The notion of the female body as the site of a political struggle rings true for my life. My perceived identity appears to have been directly connected to my having, or not yet having, an adult woman's body. For me womanhood, became the focal point that absolved me of ethnicity.

MONEY– THE ROOT OF ALL GOOD.

"The Clash of Civilizations" is a theory proposed by Samuel Huntington in 1993 that has been popularized and reinforced by endless media propaganda. In short, it positions of a vast array of diverse people as a single Muslim "them" who are deeply unlike a unified "us." In sharp contrast Zaidi (2006) notes how in Pakistan the "elite," unlike the rest of the populace, are globally *integrated* to the moneyed and seamlessly multicultural world of the rich. Wealth apparently causes color/ethnicity blindness. Paulo Freire speaks of poverty as a nationality, exemplified in a woman who categorized herself as, not American but poor (1997, p. 102). Is the corollary not Muslim but rich? Dubai, even in a post 9/11 climate it remains the fantasy playground of the rich, with over 7 million international tourists, many whom are not Arab but European and American[5]. How much truth can there be to the essentialist difference of "us not them," if it can be swept aside by cash? If Islamophobia is contingent on particular positions in a capitalist hierarchy, then it can hardly maintain reasonable credibility as a righteous ideological stance. Squires (2006) notes the complex intersections in the United States of race and class. Kincheloe and Steinberg (2007) point out that class is considered déclassé and rarely spoken of, and urge teachers to a complex awareness and a "resistance that is grounded on an understanding of the intersection of class bias with racism" (p. 19). When we compare images, for example, of the rich Arab elite with those of impoverished Pakistanis/Afghanis/other Muslims, what is immediately apparent is how deficit views of the poor (lazy, inept, etc.) combine with Islamophobia in a selective demonizing of a supposedly monolithic identity.

CONTINGENCY.

Reflecting on my own shifting place as a perceived member of "us" or "them" I am struck by the contingency of identity. Multiple variables interact with ethnicity to perpetuate inequality (Kincheloe & Steinberg, 1997). Gender, class and education are examples of variables that combined with my ethnicity to justify the ways in which I have been perceived or positioned. The paradigm that insists Islamic and Western identities are irreconcilably different is belied not only by the fact that these differences are not only *not real*, but they are also *not fixed.* Yet the impact of anti-Muslim sentiments can and does have all too real and often fixed effects not only on agency, but on life and limb. As I reflect on my own experiences of being "us" or "them" with regard to teaching I am ever more aware that the myth of "us/them" may surround us, yet it is refutable. Creating safe spaces for those with demonized identities involves commitments to an understanding of identity that refuses binary categories, and embraces complexity as humanity. I have met many teachers and students who work diligently to this end. Freire (1992/2004) notes that generally the powerless may have "no other picture of themselves other than the one imposed on them" (p.133). Amartya Sen (2006) points out that identity is always multiple, and "our freedom to assert our personal identities can sometimes be extraordinarily limited in the eyes of others, no matter how we see ourselves" (p. 60). My perceived identity, the perceived identity of Muslim friends and family (and I suspect the perceived identity of many who cross borders and cultures or who simply do not fit the stereotype), resides at the nexus of multiple intersecting selves and (literally) *appears,* resting not on a truth of difference, but rather on political, geographical, economic, gender, sexual, class contexts, and the layers of power in each of these positions.

There may be little coherency to the perceived identity of any single person, yet the desire to be seen as deserving of equal respect threads through all of our multitudes. Those who are perceived as Muslims or Arabs and who possess little in the way of economic or cultural capital are given fewer opportunities to refute negative stereotypes and to defend themselves against racism. As a child and as a non-middle-class young person I had little access to the signifiers of worth in capitalist society. As a child I was a "Nigger/Paki"; as an elderly woman I may return to that (or "terrorist" perhaps) as my default label. But for now, ironically, I struggle to not be refused a place as "one of them."

A LIFE OF DAYS.

"Allah-u-Akbar" (God is Great). The adhan (call to prayer) drifts through the warm twilight air to waft in through the windows and soak into the walls. At dawn and in the twilight, a light-shifting sky seems to repeat the call. In my heart, even as a non-Muslim, and a non-religious person, this call to prayer resonates within me as a moment of deep reflection, peace and comfort...

The moments shared here center from the everyday. The truth of everydayness, it seems to me, is erased in the portrayal of the Muslim "other." There are all too few images in the West of Muslims as embodied beings connected to time and life and able to interact in the world in ways that are sensual and loving. There is a dearth of representations for the many who are of Muslim/Arab descent or Muslim but do not make their religion or religious identity their sole or dominant identity. Fewer still are the representations of the millions of individuals or communities of Muslims who do not fit the western idea of them. But the portrayals of Muslims as a monolithic and bloodthirsty lot abound. "Days are where we live," affirms the poet Philip Larkin, where *we* live perhaps but not where *they* live. If we believe the Islamophobic discourses we are surrounded by, then we take for granted that *they* live only in ideologies and in vitriol. There is an obvious symbolic violence in denying a group the right to an embodied and complex identity. I am reminded of Shylock's famous speech in the *Merchant of Venice*, when he asks the court of Venice, as a Jew is he not, "fed with the same food, hurt with the same weapons, subject to the same diseases...as a Christian is? If you prick us, do we not bleed?" (Act III, Scene I). With the inundation of stereotypes and negative images in the post 9/11 West, Muslims (and those perceived as Muslims/Arabs/people from over there) have had little opportunity for access to a space where they too bleed when pricked, eat dinner, love their wives, admonish their children for picking leaves, and live complex and idiosyncratic lives.

As an educator, I nurture the hope that classrooms can be places where we can probe assumptions about reality, classifications, and the reasons behind them. Kincheloe and Steinberg (1997) remind us that in order to live in a humane world we must gain consciousness of how and why our "political opinions, socio-economic class, role, religious beliefs, gender role and racial self-image are shaped by dominant powers" (p. 23). There are many challenges, "the question is not how to overcome identity, but how to transform our current interpretations and understandings of them" (Alcoff, 2006, p. 287). If as teachers and students, we can sophisticate our perceptions of "Muslim/Arab/people from over there" then maybe we can work to resist the notion of "us and them" to create safe spaces for the many who live at the edges of a demonized identity, and in doing so for all of us, in all of our complexities.

DISCUSSION QUESTIONS AND EXTENSION ACTIVITIES

(1) In this chapter, Ali Khan discusses the effects of the imposition of an externally-defined, monolithic, and singular Muslim identity. Her analysis considers issues related to identity framed as binaries, such as "us" v. "them," particularly with Muslims. As a discussion exercise, create a list of the categories of your own identity (for example: woman, teacher, Jew, mother, child, etc). Which were easy to name, and which were harder? Which are visible (and thus you have no choice to reveal), and which are invisible (and thus you have the choice to conceal)? How are these labelled identities organized and represented in education? What activities and strategies have you seen or experienced that create classrooms (or other spaces) that present more complex definitions of identity (any that move beyond binaries)?

(2) Ali Khan states that womanhood "absolved" her of ethnicity (being a "woman" suddenly mattered more than being "one of them"). Discuss the statement, "Sexism can override or alternatively reinforce racism, particularly with Muslims."

(3) This chapter references the impact of class on perceptions of Muslims. Think about the idea that, "rich Muslims are exotic, poor Muslims are scary." Does this fit with images and narratives in the news, in movies, in school? Do you agree with this interpretation of the way in which Muslims are perceived of and characterized in the West? If not, how have you been able to resist the overwhelming barrage of a particular type of Muslim story? Why haven't you (and others who like you) been able to make the representations of Muslims more complex and less rooted in binaries of us/them, exotic/scary, and so on?

IF YOU LIKED THIS CHAPTER, YOU MAY ALSO ENJOY READING:

al Houseini, D. (2009). The evolution of an identity crisis. *In this book.*

Mogra, I. (2009). Being a Muslim and a headteacher: Insights from a life history approach towards accessing leadership. *In this book.*

Gottschalk, P. & Greenberg, G. (2008). *Islamophobia: Making Muslims the enemy.* New York: Rowman & Littlefield Publishers.

Jhally, S. (Director) & Earp, J. (Producer). (2006). *Reel bad Arabs: How Hollywood vilifies a people* [documentary]. Northampton, MA: Media Education Foundation.

Mohanty, C.T. (c.1984). Under Western eyes: Feminist scholarship and colonial discourses. *Boundary 2*, 12(3/13), no. 1 (Spring/Fall).

Sensoy, Ö. (2007). Social education and critical media literacy: Can *Mr. Potato Head* help challenge binaries, essentialism, and Orientalism? In D. Macedo & S. R. Steinberg (Eds.). *Media literacy: A reader* (pp. 593–602). New York: Peter Lang.

Sensoy, Ö, & DiAngelo, R.J. (2006). "I wouldn't want to be a woman in the Middle East": White female narratives of Muslim oppression. *Radical Pedagogy, 8* (1).

Shaheen, J.G. (2001). *Reel bad Arabs: How Hollywood vilifies a people.* New York: Olive Branch press.

Anti – *Obsession the Movie* and anti-Islamophobia teacher materials from the Critical Pedagogy Project, McGill University:
   http://freire.mcgill.ca/content/counter-obsession-movie-part-1
   http://freire.mcgill.ca/content/counter-obsession-movie---partchapter-2
   http://freire.mcgill.ca/content/counter-obsession-movie-part-1-materials-ii

NOTES

[1]   1995, the Alfred P. Murrah Federal Building in Oklahoma was bombed by two white militia sympathizers, Timothy Mcveigh and Terry Nichols. The attack left 800 injured and claimed 168 lives.

[2]   As of June 2008, estimates of Iraqi civilian deaths since the war vary between 92,000 (iraqbodycount.org) and over a million (justforeignpolicy.org). There are no official numbers of Afghan deaths since the US invasion, but one estimate places the figure in a six-month period (Oct, 2001-March, 2002) as over 3,000 (cursor.org). My point here is not to quote exact numbers but to question the silences that exist around them.

[3]   A core tenant of Christianity is "love thy neighbour." A fundamental understanding of Islam is of a God "merciful and compassionate."

[4]   US prisoners suspected of being Islamic terrorists are held in prisons (such as the one infamously at Guantanmo Bay in Cuba) and made to wear orange jumpsuits.

[5]   Investments in Dubailand, which hopes to outshine Disneyworld, are set to exceed the equivalent of 18 billion US dollars (ameinfo.com). Dubai's economy is built on the labor and exploitation of mostly Pakistani and Bengali migrant workers whom according to Human Rights Watch experience widespread violations of their human rights.

REFERENCES

Abukhattala, I. (2004). The new bogeyman under the bed: Image formation of Islam in the western school curriculum and media. In J. L. Kincheloe & S. R. Steinberg (Eds.), *The miseducation of the west: How schools and the media distort our understanding of the Islamic world* (pp. 43–58). Westport, CT: Prager Publishers.

Akhavan, N., Bashi, G., Kia, M., & Shakhsari, S. (2007). *A genre in the service of empire.* Retrieved December 5, 2008, from http://www.zmag.org/znet/viewArticle/2141

Alcoff, L. M. (2006). *Visible identities: Race, gender and the self.* New York: Oxford University Press.

Ali, T. (2007). *The Freire project interviews Tariq Ali.* Retrieved March 1, 2008, from http://youtube.com/watch?v=w2BuAMjMgBo

Chambers, C. (n.d.). *Dog bites. Creating a curriculum of metissage.* Retrieved May 10, 2008, from http://www.ccfi.educ.ubc.ca/publication/insights/v07n02/metissage/dogbites.html

Civilian victims of United States aerial bombing of Afghanistan. (n.d.). Retrieved June 10, 2008, from http://www.cursor.org/stories/civilian_deaths.htm

Council on American-Islamic relations, CAIR. (n.d.). *American muslim voter survey 2006*. Retrieved May 7, 2008, from http://www.cair.com/AmericanMuslims/ReportsandSurveys.aspx

Council on American-Islamic relations, CAIR. (n.d.). *American public opinion about Islam and Muslims, 2006*. Retrieved June 6, 2008, from http://www.cair.com/Portals/0/pdf/american_public_opinion_on_muslims_islam_2006.pdf

Davis, J. (n.d.). *Jayna Davis interview, Oklahoma City, AOL*. Retrieved May 7, 2008, from http://video.aol.com/video-detail/oklahoma-city-jayna-davis-interview/3473070104

Freire, P. (1997). *Pedagogy of the heart*. New York: Continuum International Publishing Group.

Freire, P. (2004). *Pedagogy of hope* (5th ed.). New York: Continuum International Publishing Group.

Giroux, H. A. (1997). *Pedagogy and the politics of hope: Theory, culture, and schooling*. Colorado, CO: West-View Press.

Giroux, H. A. (2000). *Stealing innocence: Youth, corporate power, and the politics of culture*. New York: Palgrave.

Huntington, S. (1993). The clash of civilizations. *Foreign Affairs*, *72*(3). Retrieved May 7, 2008, from http://www.foreignaffairs.org/19930601faessay5188/samuel-p-huntington/the-clash-of-civilizations.html

hooks, b. (1994). *Teaching to transgress*. New York: Routledge.

Investments in Dubailand to exceed AED 65 Billion in 18 months. (n.d.). Retrieved May 10, 2008, from, http://www.ameinfo.com/77595.html

Iraq body count. (n.d.). Retrieved June 10, 2008, from http://www.iraqbodycount.org/

Iraqi deaths estimater. (n.d.). Retrieved June 10, 2008, from http://www.justforeignpolicy.org/iraq/iraqdeaths.html

Khayyam, O. (1952). *The Rubaiyat of Omar Khayyam* (E. Fitzgerald, Trans.). New York: Garden City Books.

Kincheloe, J. L., & Steinberg, S. R. (1997). Introduction: What is multiculturalism? In J. L. Kincheloe & S. R. Steinberg (Eds.), *Changing multiculturalism* (pp. 1–26). Philadelphia: Open University Press.

Kincheloe, J. L. (1998). Addressing the crisis of whiteness: Reconfiguring white identity in a pedagogy of whiteness. In J. L. Kincheloe, S. R. Steinberg, & M. N. Rodriguez, et al. (Eds.), *White reign: Deploying whiteness in America* (pp. 3–30). New York: St Martins Press.

Kincheloe, J. L. (2004). Introduction. In J. L. Kincheloe & S. R. Steinberg (Eds.), *The miseducation of the west: How schools and the media distort our understanding of the Islamic world* (pp. 1–24). Westport, CT: Prager Publishers.

Kincheloe, J. L., & Steinberg, R. S. (2007). Introduction: The nature of class, socioeconomic context and critical pedagogy. In J. L. Kincheloe & S. R. Steinberg (Eds.), *Cutting class: Socioeconomic status and education* (pp. 3–70). Maryland, MD: Rowman and Littlefield.

Kincheloe, J. L. (2008). *Critical pedagogy primer* (2nd ed.). New York: Peter Lang Publishing.

Larkin, P. (1985). Days. In Lucie-Smith (Ed.), *British poetry since 1945* (2nd ed., p. 125). Harmondsworth: Penguin Books.

Mobilities of a "globalizing"city-state. Retrieved May 7, 2008, from http://www.dubaiphd.com/DubaiPhD.com/Research.html

Moyers, B., & Rushdie, S. (2006, June 23). *Bill Moyers on faith & reason: Bill Moyers and Salman Rushdie*. Retrieved May 10, 2008, from http://www.pbs.org/moyers/faithandreason/print/faithandreason101_print.html

Öztürkmen, A. (2005). Staging a ritual dance out of its context: The role of an individual artist in transforming the Alevi Semah. *Asian Folklore Studies*, *64*(2), 247–260.

Said, E. (1978). *Orientalism*. New York: Random House.

Said, E. (2001). The clash of ignorance. *The Nation*. Retrieved June 6, 2008, from http://www.thenation.com/doc/20011022/said

Shakespeare, W. (2000). *The merchant of venice*. Hertfordshire: Wordsworth.

Sirin, S., & Fine, M. (2008). *Muslim American youth: Understanding hyphenated identities through multiple methods*. New York: NYU Press.

Skalli, L. (2004). Loving Muslim women with a vengeance: The West, women and fundamentalism. In J. L. Kincheloe & S. R. Steinberg (Eds.), *The miseducation of the west: How schools and the media distort our understanding of the Islamic world* (pp. 43–58). Westport, CT: Prager Publishers.

Smith, L. T. (1999). *Decolonizing methodologies: Research and Indigenous peoples*. London: Zed Press.

Smith, S. E. (2007). Defeating stereotypes. *Diverse issues in higher education, 24*(17), 20–24.

Squires, C. R. (2006). *Dispatches form the color line: The press and multiracial America*. Albany, NY: State University of New York Press.

Steinberg, S. R. (2004). The bitch who has everything. In J. L. Kincheloe & S. R. Steinberg (Eds.), *Kinderculture: The corporate construction of childhood* (2nd ed., pp. 150–163). Bolder, CO: Westview.

Steinberg, S. R. (2004). Desert minstrels: Hollywood's curriculum of Arabs and Muslims. In J. L. Kincheloe & S. R. Steinberg (Eds.), *The miseducation of the west: How schools and the media distort our understanding of the Islamic world* (pp. 171–180). Westport, CT: Prager Publishers.

Stonebanks, C. D. (2004). Consequences of perceived ethnic identities. In J. L. Kincheloe & S. R. Steinberg (Eds.), *The miseducation of the west: How schools and the media distort our understanding of the Islamic world* (pp. 87–102). Westport, CT: Prager Publishers.

Sturken, M., & Cartwright, L. (2001). *Practices of looking: An introduction to visual culture*. New York: Oxford University Press.

Sen, A. (2006). *Identity and violence: The illusion of destiny*. New York: W. W. Norton and Company Inc.

US Census. (2005). *We the people of Arab ancestry in the United States: Census 2000 special reports*. Retrieved December 6, 2008, from http://www.census.gov/prod/2005pubs/censr-21.pdf

Whitman, W. (2004). Song of myself. In *Leaves of grass* (pp. 23–76). New York: Bantam.

Zaidi, A. S. (2006). Introduction. In A. S. Zaidi (Ed.), *Education under globalization: The case of Pakistan* (pp. 1–12). Islamabad: Arsha.

Zuss, M. (1999). *Subject present: Life-writings and strategies of representation*. New York: Peter Lang.

Carolyne Ali Khan
Urban Education
The Graduate Center of CUNY. New York

CHRISTOPHER DARIUS STONEBANKS

IF NANCY DREW WOULDN'T WEAR A HIJAB, WOULD THE HARDY BOYS WEAR A KUFI?

INTRODUCTION

To what extent are public schools in North America, (Canada and the US[1]), seen as inclusive by Muslims and those whose cultural identity is derived from predominantly Muslim countries (hereafter referred to as Muslims)? Given the negative representation of Islam, Muslim culture, history, as well as the current state of affairs reported by the news and the tacit acceptance and duplication of these representations in public schools, what could be said of a young Muslim's relationship with schools?

Muslims comprise the second largest religious group in Canada, with a rapidly increasing population, currently estimated at 650,000 people. Yet there are so few working in schools or studying in teacher education programs. What space, if any, has the teaching profession created, facilitated, or even allowed for Muslims to actively participate in the public school system? Is their participation in schooling present enough to see their representation within the teaching ranks? Or is there a disproportionate number not even pursuing a career in primary and secondary teaching? And if so, why not? Perhaps the relationship between our power bloc (Steinberg & Kincheloe, 1997) controlled schools, which has predominantly reflected a White, Christian world with the teacher serving as an agent of comforting reproduction for themselves, all the while ready and vigilant to civilize "others" (Harper & Cavanagh, 1994; King, 2000; Meiners, 2002; Stonebanks, 2008) and their oversimplified and monolithic understanding of Muslims have contributed to their absence.

CHRISTOPHER, MAJEED AND ABDUL

Through my experience, as a person of mixed Iranian/European descent with Muslim relatives, having worked in Canada's public schools since the early 1990s and in teacher education since the mid 1990s, this chapter explores the barriers faced by Muslim Bachelor of Education students entering the teaching profession. Within the space constraints of this chapter (which I will take eighteen words to note are in-part self-imposed by myself as one of the editors) the examination of schools in the West and their relationship with Muslims will be explored in tandem with responses from two interviews from self-described observant Muslims: Abdul[2], a pre-service teacher, and Majeed, a teacher who is a recent university

Ö. Sensoy and C.D. Stonebanks (eds.), Muslim Voices in School: Narratives of Identity and Pluralism, 169–183.

graduate of education. Given the low representation of minorities, in general, in the field of education and the criticism that could emerge for participants who agree to participate in this research, participants were sought out informally and discreetly and assured confidentiality. One important criterion was for individuals who described themselves as "practicing" Muslims. This was done not to discount the experiences of Muslims with more secular viewpoints, but to simply narrow the focus within this chapter. Moreover, I wanted to compare my own culture-oriented perspective with those of others from a more faith-based position. Originally, four interviews were arranged with two men and two women. But scheduling conflicts resulted in both women not being available for interviews.[3] It is thus acknowledged that what has resulted is a modest, and masculine (for lack of a better word) viewpoint and rightful room for other, more, and diverse perspectives should and must be forthcoming.

Both participants trace their heritage to Pakistan: Majeed born in Canada and Abdul an immigrant to North America in his late teens. Besides very brief correspondence to organize the interviews, the interview itself was the first time I had an opportunity to talk with these two men and during this relatively short time together I found the two young men (mid twenties) to be extremely pleasant. Their humour, depth of faith, intelligence, pedagogical perspectives and willingness to share their own experiences were impressive and humbling. First impression conversations centred around shared experiences: With Abdul, I discussed the joys and love of fatherhood, and with Majeed we shared our passion for our local Montreal Canadiens hockey team, at that point in the heat of a playoff run, and joked if we could possibly find something in the Qur'an to discount our team's rival, the Toronto Maple Leafs. Conversations not unfamiliar to me, but I wonder with the prevailing perceptions of Muslims how many in North America, and those working in schools in particular, would find such jovial interactions common between "people of the East." I hope this chapter and indeed the book at large contributes to a better understanding of the challenges faced by Muslims to not simply *integrate* into the teaching profession but to freely contribute and foster further dialogue between Muslim and non-Muslims in Canadian society in general, which at this point can charitably be described as strained.

MORLEY, AYAAN AND NANCY

Although academic references are always compulsory (and have been included) when speaking against the master narrative (Lyotard, 1979) or dominant memory (Kincheloe & Steinberg, 1997), these references affirm what, in many cases "we" already know; Many Muslim youth in North America struggle in defining meaning of self, religion, way of life, community and ways of knowing while being exposed to multi-media entertainment images (Shaheen, c1984, 1999 & 2001), a news media (FAIR, 2001; MacArthur, c2004) and an education system (Shah, 1996; Kincheloe & Steinberg, 2004; Stonebanks, 2004, 2008) that portray Islamic as well as Muslim culture and people in a negative manner. Turning on the evening news we see international reports predominant blaming of Muslims for the 2005 youth riots in France and the outrage and protests by Muslims across Europe regarding the Danish Jyllands-Posten's publication of unfavourable cartoons of the Prophet Mohammed. The local news fairs no better, as we hear the seemingly popular promotion of the banning of hijabs in many public spaces in Quebec, the refusal of Muslim prayer rooms in Canadian universities or the continued detainment of and accusations surrounding so-called home-grown terror plots of countless Muslims in North America and the general mounting suspicion of terrorist sympathies by Muslim youth born in Western countries. All of which have left non-Muslims confused, angry and poorly informed about their fellow citizens. They have also left Muslims to being defined almost solely by a media saturated with Muslim stereotypes of incompatibility with a Western vision of their own virtues as they continue to live under a political climate and an education system that predominantly allows no voice, contextual consideration or individuality. As Shaheen (2001) notes, perhaps no other group, save the Indigenous of North America, can currently be so easily and so acceptably maligned in the public space than those connected in some way to Islam.

Safer: (Voiceover) She is seen as a traitor to Islam, the faith she rejected as a very young woman.

            What age did you feel this was not for you?

Hirsi Ali: From very early on, I mean, I mean from the time I started reading novels of *Nancy Drew* and *Hardy Boys*, that I wanted to be like Nancy Drew, in school.

Safer: Nancy Drew would not wear a veil.

Hirsi Ali: No.

The "tongue-in-cheek" title of this chapter, is in response to the *60 Minutes* (CBS, 2005) Morley Safer interview with the Dutch parliamentarian, Ayaan Hirsi Ali, in which the sombre nature of the conversation regarding the controversial film, *Submission* (2004), she developed with Theo Van Gogh and his senseless, unjustifiable murder at the hands of a religious fanatic takes a somewhat mischievous exchange between the two as they turn to her rejection of Islam. Ali's comment that the novels of *Nancy Drew* and the *Hardy Boys* she read in school were influences in her separation from Islam and Safer's matter of fact, "wink-wink" response, a "we both know what I'm talking about" statement that "Nancy Drew wouldn't wear a veil" is another example of the acceptability of stereotypes about Muslims by those in the West. The message is that there is a fundamental incompatibility between the qualities and values of archetypal North American characters like Nancy Drew or the Hardy Boys, and being Muslim.

The general characteristics of Nancy Drew, Frank and Joe Hardy as independent-minded, curious, rational, objective, honest, determined, smart, in essence all attributes associated with positive virtues of Western youth. The dedicated solvers of mysteries, Nancy Drew and the Hardy Boys, despite their origins stemming from the 1930s and penned by Canadian Author Leslie McFarlane under a "nom de plume," still resonate with youth and adults alike and have maintained a high pop culture status, resurfacing and modernizing their formulaic format through such mediums as television, comic books, cartoon, film and even interactive computer games where one "becomes" the character. The most recent evidence of the endurance of these stories is the 2007 release of *Nancy Drew* by Warner Bros. All the while, the books, updated or original, can still quite easily be found on North American teachers' classroom bookshelves.

The intent of this chapter is not at all to discount Ms. Ali's perspectives on Islam. I am of the firm belief that all voices should be added to the dialogue, critical or supportive, for there to begin some semblance of nuance in perceptions about Muslims. At the outset of both interviews, I showed the 60 Minutes exchange to Majeed and Abdul. Majeed took a respectful, cautious yet resolute stance that, like with any other religion, people can have differing experiences that influence them. When our conversation turned to North America's popular culture demonizing Islam, Majeed brought this perception back with an individual's exposure to the religion. He said:

> I mean, it brings back the *60 Minutes* clip, what's her experience with Islam right? And how it shapes everything she does after regarding Islam, right? Everything, right? It could have been just a bad Sunday school teacher she had, and now everything is wrong with Islam, right? And she's going to make a movie to show that it's wrong. She'll read the Qur'an, with this lens and with this (lens), with these (lenses)… she's looking at Islam through that lens, right?

What has become problematic with narratives like that of Ms. Ali's is not the substance of her perspectives and experiences. Rather, it is that they are often the *only* ones ever heard or perhaps, the only one's the West *wants to hear*. It is perhaps why a comment stating that Nancy Drew wouldn't wear a veil is acceptable, but, for instance, an anti-Semitic statement that would have one point been accepted in a public setting, like, "well, the Hardy Boys wouldn't wear a yarmulke," would now more increasingly evoke a confused and incredulous response in the open forum with calls such as, "Why not? Explain yourself." There were no requests to "explain yourself" that I could find in my searches after the airing of the Safer/Ali interview.

WHO ARE THE MUSLIMS IN YOUR (TV) NEIGHBORHOOD?

The discourse about the incompatibility between being Muslim (ie "the veil") and positive archetypal North American attributes (being independent-minded, curious, rational, objective, honest, determined, smart) are acceptable and fill our North American lives at formal and non-formal levels. Like the conversation between Safer and Ali that moves from the seriousness of life and death issues to the somewhat light-hearted reference to iconic characters from pop culture, the constant barrage of this incompatibility exists for youths in North America to be consumed through the media from youth into adulthood. Whereas, for instance, Marc Brown's Arthur character, the famous cartoon aardvark on PBS channels in the United States and Knowledge Network, Radio-Canada and TVO in Canada, has adventures with central characters like Francine, who celebrates Hanukkah, and Alan, who celebrates Kwanzaa, there are no prominent characters who observe Ramadan. I guess we can just assume that Muslim youth in North America don't engage in fun adventures on the much reputed liberal airwaves of North American public television.

Yes, again, this is (partially) tongue-in-cheek, but the message that it normalizes for North American consumers of media is that the vast majority of representations are either nonexistent or, if they exist, negative. Although they represent the second largest religion in the world, in Canada and arguably in the United States, a casual glance at sitcoms and school curricula shows that Muslims are not y/our neighbours, work colleagues, spouses, classmates, teachers or even the friendly and wise elderly landlord that always seems to dole out sage advice to the protagonist in so many movies and television shows. What, then, are they – these Muslims, these "people of the East"? Review the works of Said to Shaheen and the answer becomes quite clear; they are cast as the opposite of all that is "good." In this context, a statement like, "Nancy Drew would not wear a veil" makes perfect sense; and equally makes North American television characters like the nun Sister Stephanie in *Father Dowling Mysteries*, a nun solving crimes, a "realistic" image. With this prevalent attitude in the West about what and who we see as independent-minded, curious, rational, objective, honest, determined, smart, what signals do such comments send to young Muslims who are considering the teaching profession in which, like Nancy Drew and the Hardy Boys, they are expected to be a prototypical role model for socialization and reflection of all things just and right in larger society?

First tackling the notion of the incompatibility between the positive qualities of archetypes forwarded in the North American classrooms, Abdul easily recalled numerous significant scholarly Muslim women in history, or what he called "examples of strong women":

> I've trained in theology, and you know I could tell you from history, there are many, many examples of women who were very different than what we think that a Muslim woman is; subjugated, oppressed, and all of these things.

Abdul then shifted his thoughts to the common notion that women who wear a veil later in life are somehow required to change their personality and adopt an inactive, dominated and sombre lifestyle. Reflecting on various women he knew who have recently adopted wearing the hijab, he began discussing a colleague who plays hockey:

> ...she wears a hijab and she could play ice hockey and all of that, and I saw her develop from a stage where she didn't wear the hijab, and I've seen her without the hijab, ok? That was when she came in the Muslim Student Association and all of that. Now she decided to become a little more practicing; she wore a hijab. That doesn't change her personality at all! She was playing hockey the way she was. It doesn't stop her. My wife, she's a convert to Islam, she wears the hijab, she goes skiing, she's an expert skier. She does the black diamonds [at (a significantly large ski hill)] you know? ...there's Aliya (not her real name), she's a woman in physics (related science

173

program). She used to be, she was doing her PhD in Islamic studies. She's a black belt in, in karate…I mean, if you bring all of these examples of real life in front of people, this doesn't go with the image that is projected of the Muslim woman in the media, which is a false image, clearly, because ground realities are totally different. Now, why is it projected in the media as such?

Abdul's example brings to mind recent news in Quebec in which Muslim girls wearing hijabs were denied access to participate in soccer games (Wyatt, 2007) and taekwondo tournaments (Montpetit, 2007). In these incidents young, veiled Muslim girls were taking part in activities that are associated with such qualities as competitiveness, perseverance and physical strength and skill, personal merits usually not associated with the submissive Muslim woman, but they are denied because of their "Muslim-ness."[4]

Despite personal realities, such as Abdul's example of a hijab wearing hockey player or skier, in North America simply saying "the veil" in connection with Islam immediately stirs images of oppression, hardly the enduring image of the "Western" teacher that Cavanagh and Harper (1994) criticize who is seen as "having the duty to bring civilization to the 'uncivilized'" (p. 28). With this ever present belief, how can the uncivilized Muslim be expected to bring civility to others like themselves?

WHO ARE THE MUSLIMS IN YOUR CLASSROOM?

During my teaching in the Department of Education at McGill University, on the few occasions I had students in my class who wore a hijab (or other veil) they expressed their frustrations with having to explain to their peers that this was a personal and informed decision, and, no thank you, they did not need to be saved from oppression or their ignorance. Particularly interesting about this response from power bloc pre-service teachers to their Muslim peers is that so many of them in the Montreal area attended schools during the era of religious school boards and had attended the Catholic schools (public and private) in which nuns wearing various head coverings was common. Much of their preconceived notions about what the veil meant stemmed from miseducation about Islam and their subjective assumptions on ethnicity. As Sensoy and DiAngelo (2006) describe:

> In the case of the veil, the ethnic appearance of the person wearing it, its color, and the religious iconography that may surround it all trigger different sets of cultural concepts. For example, from a mainstream Western perspective, a black veil might trigger concepts such as religious fundamentalism, mourning, and seclusion. But a black veil on a White woman (such as Mother Theresa), might trigger concepts such as sacrifice, Catholicism, and social justice. A white veil might trigger concepts about marriage, virginity, and "true" love. A veil along with a bared midriff might evoke ideas about seduction, eroticism, and entertainment. (¶ 20)

This discussion reveals that many pre-service teachers they teach hold profound stereotypes about Islam and the Middle-East. My own lived experience confirms that these kinds of stereotypes carry into school classrooms and exist even within university teacher education programs. This is a highly overlooked and under-estimated chasm of understanding between Canada's second largest religious group, those who are either considered or consider themselves Muslim and public schools, that still reproduce overtones that validate a dominant Eurocentric, Christian culture (Apple, c2004) in Canada (Rahim, 1990) and Quebec (Stonebanks, 2004, 2008). As Horton and Scott (2004) describe:

> Multicultural teacher educators strive to address the needs of all students in an educational environment that is witnessing increasing diversity in the classroom while continuing to attract a majority of its teachers from middle-class, European-American backgrounds. (¶ 9)

At a recent conference, I mentioned something to the effect that despite superficial multicultural overtures in the field of education, "there is an increasing body of writing that recognizes that teacher education in Canada and the U.S. continues to be dominated by White privilege." A colleague in the audience was quick to point out that there is not an "increasing" amount of writing about this problem of exclusion, there is *already* a large body of work concerning this dilemma. Change, in both "the field" and in academia, has yet to occur in a substantial manner that reflects, what sometimes sounds and feels like, multicultural rhetoric. In this context, how can we expect Muslims to see careers in this field as welcoming? Do they perceive that our schools are locations where they are free and encouraged to share their worldviews, beliefs and ways of knowing or do they perceive schools as a location of identity negotiation, where one's true self is always in flux to accommodate another's more dominant perspective of you (Suad Nasir & Al-Amin, 2006, Stonebanks, 2004, 2008) as the Other (Said, c1985) or, in growing instances, as the eternal Muslim "boogeyman" (Abukhattala, 2004)? Asking Abdul if he felt he was a visible Muslim and how that compared to the Hardy Boy archetype he began laughing:

> Oh, definitely! I look like one of those prototypical terrorists (starts to laugh) you have to talk to me to calm down! There's one of these comedians, Azhar Usman (…) I don't know whether you heard of him, he's a lawyer in Chicago, and he looks like me. And he did a show, "Allah made me funny," so he said, "I'm going on the airplane, you know, this person is calling his wife, he says 'honey, I might be calling you the last time!'" So, I mean yeah, I have seen that, you know, seen those looks coming from people.

Despite the assumptions made about Abdul, he maintains a positive, optimistic attitude about the future:

> I mean, anyone who looks a little bit brown and you know who have some facial hair or something like that, to, you know, "evil characters", and that is definitely there. However, I must say that young students who are sixteen years old or fifteen years old, I don't see that much from them, they're pretty open minded.

Majeed also recognizes that the students he works with are accepting of him; however he acknowledges that the experience of Muslim women could be profoundly different from his experience:

> ... to be honest, it's, it's especially true for the women who wear the hijab. For me I can wear a beard and I can blend in; the kids will say "that's a cool beard sir," "when did you grow it?" you know, in high school they say "I want to have a beard like Mr. Majeed!" and they, they talk like this, right? I'm like, "yeah, whatever," it's fine, and they don't, they don't see it as a religious thing.

Whereas Majeed's beard worn in a style quite fashionable in any North American metropolitan milieu can be seen as "cool," the hijab sets off interpretations that can be judgemental and problematic in schools. On first impressions, an observant male Muslim, such as Majeed, whose ethnicity sets him in the cast of 'other,' but whose clothing and "home grown" Canadian speech may not fit within the West's immediate stereotypes of an observant Muslim, the subject of religion may not be immediate. Majeed, who described his school experience as "multicultural" and despite recent criticisms of "food and festival" approaches to multiculturalism (perhaps also reflecting that in the absence of a curriculum that truly reflects anything other than dominant culture these activities represent, at the very least, *some* kind of inclusion) noted these efforts actually provided a connection between his own sense of belonging within the school. School in Canada was something that Majeed enjoyed; however, this did not stop him from feeling apprehension when making a decision to enter into the teaching profession:

> I wanted to be a teacher for a while, and then I did have... It's kind of hits on this, I had an apprehension because I just, like, for me, my prayers are important to me, right? Make my five daily prayers, that's important, right? I always had this in mind, you know in CEGEP when I was coming in, like I had to make my prayers when I go to my school where I work, to do my stage [field experience], and I was like, *should I apply or not*, and I kind of did other things and I came back to education after...And then it's the same thing, but I, I just, I, like it's, this shouldn't be a reason why I don't want to do the thing I want, do...Do the job I want to do?... but it bothered... it, was on my mind all the time. Every stage I had, "Okay, I got to go, I got to go. By the way, I got to go make my prayers". So, for all the stages I did, never once was there a problem. And, it kind of goes maybe back to one of the things here [at the university], people here at the school are helpful as well. At first they give you kind of a look, right? Like, "What do you mean? This is an odd request." Because I would request places to be placed, that were...I knew that there was already something set up, there was a significant Muslim population at the school, so they could accommodate...there, there was something already for them, right? So, I wouldn't have to like take my car and go to like the mosque or whatever...because like I said, we're working with "bells and a schedule".

Abdul, who noted his "visible Muslim-ness," joked how in his first year introductory course to teaching, the professor cautioned the students on the reality of judgement concerning proper attire and appearance while attending their in school field experience:

> Yeah, they always use that word, "be well groomed." As I look at myself in the mirror, I'm not well groomed according to your definition. (Starts to laugh) According to the definition centuries ago, I'm very well groomed! [My professor] used that word, "well groomed"; ok we'll do it…

Abdul, emoting confidence and comfort of self, and unlike the humourless characterizations of Muslims in Western media, sees the comedy of judgment based on appearance. On the one hand, the field of education prides itself on its "acceptance of diversity" while on the other hand, this young Muslim man has to navigate preconceived notions of a beard or clothing that he knows is sadly associated with "one of those prototypical terrorists."

Despite multiculturalism courses and its cross curricular applications being touted as centerpieces in many departments of education across Canada and the US, we are still left with realities of the field for visible minorities, like an 80% White (Clark & O'Donnell, 1999) pre-service teaching population that has seemingly remained consistent, or higher, coupled with a prevailing sense that the role of the teacher is to reproduce their own culture and knowledge (Semali & Kincheloe, 1999) while civilizing others (Cavanagh & Harper, 1994) that creates a barrier for inclusion.

The literature review on this subject reveals a small but growing number of educational researchers who have addressed the problem regarding Muslim students and the disconnect to education systems in Canada and the US; a crisis that has existed for Muslim students for many years (Stonebanks, 2004) but has intensified since 9/11. Through her own experiences as an Iranian immigrant with a young daughter in a North American public elementary school, Gerami (1998) chronicles this divide, stating there is no separation between public education and Christianity as "…(t)he Christian discourse is there and ever present …" (P. 36). Noting the particular context of vilification of Muslims in Western discourse, Gerami quotes Freebody and Baker (1985) citing that for many non-Christian children, school "… is a world in which they will always feel vaguely out of place, insecure, and perhaps inferior" (P. 34). The primary school experience (Gerami, 1998; Stonebanks, 2004) of disconnect between school and students who are Muslim or of Muslim descent continues to higher education where the student still faces stereotypes of what it means to be Muslim or, what is now loosely and widely associated with being Middle Eastern. As Majeed observes:

> To sum it up, I think that as Muslims feel more and more comfortable as students in the school environment, they will feel more comfortable and open to the prospect of working as teachers. That was certainly the case with me.

Stemming from their own encounters, Suad Nasir and al-Amin (2006) did preliminary research on the Muslim experience within campuses in the US as they

177

believed it is critical to have a better understanding of the daily lives of these students in higher education. Through their research they revealed a prevalent sense of anxiety felt by Muslim students at being hampered by stereotypes and bigotry that resulted in lowered academic achievement. Nasir and al-Amin observed that all of their participants remarked on the burden of being perceived as either the "terrorist" or the "oppressed woman" (p. 25).

Within the Quebec university context, Hoodfar (1993) scrutinized similar perspectives, with one participant in her study disclosing, "I wouldn't mind if only the young students who knew nothing about except what they watch on television demonstrated negative attitudes to Islam but sometimes our teachers are worse." Hoodfar notes that even in her position of authority as a professor, as a Canadian of Iranian descent, she could not escape the continuous construction of being the "other" and considered how then, "could young Muslim students escape it?" Drawing from socialization and "cultural capital" theories of Bernstein and Bourdieu, Hamovitch (1996) writes that in North America, the relationships students have with their schools depends significantly on their racial/ethnic characteristics. Majeed echoed this racialized dimension:

> I actually had a Muslim teacher as well...I relate back to it now because like for me, like if I saw her she was someone like me who was there right, kind of thing? Somebody who, I mean she was actually not born here, right? So now sometimes I notice that with students, right? Because there is like one brown kid in the class, and I'm brown, without even saying anything we have some sort of connection, right? And, and it happened during one of my field experiences as well, the, the teachers I was working with, they noticed that too you know? Some of these kids that are usually a bit quieter when I am around they have a connection with you, right? And if you use it correctly, use it positively; it can make a difference.

Given these experiences, could it be argued that Muslims are receiving the message that there is an incompatibility between the qualities and values of the archetypal role-model of teacher and their religious beliefs and/or culture? If these attitudes towards Muslims exist in our schools, what signals do they send to young men and women who are thinking of entering the teaching profession in which being a prototypical role model for socialization and reflection of "larger society" plays a pivotal function? – not to mention to young Muslim school children? Apple (1996) notes that educational research was initially championed as giving a voice to the unheard or silenced, but continues to be overwhelmed by a narrative on schools that are consistently White, essentially reaffirming the power-bloc's master narrative. Common are the non-power-bloc perspectives that serve to fuel the West's master narrative as the Muslim woman as "victim" and her gender counterpart as "misogynistic Middle Eastern man"; the stories that are touted as broad generalizations of what it means to be the other and in need of, consciously or not, the civilizing of the West. They are the enduring and increasingly well received master tales that Akhavan, Bashi, Kia and Shakhsari (2007) define as "a genre in service of empire" (¶1):

These women's memoirs—perhaps best represented by Azar Nafisi's *Reading Lolita in Tehran* (2003), and Roya Hakakian's *Journey to the Land of No* (2005), with their mutual roots in Betty Mahmoody's *Not Without My Daughter* (1988)—have assumed center-stage in appropriating the legitimate cause of women's rights and placing it squarely in the service of Empire building projects, disguised under the rhetoric of the "war on terror" (Ibid. ¶1)

The analysis of Akhavan et al. is that the similar memoirs they refer to make moral arguments for aggression on "Muslim nations", in this case, Iran. Iran, we can never forget because we are reminded so often, has had its story written for it by the most powerful nation in the world, and has been cast as a member of the "Axis of Evil". What stands out about the narrative stories that Akhavan et al. refer to is not the quality or accuracy of the work, rather it is the overwhelming presence it has in the consciousness of countries like Canada and the U.S. No other counterstories, save perhaps the much more nuanced, but still framed in a manner which is read by Western readers as the Middle-East as a "problem", *Persepolis* (Satrapi, c2003), shakes the tale of the monolithic Muslim world. For those of us of Middle-Eastern origin living in the West, these are unwavering narratives about self thrust upon us by members of the power-bloc that seem unwilling to hear alternative accounts of current life, history or hopes for the future. Akin to Hoodfar's experience of such statuses as "professor" not making one exempt to having one's identity constructed by members of privilege, it is a common occurrence that one of the many negative roles of the "misogynistic Middle Eastern man" is ever present in my adult life. To be rid of it, means to deny my heritage and embrace being civilized by those in the West, like teachers, who have the sanctioned power to do so. In this story it makes sense, once again, that a young girl or boy who wants to aspire to being positive role models must cast aside the backwardness of Islam, of being Muslim, of their cultural inheritance. Yet for all the incompatibly between Nancy Drew and the hijab, counterstories emerge and exist that suggest otherwise. For example, historian and columnist Guha (2004) writes:

I was on the pavement in Flora Fountain, searching for treasures in what is now…the best second-hand book bazaar in the country. At one stall I saw two ladies, in burkhas, escorting a little girl, dressed in a skirt. The girl stopped low and selected a book to buy. It was, I noted with interest, a work by the well known American children's writer, Carolyn Keene, creator of Nancy Drew. With a laugh and a smile the ladies took out their purses and granted the child's wish. One news report, and a single, isolated incident — but from what I learn from friends in the education movement, these instances are rather typical. (¶10)

Women wearing burqas, perhaps the "mother of all" symbols of repression in Islam for the West, and they are purchasing a Nancy Drew book for a little girl. As Guha states, it is perhaps "one news report, and a single incident," yet perhaps more typical than thought and certainly more so than we are led to believe according to Western media portrayals of Muslims, especially Muslim women wearing burqas.

HER FIRST LESSON

When Majeed and I discussed the various veils that Safer and Ali could have been referring to, we discussed the probability that they were referring to a style of veil like the face covering niqab or the burqa, rather than the headscarf. I questioned Majeed, who had now had a couple of years of experience teaching, whether a person wearing such clothing could effectively teach in a Canadian or U.S. classroom. Would, as stated by the former U.K. foreign secretary, Mr. Straw, wearing the face veil be "...bound to make better, positive relations between the two communities more difficult" (BBC, c2006, ¶ 5) and would it cause too much confusion amongst students unfamiliar with such beliefs? With his own matter of fact, "wink-wink" response, Majeed simply said: "That's probably going to be her first lesson."

DISCUSSION QUESTIONS

(1) Stonebanks argues that the absence of Muslims and peoples of the Middle East in popular media (including television shows for children) as positive and recurring characters are significant absences. How might the absence of such representations influence the identity and self-image of Muslim children? What lessons does it teach non-Muslim and non-Middle Eastern children about the world they live in? Is this absence something teachers and schools should be concerned about?

(2) Majeed stated that he believes a face covering niqab or the burqa would not be an insurmountable obstacle for a Muslim teacher and her students. With consideration to public schools in your context, discuss what possible ramifications would occur if a Muslim teacher wore a niqab or a burqa in the classroom. Moreover, what would happen if a student teacher wore a niqab or a burqa at your local university that has a teacher accreditation program? And how would your responses connect with your public school's or university's policies on diversity?

(3) Find eight different photographs of children that focus primarily on their faces (similar to what you would find in any elementary school yearbook or class picture). Make sure the photo has no visual cues that would lead the viewer of the image to make quick conclusions (such as a photo of a child with a black-eye who is crying). Post the photos so they are easily seen (Bristol, Keynote, or PowerPoint) and write a name, a country (or countries) of heritage that is often associated with Muslims as well as their age under each photo (like, Amir-Hussein, Iran, 12 years old). Organize students into eight groups and assign a child-photo to each group. Using their imagination, tell them that this is a child that has been in their fictional classroom for six months and have them describe him or her. Give them ten minutes to come up with a description and have them present their students to the rest of the class. Typically, pre-service teachers and teachers will make every effort to describe these children as they would any other child in their classroom; careful to avoid stereotypes associated with Islam. In a short period of time, this exercise reveals that more humanity and depth has been given to these *imaginary* children

than Western television and film has given since its inception. To demonstrate this, in their same groups, challenge them to come up with a list of eight recurring and positive Muslim or Middle-Eastern child characters from television or film. You may want to follow up this activity with the *Scarves of Many Colors: Muslim Women and the Veil* (Bigelow et al., 2000) curriculum.

IF YOU LIKED THIS CHAPTER, YOU MAY ALSO ENJOY:

Ali, T. (c2003). *The clash of fundamentalisms: Crusades, jihads and modernity.* New York: Verso.

Cortés. C. E. (2000). *The children are watching: How the media teach about diversity.* New York: Teachers College Press

Said, E.W. (c1998). "Islam Trough Western Eyes". *The Nation.* [www document] URL http://www.thenation.com/doc/19800426/19800426said

Sensoy, Ö. (2007). Social education and critical media literacy: Can *Mr. Potato Head* help challenge binaries, essentialism, and Orientalism? In D. Macedo & S. R. Steinberg (Eds.). *Media literacy: A reader* (pp. 593–602). New York: Peter Lang.

Steinberg, S. R. (2004). Desert Minstrels: Hollywood's Curriculum of Arabs and Muslims. in J. L. Kincheloe and S. R. Steinberg (Eds.) *The Miseducation of the West: The Hidden Curriculum of Western-Muslim Relations* (pp. 171–179). New York: Greenwood Press.

NOTES

[1]   With particular focus on the province of Quebec.
[2]   Both names of interviewees have been changed.
[3]   I would like to thank Bishop's University's Senate Research Committee for their financial support of this study.
[4]   The argument has been made that these decisions to exclude these children are based on "universal rules" or to avoid possibilities of injuries.

REFERENCES

Abukhattala, I. (2004). The new Bogeyman under the bed: Image formation of Islam in the western school curriculum and media. In J. L. Kincheloe & S. R. Steinberg (Eds.), *The miseducation of the west: The hidden curriculum of western-muslim relations* (pp. 153–170). New York: Greenwood Press.
Akhavan, Bashi, Kia, & Shakhsari. (2007, February). *A genre in the service of empire: An Iranian feminist critique of diasporic memoirs. ZNET.* Retrieved March 15, 2007, from http://www.zmag.org/content/print_article.cfm?itemID=12010&sectionID=1
Apple, M. W. (c2004). *Ideology and curriculum.* New York: Routledge Flamer.
Apple, M. W. (1996). *Cultural politics & education.* New York: Teachers College Press.

British Broadcasting Corporation News. (2006, October). *Straw's veil comments spark anger.* Retrieved April 8, 2008, from http://news.bbc.co.uk/2/hi/uk_news/politics/5410472.stm

Cavanagh, S., & Harper, H. (1994). Lady bountiful: The white woman teacher in multicultural education. *Women's Education/Des Femmes, 11*(2), 27–33.

Clark, C., & O'Donnell, J. (1999). Rearticulating a racial identity: Creating oppositional spaces to fight for equality and social justice. In C. Clark & J. O'Donnell (Eds.), *Becoming and unbecoming white: Owning and disowning a racial identity* (pp. 1–9). Westport, CT: Bergin & Garvey.

FAIR (Fairness & Accuracy in Reporting). (2001). *This isn't discrimination, this is necessary. Beware the Arab-looking.* [www document] Retrieved September 17, 2006, from http://www.fair.org/index.php?page=1081

Freebody, D., & Baker, C. D. (1985). Children's first schoolbooks: Introduction to the culture of literacy. *Harvard Educational Review, 55*(4), 381–398.

Gerami, S. (1998). Christianity in public schools: Perspective of a non-Christian immigrant parent. *Early Child Development and Care, 147*, 33–34.

Guha, R. (2004, July). New aspirations – Things are changing in education, and not always expectedly. *The Telegraph.* Retrieved April 15, from http://www.telegraphindia.com/1040724/asp/opinion/story_3524247.asp#

Hamovitch, B. (1996). Socialization without voice: An ideology of hope for at-risk students. *Teachers College Record, 98*(2), 286–306.

Hoodfar, H. (1993). The veil in their minds and on our heads: The persistence of colonial images of Muslim women. *Resources for Feminist Research, 22*(3/4), 5–18.

Horton, J., & Scott, D. (2004, Summer). White students' voices in multicultural teacher education preparation. *Multicultural Education.* [www document] Retrieved May 19, 2008, from http://findarticles.com/p/articles/mi_qa3935/is_200407/ai_n9414143

Kincheloe, J. L., & Steinberg, S. R. (1997). *Changing multiculturalism.* London: Open University Press.

Kincheloe, J. L., & Steinberg, S. R. (Eds.). (2004). *The miseducation of the west: The hidden curriculum of western-muslim relations.* New York: Greenwood Press.

King, J. E. (2000). White teachers at the crossroads. *Teaching tolerance.* [www document] Retrieved May 11, 2008, from http://www.tolerance.org/teach/printar.jsp?p=0&ar=174&pi=ttm

Lyotard, J. F. (1979, c1984). *The postmodern condition: A report on knowledge.* Minneapolis, MN: University of Minnesota Press.

MacArthur, J. R. (c2004). *Second front: Censorship and propaganda in the 1991 Gulf War.* USA: University of California Press.

Meiners, E. R. (2002). Disengaging from the legacy of lady bountiful in teacher education classrooms. *Gender and Education, 14*(1), 85–94.

Montpetit, J. (2007, Apr 15). Quebec martial arts team protests hijab ban. *The Star.* Retrieved June 3, 2008, from http://www.thestar.com/article/203338

Rahim, A. (1990). Multiculturalism or ethnic hegemony: A critique of multicultural education in Toronto. *The Journal of Ethnic Studies, 18*(3), 29–46.

Said, E. G. (1978, c1985). *Orientalism.* Harmondsworth: Penguin.

Satrapi, M. (c2003). *Persepolis.* New York: Pantheon Books.

Semali, L. M., & Kincheloe, J. L. (Eds.). (1999). *What is indigenous knowledge? Voices from the academy.* New York: Falmer Press.

Sensoy, Ö., & DiAngelo, R. J. (2006). "I wouldn't want to be a woman in the Middle East": White female narratives of Muslim oppression. *Radical Pedagogy, 8*(1).

Shaheen, J. G. (c1984). *The TV Arab.* Bowling Green, Ohio: Bowling Green State University Popular Press.

Shaheen, J. G. (1991). The comic book Arab. *The Link, 24*(5), 1–11.

Shaheen, J. G. (2001). *Reel bad Arabs.* New York: Olive Branch Press.

Shah, U. (1996). Creating space: Moving from the mandatory to the worthwhile. In L. Beyer (Ed), *Creating democratic classrooms* (pp. 41–61). New York: Teachers College Press.

Stonebanks, C. D. (2004). Consequences of perceived ethnic identities (reflection of an elementary school incident). In J. L. Kincheloe & S. R. Steinberg (Eds.), *The miseducation of the west: The hidden curriculum of western-muslim relations* (pp. 87–101). New York: Greenwood Press.

Stonebanks, C. D. (2008). Politicized knowledge to standardized knowing: The trickle down effect in schools. In N. Denzin & M. Giardina (Eds.), *Qualitative inquiry and the politics of evidence* (pp. 250–269). California, CA: Left Coast Press.

Stonebanks, C. D. (2008). An Islamic perspective on knowledge, knowing and methodology. In N. Denzin, Y. Lincoln, & L. T. Smith (Eds.), *Handbook of critical and Indigenous methodologies* (pp. 293–321). California, CA: Sage Publications.

Suad Nasir, N., & al-Amin, J. (2006, March/April). Creating identity safe spaces on college campuses for muslim students. *Change, 38*(2), 22–27.

Submission [transcript]. "60 Minutes." CBS television. March 13, 2005.

van Gogh, T. (Director). (2004). *Submission.* [Film]. Netherlands: VPRO.

Wyatt, N. (2007, February 26). Rules forbid hijab, says Quebec Soccer Federation. *The Star.* Retrieved June 3, 2008, from http://www.thestar.com/News/article/185923

IMRAN MOGRA

BEING A MUSLIMAH AND A HEADTEACHER

Insights from a Life Story Approach towards Accessing Leadership

INTRODUCTION

This chapter provides selected outcomes from a larger empirical study undertaken in Birmingham primary schools in the West Midlands conurbation of the United Kingdom. A life story approach was adopted in order to explore the career and life experiences of Muslim teachers employed by the state. The project provided participating teachers an opportunity to reflect on their experiences within schools. It was anticipated that a better understanding of the experiences of some Muslim teachers and their contributions in educational settings could be gained and that such an understanding would allow for implications to be drawn for those working in the field of primary education.

As researcher, this study also offered an opportunity to me to reflect on my own life story and its relation to my career and life working in education in state schools. I have served inner city schools of Birmingham mainly in two capacities: as a governor and teacher. Currently I am a teacher educator and in my capacity as a faculty based tutor I supervise post graduate and undergraduate students during their teaching practices. This role provides me with an opportunity to work in some schools across the city and beyond and establish relationships with a range of teachers from various backgrounds and experience their ethos. Occasionally I meet Muslim teachers in schools. The recruiting and retaining of ethnic minority teachers has been an ongoing concern in the UK for over two decades. Through such involvements and experiences I have also become conscious of their upward mobility and progression within the hierarchy of schools. As a person whose parents are of Asian descent who settled in Africa I conducted thirteen in-depth life story interviews with Muslim teachers. At the outset I was expecting Muslim teachers from diverse backgrounds through happenstance and snowballing sampling methods to be contacted. However, possibly due to the demographic population of Birmingham, Muslim teachers predominantly from Pakistani (8), Bangladeshi (3), East African Indian (1) and a North African (1) backgrounds featured in the research. They were nine females and four males and all were promised anonymity. I wanted to gain insights of their experiences, whether cultural or religious, from a more faith-based perspective of my own and to explore among other interests what they understood by a Muslim teacher and their spirituality so that the influence and the role of faith became evident.

Ö. Sensoy and C.D. Stonebanks (eds.), *Muslim Voices in School: Narratives of Identity and Pluralism*, 185–201.

Research studying the life, career and experiences of Black and Asian teachers has been approached predominately by race, class and gender centred models. The religious and faith dimension of teachers and the role it plays in their lives remains an under researched area. As a Muslim, male, teacher educator, I attempt to add such a perspective to existing literature through the exploration of two life stories. The emerging data I gathered demonstrates how understanding an individual's life and career experience depends significantly on understanding the wider life history within which it is placed. The implications of appreciating this are explored through the discussion of the life stories of two participating Muslimah teachers: Fatimah and Zaynab. A description of the nature of the professional school experience is shared in order to show what was accessible to them in advancing their careers and how their characters assisted them in mapping different roads to achieve and aim for headships following critical times.

These Muslimah teachers encountered barriers at various stages in their schooling and careers. Fatimah, occasionally, had to survive in a hostile staffroom and school environment and the Islamophobic taunts by a colleague. She encountered a barrier to her progress when her evidence based portfolio was unaccepted which made her professional advancement difficult. A Muslimah head teacher, Zaynab, was at the receiving end of derogatory racial terms in her childhood. Apart from such overt and wounding racism she was subjected to institutional racism and denial of her dignity and self respect by her teacher. The sense of injustice and unfairness lives with her to this day. The experiences of these two teachers were racially and religiously affected, and I was deeply interested in their lives to facilitate an opportunity to have their voices heard thus empowering them. In addition, to explore what it felt like to be a Muslim teacher in the context of a society and an educational system which is structured by class, gender, and race and where religion, in some quarters, in particular Islam, is under scrutiny and contempt. Life stories advocate such voices to be accepted as authentic and legitimate. This chapter begins with a discussion on the potential of using life story method in gaining an understanding of the meaning that teachers attach to their actions and events with reference to some leading researchers in this field. The chapter ends with some reflections based on insights gained from the study.

BIOGRAPHICAL METHOD

In collecting biographical data, the various forms and varieties of the biographical method have included life history and life story (Denzin, 1989). The core of the biography is the text by the storyteller as well as the biographical narration that emerges from the interaction in the telling. Therefore the telling itself is part of the emergence of the life story. Hence in telling the narrative the life story becomes concrete. The biographical method focuses on the individual, it is particularistic and the notion of time is central to the narrative analysis as there will be different versions of any life due to the varied experiences that people have and due to the way in which they tell their story.

Three differing approaches to biographical research have been identified: the realist, neo-positive and the narrative approach (Miller, 2000). According to Miller (2000), the realist approach subscribes to the techniques of grounded theory and is "based fundamentally in processes of inducing concepts from empirical data." The neo-positive approach emphasises the "empirical testing of pre-existing conceptual frameworks," whereas, the narrative approach centres upon "the process of constructing a view of reality that is carried out jointly by the researcher and the interviewee" (p. ix). Researchers can be eclectic in the techniques they apply. However, each approach has its own core insight that it brings to the biographical perspective. This study privileged the narrative approach because storytelling allows a person to retell events that have had significant impact upon them.

Life Stories and Teachers

The popularity of life stories has grown in a variety of social science disciplines. An international perspective from researchers committed to enhancing the lives and work of teachers has been collected by Day, Fernandez, Hauge, and Møller (2000). Some researchers apply the terms *life history* and *life story* interchangeably (Bryman, 2001) while others (Denzin, 1989; Goodson and Sikes, 2001) make a distinction and advocate that a *life story* can be conceived as a narrative, an individual's reconstruction of what is considered significant in his or her life, whereas a *life history* is likely to be co-constructed with a researcher using a range of data sources and moves through stages of interpretation so that the narrative becomes contextualised and theorised.

One of the reasons for the use of the life history technique in diverse fields is its flexibility and adaptability (Hitchcock and Hughes, 1995). But, Thomas (1995) reminds us that the story by a teacher cannot be considered "as typical or representative," nevertheless, "within each individual narrative, there will be episodes, experiences and emotions with which teachers can readily identify" (p. xiv). In addition, through the analysis of individual lives, the relationship between social forces and personal characters are explored. The life story can also reveal how an individual enters a community and matures within a community. Although the individual is significant, the individual does not exist in a vacuum and hence the study of individual life stories without reference to the community to which individuals subscribe to would be incomplete. al-Zeera (2001) argues that looking at narratives whilst ignoring the shared history of a community and the wider narrative context "is both misleading and pointless" (p. 5). For Muslims, if the personal and separate stories of Muslim individuals are shared and shaped by the larger Islamic narrative context, these stories can provide the new generation with a wealth of personal experiences to relate to and thereby encourage them to reflect on their personal experiences and place them in the larger Islamic context (al-Zeera, 2001).

In this chapter, life history and life story are used interchangeably since these narratives were based on interviews as well as on the respondents telling their own story about their lives. Therefore, life stories can be important in studying educational institutions and the changes occurring over time, in knowing about integration and assimilation, and in acquiring a contemporary insider view of a religion or culture. Two such life stories will be presented in the remainder of the chapter.

THE STORY OF FATIMAH

Fatimah was born in Pakistan and came to England as a graduate student. She is fluent in English, Urdu, Persian, Arabic and Punjabi and was interviewed on a day when it was raining. She had dressed casually wearing jeans, a jumper and a loose head scarf.

Early life

Reflecting on her childhood, she expressed fond memories. Religion was nominal in her family, limited to the extent of following elementary rules of Islam. She attended a convent school run by American missionaries and was tutored at home for the Qur'an. She recalled her childhood days:

> I think it was wonderful. Although we weren't really religious but that culture and moral were very important. Such as: following the basic rules of Islam, respecting the elders, being honest, and truthful. These things were very very important in my family and they still are I think.

At the age of 19, in 1993 she visited Birmingham and her first task was to familiarise herself with the routines and way of life in England. Subsequently, in 1995 she enrolled for a master's degree programme at a local university. Until her arrival in Birmingham, she revealed:

> Religion as such it wasn't very important when I came to England as I said earlier on. I discovered that something needed to be done. At that point I started having my scarf. That was my first experience in England.

Schooling

Her earliest memories of schooling in Pakistan were pleasant. She remembered that as soon as she walked into class her teacher would welcome her with a big smile. She remembered that her teacher wore red lipstick. Fatimah, thereafter, desired for "the whole of the first year," to sit on the teacher's chair knowing well that it was not for her. In secondary school she had happy memories of her favourite teacher who she considered intelligent and encouraged all of her students to do well. This teacher was prepared to listen, communicate and share jokes instead of being the stonefaced, order giving stereotype of the stern, top down authority figure.

These observations and experiences were imprinted on her self because in later life, as a professional, she was adamant about not being a strict teacher. In addition, she recognised the importance of relating to pupils and building positive relationships. It was, therefore, unsurprising that her first senior post was in the Foundation Stage.[1]

However, whilst in Pakistan she had never wanted to be a teacher. She studied mathematics, statistics and economics and aspired to be employed by a bank as she had observed her father often dealing with figures and counting money.

Her primary reason for coming to the U.K. was to visit her brother who was attending a boarding school. Her own dislocations in the first fifteen months in Birmingham were amplified when she first met her brother:

> When I saw him he couldn't speak to me because he didn't understand Urdu language at all. And that was very hurtful for me. I used to sit at home and look at him and he would look at me. And I said that's not right. I am going to stay here and teach him and make him communicate with me and with the rest of the family. So I stayed although it was very hard because there was a gap of 13 years. He was like a *gora* [white person] his thinking was totally different and he wasn't an Asian [gestures her face] he was very Westernised although very strict Muslim but different values and cultural beliefs. That was the reason I stayed in first of all.

At University

As her brothers and sisters had, she aspired for a master's degree, and therefore, attended a local university, with some initial apprehensions about plunging straight into a British university. Here she was exposed to the hostile nature of debates and criticism from some missionary experts and therefore defined her "real" Islam against this background. But it is in this context that she discovered her religion and what she believed Islam was really all about. She appreciated the close contact with tutors and spoke highly of a lecturer who enlightened her to other aspects of Islam, which she had been unaware of "because Islam in Pakistan is totally different than the Islam in Britain." She saw a spectrum of Islam: from a cultural and moral phenomenon to a complete way of life.

Following her master's degree, she enrolled for the Post Graduate Certificate in Education course and described this experience as "horrible." She thought the college had been racist and picked on those perceived to be weak. The college, having had an unsatisfactory inspection from the Office for Standards in Education (Ofsted) was attempting to prove to them that they were serious about raising standards. She recalled:

> I remember one discrimination by a teacher who I will probably never forgive. Her name is Mrs Smith she is still working at Hilltop College [both are pseudonyms]. I did all the display work in the classroom. The headteacher of that school and the deputy came and said well done to me you have really worked hard. But that woman said, "oh I like your work" and that's it. She did not mention it in her writing. I always felt that they are saying one thing verbally but they never put it down on a piece of paper.

In addition, she recalled a negative experience relating to one of her assignments receiving a poor mark, which after much deliberation and evidence forced the faculty to rescind their assessment.

Teaching Practice

After qualifying to teach, she took on supply teaching. At a school, she was accused by a parent of bruising a child. The headteacher confided in her by indicating that the child's parents had a history with social services, prison, and history of drug abuse. At this stage Fatimah was unaware of union support that she could request. In retrospect, she felt more could have been done by the supportive head by involving other people in the process. This experience, in a predominantly white school, dispirited her so much so that she questioned the very profession of teaching, feeling despondent and disillusioned.

She then accepted a post in a Church of England school unaware that some people in that area were sympathizers of the British National Party. She suffered racist name calling such as "Paki" and verbal abuse such as "b-i-t-c-h"[2] from some of the children. At the end of the year although the teachers and the headteacher were very supportive over what had happened, she left due to some of the children and parents. Thereafter, she visited other schools and arrived at a multifaith and multicultural school and readily accepted an appointment there. Happily settled and making a positive impression she narrated some students' responses to her:

> I've had children they would sometimes come to me and say "mum." You know they could see me as not a blonde person with blue eyes sitting in the chair.

Although she joined a school that had three other female Asian teachers and a male Asian teacher she nevertheless felt "it was a very different air." She found it difficult to attend staff meetings. This was not the result of her own inadequacy, but, rather, it was due to the way other colleagues made her feel whilst she was in the staffroom. This was of paramount worry and it took some time to become assertive in the staffroom.

In School

This was her first school where there was a significant representation of minority ethnic children. She was stunned to hear Muslim songs played during assembly as she did not expect such in British schools. She enjoyed the ethos and the community spirit that existed there. She expressed her feelings in the following words:

> I really enjoyed working with parents and the children because I felt that I had more respect from the children. I felt they were my family and my children and I am working in my own home.

Consequently, she was motivated further and could address more needs of more children based on the good knowledge that she possessed about their background and understanding their religious beliefs and culture revealing parallel dynamics of enthusiasm and idealism about teaching as expressed by other Black and Asian teachers (Osler, 2003). However, in terms of professional development the school was disappointing and she revealed that the school did not bother to send her on any courses that were crucial for updating her knowledge. Even though her many requests were documented in her performance management reviews she was left to her own devices to find the time and ways to learn. The school was constrained by the budget and staff absences. She rationalised such practice:

> I think if you are a white person or English person or somebody's favourite you will be absolutely fine. You will go on courses. You will go on training.

Professionalism and Islamophobia

She shared another incident of powerlessness and lack of status, revealing:

> A teacher approached me. He used to be taken as if he was a funny man but I don't think he was funny. He was very rude, very disgusting and he was a disgrace to his own faith. I think there was a bomb scare in Birmingham. I was standing waiting for a senior manager to see me. He came to me and started to talk to me and another teacher. And I said what happened? The other teacher was saying I have to phone my daughter because she was going to go to the city centre and there has been a bomb scare. He said there is a bomb planted in Birmingham. You must have known about it wouldn't you? These were the exact words that came from his mouth. I had the shock of my life and I thought he is standing in a school and he is working at the same level as me and he doesn't have any respect for me. So I approached the senior manager instead of dealing with the child's problem at that time. I felt I was going to scream. I would have given him a *thappar* [slap] on his face but I didn't. I spoke to the senior manager obviously he said, and these were his words, "I have heard lots of complaints about him. He is really out of hand. He should not be saying these things to you at all because this was not the first occasion." Then the headteacher came to me straight away. She spoke to me and she said I have heard what he said to you. And again it was all swooped under the carpet no action were taken – a little comfort will do. Well I think I was foolish I should have reported it to the governors maybe I was a coward.

The visible religious identity is apparently affecting life opportunities of both male and female Muslims. Prejudice, stereotypes, media portrayal, unfounded fear about life style influences are realities for some Muslims. Whilst some Muslims face barriers based on misconceptions and a lack of knowledge of visible Islam the reality is much more complex (Jawad and Benn, 2003; Osler, 2003). Race, gender, culture and religion are interwoven and often difficult to untangle.

Promotion

The accounts of difficulties experienced by Black and Asian teachers have been recorded by Henry (1991), Ghuman (1995), and Muslimahs by Osler (2003), and Benn (2003). Fatimah spent many years in this school and would have stayed longer because she loved it and never looked for financial gains but a "terrible" incident happened again. Her line manager having examined her performances declared that all her targets were met but rejected her threshold application. No explanation was offered upon enquiring. She was prepared to accept rejection on budgetary limitations but was vehemently opposed to let it be a reflection of her work. She remembered:

> I said if you turned round and said there is no money in the budget I will accept that. But don't tell me you haven't worked hard enough for threshold [in my subject area]. And then I said okay if you don't want to listen to me let us arrange a meeting and sit down together and go through all the work that I have done without you lot paying me anything.

Three meetings were arranged and each time her line manager failed to attend. Eventually she encountered the head and requested an explanation. Surprisingly, the headteacher claimed her work to have been insufficient. Fatimah challenged the head offering all the evidence for the ten projects she had undertaken and the awards achieved. On that day she finally decided that that school was not the place for her to be in anymore. She was certain there would be other schools who would appreciate her initiatives, and consequently, with "a brilliant reference from her headteacher," who oddly, did not want her to leave. She was successful in her first interview in eight years.

By mustering her achievements, experiences and her own religio-cultural identity, at the time of the interview, Fatimah achieved a senior manager's post leading the Foundation Stage. She is ambitious and is aiming to be a head in the next five years. She is actively seeking promotion in her current school and around the city.

Fatimah commented on some of her personal characteristics that she thought marked her as a successful teacher: determination under adverse colleagues, her capacity to respond to school initiatives to support the school development plan and positive relations with children and parents.

Fatimah subscribed to the view that intrinsic motivation for promotion was more powerful than extrinsic. She clearly amassed evidence of activities that she had undertaken and demonstrated a clear impact upon children's learning and standards but when these were not acknowledged she was pushed to consider an alternative school. She resisted compromising this significant contribution on her part to the school community. She viewed her involvement in teaching as an enjoyment and a very rewarding experience. Fatimah considered teaching as a respected profession. Occasionally, she has had to say to herself teaching is only a job and to take things sometimes with a pinch of salt to encourage herself. Her new post has raised her self-esteem and confidence and has given her an opportunity to adopt an assertive identity that allows her to participate in new learning initiatives and to explore activities that have a direct impact on children's learning and achievement.

THE STORY OF ZAYNAB

Early Life

Zaynab was born in Pakistan and is a mother of two. She was interviewed on a day when it was cold and dry, about her journey into headship at her school in a community room dedicated for parents and staff. She accompanied her parents to England at the age of four and was raised in "quite a religious home in terms of high standards and morals" with a strong work ethic. She grew up in an atmosphere which reflected beliefs and ideals centred on striving to succeed and living within the parameters of faith. Unsurprisingly, her parents encouraged learning, promoted the respect of teachers and were very supportive of the school even though her mother could not speak any English:

> We did have a work ethic in our house. You know my dad used to say: you are here work hard and do your best but remember your identity and who you are. So that's been very strong in my own personal development.

Her mother was a stable influence in terms of high moral standards, expectations and a driving force to set expected behaviours. Such attitudes had a lasting impression on Zaynab's personality.

Schooling

Reflecting on her first memories of schooling in a suburb of Birmingham, Zaynab portrayed successful study and happy days. Three essential factors within a classroom made this possible: a play-based curriculum, feeling very comfortable in class and teachers taking an interest in new arrivals without any English. She felt "taken under their wings" and fondly recalled their visits to her parents. Significantly, she recollected her parents giving her teacher a *sari* as a wedding gift. For Zaynab these were profound moments and inspired the nature of relationship she was to establish, as a head, in her school in later life.

However, these positive experiences in primary school were short lived and dramatically changed once her parents moved to Solihull for a short period. Zaynab revealed that since some children had never seen a brown face, it was common in her days to be "called Paki, chocolate face, wog and go back home." Such racist abuse in schools is well documented (Troyna and Hatcher, 1992; Gillborn, 1995). However, for some Muslim children today, Islamophobia is their regular experience and such racial/ethnic taunts, a regular source of anxiety (Din, 2006).

By not dealing with the issue, her teachers let her down – telling her instead to ignore it. This painful encounter had irreversible effects and a very strong influence on her perceptions of unfairness and injustice. She recalled:

I don't think the teachers really dealt with it. They told me to ignore it. I think that had a very strong influence on me in terms of unfairness and injustice. Only one or two teachers stuck out who actually taught the class that what they were doing was wrong.

Probing her further about life in school, she unhesitatingly revealed two more painful incidences. Initially, she dropped her face and then spoke in the following words:

I remember going to my class and the children staring at me and I don't remember the teacher making me feel welcome. I do remember wanting to go to the toilet and she wouldn't let me go so I wet myself in the class. That has lived with me as well. But I remember her saying to me you haven't brought your t-shirt. You can go out with nothing on. When I think about that it actually makes me cringe. My parents, you know, whether I went home and told my parents I couldn't remember. But I remember that experience because she did two things to me that were very detrimental.

These unforgettable encounters were adverse to her human dignity and according to her demonstrated a complete oblivion to the feelings of a child. However, she found faint comfort in a few English friends who pitied her and invited her to their house to play.

Later, having completed half a year of secondary school in Solihull, she then moved to an inner city girl's school and found the staff there to be very supportive and unsurprisingly she was really successful:

I actually moved from half a year in secondary school in Solihull to a secondary school in Bordesley Green. I think that is where I flourished really because I took the year exams, came top of the class. My parents put a tutor in for me and I think I began to have a belief that I could aspire.

In particular, the attitude of key persons, some of whom have become life long friends, such as her religious education teacher, the then-new headteacher and form tutor contributed to her success. She was good in gymnastics. Zaynab proudly celebrates the fact that she was probably the first Muslimah to participate in a residential week.

Professionalism

A mixture of factors contributed to her becoming a teacher. Encounters with career advisors have not always been positive for minority ethnic students (Ranger, 1988; Parker-Jenkins, et al., 1999; Osler, 2003; Arora, 2005). But Zaynab was indebted to her careers advisor who steered and reassured her of her capability to become a teacher. Thus, she believed in herself and applied for her first interview.

Being the eldest of six children and naturally looking after them she often encouraged her siblings to do well and join her in university. A cultural trend was occurring: the respect of the elder sister – so they listened to her and during the holidays she taught them English and mathematics followed by *suparah* [portions of the Qur'an] lessons ensuring they never sat around lazily. These were probably coupled with "the cultural expectations of the *baji* – the older sister." She took this coaching very seriously and perhaps it was a natural progression to becoming a teacher.

Muslimahs have experienced feelings of isolation, disillusionment, disadvantage, victimisation and being de-skilled which coupled with having a Muslim identity adversely affected their professional development (Benn, 2003). Zaynab apparently had a positive experience. She praised a college of higher education where she attended to train as a teacher in the following words: I read Catholic Christian theology and was encouraged to study my own religion at another centre too. She marvelled at the college for this arrangement describing it as being "the best thing." She recollected positively her teaching placements in a girl's only, a co-educational and a Church of England school:

> Yes I was very fortunate. I went to Lowland College (pseudonym). I had an excellent department. They really encouraged me and it is a Catholic college and I went to read theology. They said to me this is Catholicism: Catholic Christian theology. You must also learn about your religion and they did the best thing. They sent me to the centre for the study of [title]. I went to Riverside campus (pseudonym) part of the Lakeside University (pseudonym) and there was a lecturer there called Mr. Reader (pseudonym), he was fantastic. He was my tutor for the 2 years so I learnt about my religion in depth.

After graduating, in September 1982, she was appointed to her first post in a secondary school teaching Religious Education (RE). During that time there were relatively few Muslim RE teachers. Again remembering fondly the head of department who anchored and steered her in the right direction she settled well – a sign of self- confidence that can develop through positive leadership (Benn, 2003). Within two years she gained promotion in Section 11 teaching multiculturalism. This was a huge risk both economically and professionally. Black teachers, working in such sections, often experienced marginalisation and a lack of status (Brar, 1991). Nevertheless, Zaynab spent the next 12 years in Section 11 working in a variety of schools including special schools doing what she thought was an urgent need for her community and wider society.

In 1997, interestingly, she moved to teach at the very school that she had attended as a child. There, she first applied for a mainstream job, which subsequently, enabled her to take a senior post for the first time as a head of Foundation Stage. She remained in that school until 2004 when in Easter a post for an assistant headship arose.

As a member of the senior leadership team she applied but was unsuccessful and "somebody very junior" to her got the job. This was hugely upsetting for Zaynab because it was the first time she had experienced "failure." She explained:

> Well at the time I was very upset about it. I have to be honest because I think one of the things that I do do, I do speak my mind. I am not saying I am rude

but I do speak my mind. I think I do say in the polite and courteous way because that is the sort of vision I am trying to set in this school. But I think, I don't really know, but I did feel that the head perhaps didn't want me because I didn't always keep quiet or just agree, you know. I often used to question about whether we were meeting the needs of the Asian children. I used to question. Sometimes when we had students in from colleges and I used to notice that some of the teaching assistants, some white teaching assistants were not very nice to them. I used to say to my head people can't be allowed to behave like this.

But soon after this, the Local Authority approached her to assist a school in serious weaknesses. Again, she took a risk with an aim to assist others. And so, in September 2004, she was an assistant head with specific responsibilities for the Foundation Stage, English as an additional language and attendance.

She was highly committed to the school and contributed in getting it out of serious weaknesses with Ofsted commending her work. But success was short lived. Probably her most challenging experience as an adult was to follow:

But then I hit a problem in that school. The head began a system of criticism against me. I think it is probably to do with the fact that you know sometimes these things happen to you. You think oh. You know. I don't really suffer unprofessionalism and bad behaviour. I don't tolerate it not even in a head teacher. I won't tolerate if its injustice. I think that goes back to my own upbringing. When you see such bad injustices, I don't like to see people crumbled or trodden on or spoken about in a way that doesn't help anybody. So I think what happened was that I got on very well with the staff and then she used to say to me you are too friendly with the staff. You need to go out there and become a nasty person basically. I turned round and said to her I can't do that. That's not how I was brought up so I can't do that for you.

The school went through a period of turmoil and subsequently she left the school, having discovered the following:

I found out that she was having people say things about me and write things about me. When I heard that again its injustice isn't it. I couldn't defend myself. I did go to her and say, "if there is anything I'm doing that is not right. I would like you to tell me so I can put it right". But I think she was playing games and basically she would. It's a long story but a lot of the staff were involved in complaints and *I* felt that I couldn't stay in the school for my own career. I felt that she was going to sabotage my reputation which I had worked hard to build. I'm not saying I'm all good or whatever. But what I am saying is I can't have lies being compromised. So I had to go to my union and they supported me and the rest of the staff because it wasn't just me. So that was a story in itself. But while I was at the school I thought right I can't stay here. I don't know what is gonna happen to her because life was very difficult for me. I don't even think about the days when I had to drive into school do a days work and have her watching me, sending people into my class, asking for things and being generally very unprofessional.

Although she had aspired to become a head she had not planned for it at that stage. She was between 40-42 thinking:

> Naah can't do it. I'm getting older now and it's probably far too much work. I don't know everything. I'm good at what I do. I'll stay doing this Assistant Head.

But when these problems started she had to make quick decisions. Her dilemma was whether to apply for the deputy's post in a troubled school or to move to an unknown school. When Osler interviewed Afro Caribbean and Asian teachers, she was surprised to find the extent to which some of them drew on religious tradition, personal faith and beliefs to rationalise and gain support to cope and achieve 'career success' (Osler, 2003, p. 154). Similarly, Zaynab drew on her religious tradition, faith and belief to explain and support her in achieving career success:

> I dunno I think actually for me it's a personal thing. I think well I don't know. I have to be honest with me I think God guides you. I think He guides everything if you read *namaz* prayers. And if you are, if you try and live a life where you don't do anything bad to other people I do have other people's interest. I do care about how other people are treated and how their characters are formed and how you try and support people. I have to honestly say I've never gone out and actively done anything to anybody. I just wouldn't do that and it goes against my own moral upbringing.

Being in her mid career, perhaps this was an element of a self-renewal process whereby she was searching new opportunities and tasks, rather than adhering to known and safe grounds (Hudson, 1991). Having resolved her dilemma she applied to a school giving it "the best shot" otherwise she thought what "I will learn from it, is what the interview is like. If I find it really hard then I know I'm not ready. Yeah."

Soon after her appointment as a headteacher, unknown to her, her previous head resigned simultaneously. Consequently, she sometimes thinks she should have stayed there and achieved promotion in a more comfortable way and in a way more suited to how she would have liked it to have been.

As for her vision for schools in 21st Century Birmingham she sees schools as places where teachers care considerably about pupils' personal, social and emotional well being and thereafter ensure that children are given high quality education.

CONCLUSION

In relation to accessing leadership in primary schools there is a disproportional under-representation of head teachers from the ethnic minority communities in Birmingham. Only 1.5% of Head teachers have BME backgrounds. In other words, at the moment this represents only 24 out of 452 heads" [sic] (NCSL, 2007). Only time will tell the impact of the National succession consultants who will be working with local authorities to identify priorities and future steps to inspire potential head teachers. Currently, anecdotal evidence reveals that there are only four Muslim head teachers in the primary schools of a city that has a Muslim population of about 52,163 (37.2%) of children aged 0-15 (BCC, 2001). It is surprising that leadership representation remains low. Positive and concerted efforts running in parallel with implementing policies would assist in creating a leadership that reflects all communities and faiths. Life stories may challenge the negative representation of Islam and Muslims in the UK and beyond. They may give illustrations of ways of overcoming these barriers but also illuminate ways in which structural support and individual agency has been used to succeed and overcome stereotypes.

The perceptions of these two teachers may well be shaped by their respective attitude towards their religiosity even though their life stories have illuminated similarities in their faith, gender, ethnic and professional background. The narratives of Zaynab, who had a religious upbringing and attended public schools in UK, and Fatimah, who was brought in a more culturally orientated family and attended an American convent school, are interesting as they reflect the individual choices that they made. As an adult, Zaynab does not appear overtly Muslimah and received considerable support during her journey to headship. On the other hand, Fatimah wears a scarf, is subjected to Islamophobic taunts, experiences challenges in her contributions being acknowledged and rewarded. Nevertheless, perceptions of Muslim women and men could influence some members of staff in schools in providing them the status and power that they deserve. Significantly, both are willing to serve across the city and not only in schools that are in special measures, or considered 'tough,' or located in inner city areas, or heavily populated with Muslim children. On the other hand, whilst both can be considered successful in their careers, worryingly, they would not recommend teaching to their relatives or friends.

In her story Fatimah discusses a complex set of identity positions and therefore religion is not the only factor in explaining her life experiences. Depending on the context she sometimes forefronts her gender, ethnicity and country. In fact she also makes use of class/caste when referring to herself as a daughter of a *choudhary* (landlord). Nevertheless in understanding the sophisticated nature of prejudice Fatimah was apparently hit hard with internal matters. She was unable to attend courses, her status was devalued and she had little autonomy in the face of bureaucracies within her school. She expressed her frustration over her inability to influence the decision making process and disenfranchising experience caused her to leave. The loss of status, her feelings of powerlessness in addressing Islamophobic tendencies, lack of recognition of her contributions, insufficient administrative support and limited opportunities for professional development had an impact on her at this school. However, moving onto another school she asserted her aspiration for empowerment where she had demonstrated her desire to develop her competencies in believing that she had the knowledge and skill to improve the school. In turn, the positive response from her current head teacher suggests that the school is empowering her as she is attending courses, sharing her expertise and demonstrating her competency and has offered herself for promotion.

Some Muslimah teachers experience prejudice, ridicule and hostility in their work place and in society but such attitude does not deter some of them from continuing to serve the community and fulfil their professional duties. Others unfortunately are pushed to consider alternative careers. Fatimah and Zaynab feel they are having a positive influence in their respective communities and their contributions are having an impact on children and school achievements. Hence there is a sense of empowerment for them. In the context of promoting values of respect, tolerance, justice and harmony, the significance of the value of every teacher needs to be demonstrated to children. They need not only learn that teachers are role models but they should experience the fact that just as every child matters, every teacher matters too!

DISCUSSION QUESTIONS AND EXTENSION ACTIVITIES

(1) Mogra argues that micro-aggressions experienced by Muslimah (Muslim women) such as the attitudes and perceptions of co-workers, can contribute to a minimizing of their contributions to the school. The flip side of this argument is that there are people for whom micro-advantages result in rewards that are accrued due to the attitudes and perceptions of co-workers towards certain groups. Identify examples of how both these occurrences take place for the two teachers discussed in this chapter, and also in your school/context.

(2) There are usually a few explanations for why teachers from minoritized communities do not enter the school profession. Sometimes mainstream teacher education programs claim that they would welcome minority teachers, but that there is a culture among minorities that does not value teaching as a profession. On the other hand, many teacher education students from minoritized backgrounds argue that schools are not welcoming places for minorities. Consider, did you have any Muslim teachers when you were in school? How might your own experiences as well as the experiences of Zaynab and Fatimah as described in this chapter, help you explain these differences?

(3) In this chapter, Mogra argues that life histories play an important role in the experiences of Muslim teachers in school. How are (personal) life-histories connected to (group-based) social, public, and political histories? Consider the ways in which Zaynab and Fatimah's (and other Muslim teachers') personal histories have shifted and morphed with particular political, social, and public historical events (such as 9/11). Consider also your own personal life stories, and how they relate to social, public, and political events of the time. What are the implications of the patterns in your response for public education?

IF YOU LIKED THIS CHAPTER, YOU MAY ALSO ENJOY READING:

Abdurraqib, S. (2009). On being Black and Muslim: Eclipsed identities in the classroom. *In this book.*

Stonebanks, C.D. (2009). If Nancy Drew wouldn't wear a hijab, would the Hardy boys wear a kufi? *In this book.*

Abbas, T. (Ed.), (2005). *Muslim Britain: Communities under pressure.* New York & London: Zed Books.

Gordon, J. (2000). *The color of teaching.* New York: Routledge.

Henry, A. (1998) *Taking back control: African Canadian women teachers' lives and practice.* Albany: State University of New York Press.

McCarthy, C., Crichlow, W., Dimitriadis, G., & Dolby, N. (2005). *Race, identity, and representation in education* (2nd ed.) London: Routledge.

NOTES

[1] Foundation Stage is the period of education from age three to five.
[2] Fatimah spelt out the word

REFERENCES

Arora, R. (2005). *Race and ethnicity in education.* London: Ashgate.
BCC. (2001). *2001 Census population in Birmingham: Religious group profiles.* Demographic Information Service, Planning Strategy, Development Directorate, Birmingham: Birmingham City Council. Retrieved December 18, 2007, from http://www.birmingham.gov.uk/Media?MEDIA_ID=116871
Benn, T. (2003). Muslim women talking: Experiences of their early teaching careers. In H. A. Jawad & T. Benn (Eds.), *Muslim women in the United Kingdom and beyond: Experiences and images* (pp. 131–150). Leiden: Brill Academic Publishers.
Brar, H. S. (1991). Unequal opportunities: The recruitment, selection and promotion prospects for black teachers. *Evaluation and Research in Education, 5*(1&2), 35–47.
Bryman, A. (2001). *Social research methods.* Oxford: Oxford University Press.
Day, C., Fernandez, A., Hauge, T., & Møller, J. (Eds.). (2000). *The life and work of teachers – International perspectives in changing times.* London: Falmer Press.
Denzin, N. K. (1989). *The research act: A theoretical introduction to sociological methods* (3rd ed.). New Jersey, NJ: Prentice Hall.
Din, I. (2006). *The new British: The impact of culture and community on young Pakistanis.* Aldershot: Ashgate.
Ghuman, P. A. S. (1995). *Asian teachers in British schools.* Clevedon: Multilingual Matters.
Gillborn, D. (1995). *Racism and antiracism in real schools.* Buckingham: Open University Press.
Goodson, I. F., & Sikes, P. (2001). *Life history research in educational settings.* Buckingham: Open University Press.
Henry, D. (1991). *Thirty black in British education.* Sussex: Rabbit Press.
Hitchcock, G., & Hughes, D. (1995). *Research and the teacher.* London: Routledge.

Hudson, F. M. (1991). *The adult years: Mastering the self renewal*. San Francisco: Jossey and Bass Publishers.

Jawad, H., & Benn, T (Eds.). (2003). *Muslim women in the United Kingdom and beyond: Experiences and images*. Leiden: Brill Academic Publishers.

Miller, R. L. (2000). *Researching life stories and family histories*. London: Sage Publications.

NCSL. (2007). *Leadership succession planning*. Retrieved December 18, 2007, from http://www.ncsl. org.uk/media/8E2/2A/leadership-succession-birmingham-an-overview.pdf

Osler, A. (2003). Muslim women teachers: Life histories, identities and citizenship. In H. A. Jawad & T. Benn (Eds.), *Muslim women in the United Kingdom and beyond: Experiences and images* (pp. 151–169). Leiden: Brill Academic Publishers.

Parker-Jenkins, M., Hartas, D, Irving, B. A., & Barker, V. (1999). Inclusion, exclusion and cultural awareness: Career services supporting the career aspirations of muslim girls. *European Educational Researcher*, 5(2), 5–16.

Ranger, C. (1988). *Ethnic minority school teachers, a survey in eight local education authorities*. London: Commission for Racial Equality.

Thomas, D. (Ed.). (1995). *Teachers' stories*. Buckingham: Open University Press.

Troyna, B., & Hatcher, R. (1992). *Racism in children's lives*. London: Routledge.

Zeera, Z. (2001). *Wholeness and holiness in education*. Surrey: The International Institute of Islamic Thought.

Imran Mogra
Faculty of Education, Law and Social Sciences
Birmingham City University, UK

BIOGRAPHIES OF CONTRIBUTORS

Samaa Abdurraqib, PhD (ABD)
Samaa is a doctoral student and union activist at the University of Wisconsin-Madison. She is mere months away from completing her PhD in English literature and Women's Studies. Her research focuses on diasporic women and their relationships to homes and homelands. Her article "*Hijab Scenes*: Muslim Women, Migration, and Hijab in Immigrant Muslim Literature" was published in a 2006 special issue of *MELUS*. She was born in the Northeastern U.S., but has spent the majority of her life living, studying, and working in the Midwest. She spends a lot of time wishing her cats could finish writing her dissertation.

Mona M. Abo-Zena, EdM
Mona is a doctoral student in the Eliot-Pearson Department of Child Development at Tufts University. Her main research and teaching interest is promoting positive outcomes for children and families in a range of educational and community settings; she has particular interests in religious minority youth. She earned her BA in sociology from the University of Chicago and her EdM from Harvard University Graduate School of Education. She has over fifteen years of teaching, administrative, and board experience in public and Islamic schools.

Dalia al Houseini, BA
Dalia is a recent graduate of Communications from Vancouver BC. Upon graduation she decided to pay the closest thing to her hometown a visit, and thus currently resides in Amman, Jordan. There, she is working to gain field experience and re-connecting with her culture. She hopes to have a 15 page CV that includes a Masters, PhD and a position as a CEO/GM. She does not function without music.

Seema Imam, EdD
Seema is an associate professor in the Faculty of Elementary and Middle Level Teacher Education at National-Louis University in Lisle, Illinois. She has devoted her life to a variety of Muslim community development issues, activism, and Islamic education. Seema served five years as a founding principal of an Islamic School, provides expertise on curriculum projects, and teacher professional development in the states and overseas. She and her teenage son are co-authoring several children's books hoping to normalize Islam and Muslim practices. The first book, *I am Listening*, depicts a public school teacher wearing hijab. Seema is the Chair of the University Senate at National-Louis University and a board member of the Islamic Schools League of America.

Carolyne Ali Khan, PhD (ABD)
Carolyne is a PhD student in Urban Education at the Graduate Center, CUNY, New York. She is also a teacher at Community Prep High School, and currently

teaches in the Educational Foundations Department at Hunter College. She received her BA in Anthropology from the American University in Cairo, Egypt, and her MA in Education from the University of Bath, England. In addition she has been a teacher and/or student in Germany, the United Kingdom, Japan, Ghana and Pakistan. She is excited to have a forthcoming article the journal *Qualitative Inquiry* and chapters in *Boy Culture: An Encyclopedia* (Greenwood). As an avid rollerblader she skates everywhere (and there are rumours that she doesn't actually have feet).

Shaza Khan, PhD (ABD)
Shaza is a PhD Candidate at the University of Rochester. Her dissertation research centers on the adolescent development and identity formation of Muslim American youth. Her focus on positive youth development and youth programs highlights her belief that youth have the potential to make meaningful contributions to society, and further, to change the world. Shaza has worked as an educator in Islamic schools and youth programs for the past ten years, most recently serving as an assistant director at a summer camp. She has published in *Islamic Horizons* and contributed book reviews for the *American Journal of Islamic Social Sciences* and *Intercultural Education*. As a native of Rochester, NY, she is a small-town girl at heart, but Chicago, IL is also starting to grow on her, where she lives with her husband Zain Ghani and one year old son Aayan.

Shabana Mir, PhD
Shabana is an assistant professor at Oklahoma State University. Her dissertation, *Constructing Third Spaces: American Muslim Undergraduate Women's Hybrid Identity Construction* won the Outstanding Dissertation Award for 2006 from the Council on Anthropology and Education (American Anthropological Association). She was a Visiting Researcher at Georgetown University and a Research Affiliate at the Pluralism Project (Harvard University). She has worked and studied in Pakistan, the U.K. and the U.S. She has contributed chapters to *Comparative Education: the Dialectic of the Global and the Local*, *Nurturing Child and Adolescent Spirituality* and *The Encyclopedia of Islam in America*. She has been published in the *Journal of Religion*, *Anthropology News*, the *Chronicle of Higher Education*, the *American Journal of Islamic Social Sciences*, *Q-News*, *Encyclopedia of Islam in America*, *Encyclopedia of Modern Asia* and on the Internet. She lives in Stillwater, Oklahoma with her husband Svend and daughter Raihana.

Imran Mogra, PhD
Imran is a senior lecturer in the Faculty of Education, Law and Social Sciences at Birmingham City University. He has published several papers on onomastics with particular reference to primary school children. He has also designed and delivered, nationally, a madrasah teachers' training program. Currently he is exploring the perceptions of trainee teachers about Collective Worship in State schools of England and Wales. When it is comes to washing his car he is pretty laid back!

Younes Mouchid, PhD
Younes is an Associate Professor of International Studies and Director of Degree at a Distance Programs at Cogswell College in Sunnyvale, California. Initially trained as a Journalist and a Linguist, Younes published over 25 editorials in the Moroccan newspaper *L'Opinion*, served as editor of *Newsweek* in Arabic between 2002 and 2005, and authored several chapters addressing a variety of issues in Arabic linguistics in *Current Issues in Linguistic Theory*. With a Fulbright Scholarship awarded by the Moroccan-American Commission for Educational and Cultural Exchange, He then earned a PhD in International Development Education from the University of Southern California where he focused his research on higher education reform and globalization in the Arab world. Younes has contributed to the journal *Science Letters*. His current teaching and research interests revolve around co-relational topics in Middle Eastern Studies and Peace Education. His goal is to create teaching and textual nuggets deriving "directly" from the perspective of people and native scholar of the Middle East and "free" from Orientalist and Zionists perspectives and narratives. Younes is an avid cyclist and swimmer and serves the beautiful Clairemont Resort in the Hill of Berkeley as a Fitness Instructor.

Nawell Najib Mossalli, EdD (ABD)
Louisiana Tech University, USA
Nawell currently resides in her hometown in Jeddah, Saudi Arabia while completing her doctoral dissertation in Educational Leadership from Louisiana Tech University. As a Vice Principal at a local private girls' school and evaluator for CITA, an accreditation agency, she continues to strive to promote authentic teaching to foster student-centered, multiculturally rich learning environments. Nawell's publication of "The Gum Box Girl" in *The Delta Journal* in 2002 inspired her to explore her hobby of creative writing. When she is not busy exercising her passion of training educators through workshops and seminars, or playing mom to her three adorable children (all under the age of six!) she still finds the time to write short stories and consistently freelance for a Saudi magazine geared towards students. *Design Magazine* is presently distributed throughout the kingdom, Dubai, London and will become available to US readers by the end of 2009. In her current project, Nawell is editing a study guide (with N. McJamerson) based on the Academy Award winning motion picture *Crash* as a tool to assist educators and their students to reflect on racism and explore personal prejudices.

Barbara Sahli, BA
Barbara provides educational outreach on understanding Islam and Muslims, working particularly with students and teachers. Through speaking, writing, and educating, she is committed to using her voice to change perceptions about Islam. She co-authored a chapter for the 2009 volume, *Educating the Muslims of America* (Oxford University Press), documenting the educational encounters between Muslim and non-Muslim students that she has coordinated for a decade. She has also taught reading and language arts to middle school students at the Islamic

Academy of New England in Massachusetts, and she and her students contributed articles about Islam that were featured in *The Boston Globe* and *Saudi Aramco World*. She earned a BA in psychology (back in the days of the electric typewriter) and is hoping to pursue a graduate degree.

Özlem Sensoy, PhD

Özlem is an assistant professor in the Faculty of Education at Simon Fraser University. She is author of the forthcoming book *Learning to Teach about Culture and Society*. She has contributed chapters to the books *Social Studies and Diversity Teacher Education* (Routledge), *Media Literacy* (Peter Lang), *Diversity and Multiculturalism: A Reader* (Peter Lang), *Rethinking Knowledge on Global Societies* (Information Age Publishing). She has also contributed to journals including *Rethinking Schools, Phi Delta Kappan, Taboo: A Journal of Education and Culture, Radical Pedagogy, Gender & Education,* and *Discourse: Studies in the Cultural Politics of Education*. She has studied and taught in Turkey, the United States, and in Canada. She lives in and works in Vancouver B.C. and on some days, seems to end up wearing mis-matching socks.

Christopher Darius Stonebanks, PhD

Christopher is an associate professor in the School of Education at Bishop's University. He is the author of *James Bay Cree and Higher Education: Issues of Identity and Culture Shock*, and with J.L. Kincheloe & S.R. Steinberg, *Teaching Against Islamophobia*. He has contributed chapters to books such as *Handbook of Critical and Indigenous Methodologies* (Sage Publications), *Qualitative Inquiry and the Politics of Evidence* (Left Coast Press) and *The Miseducation of the West: The Hidden Curriculum of Western-Muslim Relations* (Greenwood Press). His contributions to journals include *Taboo: A Journal of Education, Studies in Symbolic Interaction* and the *International Review of Qualitative Research*. He lives and works in the Eastern Townships of Quebec and on cold winter nights can often be found yelling encouragement to his beloved Montreal Canadiens, convinced they can hear him through the television.

Christina Safiya Tobias-Nahi, MA, EdM

Christina Safiya Tobias-Nahi is Director of Public Affairs for Islamic Relief USA in the greater DC area. She has taught comparative religion, and religion and politics at Tufts University, where she participated in setting up an interfaith youth program, and has worked with the Islamic Legal Studies Program and The Civil Rights Project, both at Harvard University. Tobias-Nahi received an MA in International Relations from Boston University-Paris Overseas Graduate Center and lived many years in France. She also earned an EdM from Harvard Graduate School of Education and was asked to write a reflective piece about 9/11 for the Boston Globe. Christina has co-authored a chapter in *Invisible Children in the Society and the Schools* (Lawrence Erlbaum), and a chapter in *Educating the Muslims of America* (Oxford University Press). While her interest has been primarily focused on Muslim children in America she has been selected to be a global consultation member in Turkey in Spring 2009 with the Inter-Agency Network for Education in Emergencies. She is also a soccer mom.

Lightning Source UK Ltd.
Milton Keynes UK
13 January 2010

148494UK00001B/97/P